SINGING I GO

"I will sing of mercy and
justice;
To You, O Lord, I will sing
praises."
Psalm 101: 1

Beryl Sand

Singing I Go

Beryl Ramsey Sand

Quiet Waters Publications
Bolivar, Missouri
2001

For information contact:
Quiet Waters Publications
P.O. Box 34, Bolivar MO 65613-0034.
E-mail: QWP@usa.net.
For prices and order information visit:
http://www.quietwaterspub.com

Front cover design by Gary Froiland

ISBN 1-931475-02-4

CONTENTS

Singing I Go

Eliza E. Hewitt

William J. Kirkpatrick

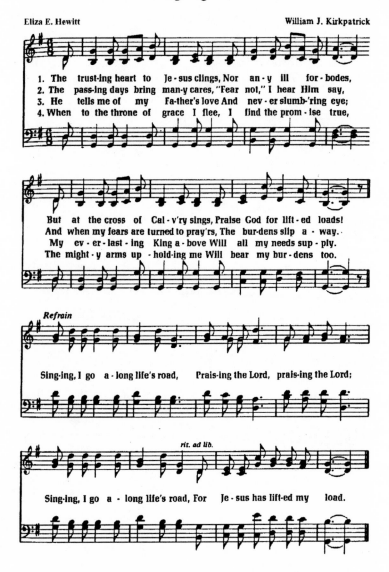

1. The trust-ing heart to Je - sus clings, Nor an - y ill for - bodes,
2. The pass-ing days bring man-y cares, "Fear not," I hear Him say,
3. He tells me of my Fa-ther's love And nev - er slumb-'ring eye;
4. When to the throne of grace I flee, I find the prom - ise true,

But at the cross of Cal - v'ry sings, Praise God for lift - ed loads!
And when my fears are turned to pray'rs, The bur-dens slip a - way.
My ev - er - last - ing King a - bove Will all my needs sup - ply.
The might - y arms up - hold-ing me Will bear my bur - dens too.

Refrain

Sing-ing, I go a - long life's road, Prais-ing the Lord, prais-ing the Lord;

rit. ad lib.

Sing-ing, I go a - long life's road, For Je - sus has lift-ed my load.

FOREWORD

My first memory of Lloyd and Beryl Sand was as a single missionary teacher in Cameroon riding their "ambulance." I was seriously ill with hepatitis. The only doctor was three hours away and Lloyd and Beryl caringly brought me to him. As I lay on a kapok mattress in the back of the covered truck, drifting in and out of consciousness, I thought, "It's too soon do die." I recovered and a year later married Walter Trobisch from Germany.

In July of 1953, Walter and I arrived together in Cameroon where we were to be the first resident missionaries in Tchollire. After a hard trip, we arrived there—tired, thirsty and discouraged. Again it was Lloyd and Beryl who had gone ahead and prepared the way. They helped us through those first days with sound advice and encouragement before they left for a well-earned furlough.

We have just received the news, as this book goes to press, that Lloyd has arrived at his heavenly home. We can hear his Master saying, "Well done, thou good and faithful servant."

Thank you, Beryl, for sharing your story and the song in your heart with us all.

Ingrid Trobisch-Youngdale

PREFACE

Before I went to Africa, I was often invited to speak about my call to mission service and also to sing. After one such appearance, a woman came up to me with the remark: "Are you actually going to go to Africa and bury your talents?"

After I had been in Africa a while and had learned some of the Gbaya language, I discovered that the word "bury" and the word "plant" were both the same. So, in using my musical talents in conjunction with my missionary work, I was actually planting something which I expect to continue to grow long after my time of service there had ended.

Since our return from Africa, when sharing with friends in congregations in the U.S., people have often said, "You should write a book." The time allotted for a talk is never long enough to cover the many fascinating things we had experienced during our time spent in Africa.

From the early days of our stay in Africa, I had this very thought in the back of my mind, so whenever I wrote letters to anyone, I saved a carbon copy of the letter. These copies accumulated over the years, and when we came back to the U.S. to retire, we kept most of them in a beaten-up, rusty, old metal trunk which we always called a "canteen" out in Africa.

Some time after our house burned down in January of 1984, I was pleasantly surprised to find that canteen in one of the outbuildings on the farm, a little building that Mother had called the "nut house" because she had kept black walnuts there when she and Dad lived there.

Somehow, finding that my carbon copies had survived the devastation of the fire clinched my somewhat nebulous resolve to write "the book." This, together with additional evidence, led me to feel that God was nudging me to undertake the task.

He gave me an inspiring verse (I Chronicles 28:20): "Be confident and very determined. Start the work and don't let anything stop you. The Lord God will be with you. He will not abandon you, but He will stay with you until you finish the work to be done..."

I also found these quotes to be urging me forward:

The Aug.1998 Readers'Digest, "Quotable Quotes," p.61: "MUSIC IS THE SOUNDTRACK OF YOUR LIFE" Dick Clark;

"You have to be first, best, or different:" Loretta Lynn.

"What is a vision? It is a compelling image of an achievable future." Laura Berman Fortgang, "Take Yourself to the Top"(Warner)

In keeping with the title of this book, *SINGING I GO*, I have tried to choose the title of some old, favorite hymn to head each chapter.

ONE
The Beginning
"On Our Way Rejoicing"

It was a chilly, gray morning in November, 1943. A group of young people from Bethel Church stood on the railroad platform in Clear Lake, Iowa, along with my parents to see me off on the first leg of my journey to serve the Lord in Africa. My thirteen pieces of freight baggage had gone on ahead, so Dad helped me onto the passenger car with my hand luggage. I don't remember what went through my mind as the train pulled out of the station, but it was not fear, even though I knew World War II was still raging in Europe and Asia. This was what I had been preparing for most of my life, especially since the night I had recommitted my life to the Lord and announced to my parents that the Lord had called me to serve as a missionary in Africa. "Oh," Dad responded. "Before you were born, I prayed that one of my children would be a missionary!"

My parents and my church had prepared me well for that day. As long as I could remember, there had been visiting missionaries coming to our country church, and usually they would be invited to our home. Mom would say, "While I prepare the meal, you entertain the guest." So I was like Mary, sitting at the feet of Jesus, soaking up information from many lands. Then, during our family devotions, the names of these missionaries would be added to our prayer list. Many years later, a former missionary to China told me that Dad had given him a check for five hundred dollars to build a chapel.

During the summer of 1943, Rudolph Steffenson, a single pastor working in Poli, in North Cameroon, had died. He was also a "shirt-tail relative," with roots in Lake Mills, Iowa. I felt that, in some way, I was replacing him because it was about that same time that I was officially accepted as a missionary by Mr. Gunderson. So, when I completed my student work at the Swedish Hospital School of Nursing in early September, I went home to shop and

THE EXPLANATION OF THE COVER DRAWINGS

The steamship on the extreme lower left corner represents the Portugese boat on which Laura Burton and I embarked from the port of Philadelphia to start on the long voyage to the port of Banana, a tiny town on the west coast of Africa. You will read about that on page 16.

The photograph which is super-imposed on the outline map of Africa is that of our International delivery truck in which we were about to leave Baboua, in the Central African Republic, to begin a new work in the Rei Bouba territory in northern Cameroun, recorded on page 89. In that picture, Carole, Linnea, and Wanda were little. Mark was not born yet. In the picture, the African standing next to Lloyd was Paul Sippison, the catechist (church leader) at Baboua. Behind the car one can see a crowd of Gbaya friends who had gathered to see us off with prayers and singing.

On the extreme lower right corner of the cover, is depicted an old African chief who was being conducted to heaven by two angels. The story is the climax of the last chapter, on page 209. The first time I saw that drawing, I thought the artist had depicted Abraham wearing wings, but if you look closely, you will see that it is the right wing of the left angel which is overlapping Abraham's shoulder.

pack. Friends at my home church gave me a "shower," just like they did for girls who were getting married.

Dear friends of our family, James and Viola Dalby, invited me to their house one day after finding out about my acceptance. Viola was dying of cancer, and she wanted me to have her little, portable folding organ to take along to Africa. Thelan Elthon, in Fertile, Iowa, made a sturdy plywood case for the organ, as well as two other plywood boxes for packing. We made numerous trips to sales to find good, old trunks. By the time I was ready to go, I had thirteen pieces of freight baggage, including a twin-sized rollaway bed, which was crated. This was all shipped to a warehouse near the pier in Brooklyn, where it was stored, awaiting our sailing date.

When the train rounded a bend, and I could no longer see the group on the station platform, I shed a few tears. They were not tears of grief, rather of excitement, to think that I was actually on my way at last!

The train took several hours to get to Chicago, where I was to meet Laura Burton, a nurse from Minneapolis. She had already spent one term of service in Africa and would be my "big sister" who would get me to our "field."

When I alighted from the train, Laura was there waiting for me. We took a cab to the Lutheran Deaconess Home where the deaconesses were expecting us. We spent several days in Chicago. I soon realized that I had made a mistake in bringing only my light spring coat. The "Windy City" was true to its name, and the wind was cold! But wasn't I going to Africa? Surely I wouldn't need my winter coat there. How wrong I was!

After a few days, we took a train again on a journey of three days and nights to get to Brooklyn, N.Y. There, too, the Lutheran Deaconess Home was our destination. Laura and I had been commissioned under the Sudan Mission, also known as the Gunderson Mission which was founded by Mr. A. E. Gunderson, and that we were "faith missionaries," having no guaranteed salary. Our financial contract was summed up in the words of Phil.4:19: "My God will supply every need of yours according to His riches in glory in Christ Jesus." Most of our friends and relatives knew about this principle, too, so many of them contributed to our needs for equipment, baggage, and train fare. Our address in Brooklyn became common knowledge, so the mail often brought us checks to meet our needs and to buy the steamship tickets to Africa. The precious sisters didn't know when they ushered us into their guest room that we would be occupying it for nearly four months. These saintly ladies, many of whom were retired missionaries, knew of our lack of ready funds, and they did not charge us. They also provided our meals in the hospital dining-room. That was missionary work!

TWO
Wait a While
"Great Is Thy Faithfulness"

One who has not traveled during wartime cannot imagine the complications and frustrations involved. Being in New York was an education in itself, though. One day, when we emerged from the subway exit on Wall Street, I looked up in open-mouthed wonder at the skyscrapers looming above us. Laura was a bit embarrassed, wishing I wouldn't act like a country hick. We soon found out that we would spend many days in New York.

Since World War II was raging in both the European and Asian theaters, all transportation had been taken over by the military, and, of course, there was no airline service. We heard that there were Norwegian freighters who still stopped at African ports. They had room for only eight to ten passengers, and frowned on taking women, "except perhaps doctors or nurses." That gave us hope, since we were both nurses. But when we asked for passage, we were warned that "it is up to the discretion of the captain."

Though our American passports were valid, we needed a visa for whatever country we might visit en route to Cameroon. Because of the uncertainty of the times, these visas were issued for only one month at a time, which necessitated frequent renewals. From time to time we were informed about something in our baggage for which we needed a special export license. This included our cameras—for which we were not permitted to carry film!

One day, on one of our forays to Manhattan, someone told us that all printed matter which we were planning to take with us must pass censorship. In other words, it had to be brought to a certain office to be examined. Back home, when I was packing, someone had advised me to distribute my printed matter among my various trunks, etc., for safe transport. So, in order to comply with these rules, we had to go to the pier warehouse, select our freight baggage, and have it all hauled to the Deaconess Home. We were permitted to put it in a basement store room, where we painstakingly opened each box and trunk, and removed all books and printed matter. I put mine in a big suitcase; Laura packed hers in a box. We chose a time of day when we expected that subway traffic would be light, and we carried our packages to the censor's office. We had to leave them there for a week, and when they had gone over and approved everything, they put a lead seal on it. We could not replace the items in our trunks, but had to transport them to Africa as they were, sealed up by the censors.

The subway system in New York is very interesting, and at that time, it was safe. We had taken so many trips on it during our stay that, by the time we left, we knew New York like the back of our hands!

Having graduated from the Lutheran Brethren Academy in Grand Forks, N.D., I had friends at the L.B. church on 59th Street in Brooklyn, and I joined the choir there. Olaf Spinnanger, the choir director, had married one of my friends from Grand Forks, and one cold January Sunday I accompanied him on the long ride to visit them in their home in New Jersey. The 59th Street Church still had many Norwegian members, so we sang some anthems in Norwegian. Some strains of a couple of those songs often come back to me yet.

Christmas in Brooklyn was something else! Though it was wartime and rationing was in effect, the clever Scandinavian ladies managed to scrounge ration tickets so they could have plenty of the necessary sugar and butter for their Christmas goodies! We "missionary ladies" were their special guests, as were whatever "soldier boys" who happened to be on furlough or holiday leave. I remember one young man, obviously from Brooklyn, who talked about the military camp being "so cold that the erlboyna froze up!"

Laura and I made the acquaintance of a young deaconess, Sr. Mildred, from one of the Lutheran churches in the area who knew her way around in the cities. On New Year's Eve, she took us to Radio City Music Hall, where we enjoyed a performance of the Rockettes. For my birthday, they took me to Madison Square Garden, where the Norwegian ice-skating star, Sonja Heiny, was performing.

On the walls of the subway cars were many advertisements. One day I noticed an ad for the Berlitz School of Languages. Most of our missionaries, when first preparing to go to work in Cameroon, spent time in France studying. With the war on in France, though, I could not go there. While I was thinking about the possibility of taking some French lessons at the Berlitz School, a check for $100 came from a friend which I felt free to use for this purpose. The time of our departure was actually drawing near by then, but I did manage to take ten lessons which were of a very elementary, introductory nature. They gave me a good start.

THREE
Ship Ahoy!
"Count Your Blessings"

At last, after nearly four months in Brooklyn, we received word that our sailing date had been set for March 1st, 1944, embarking from Philadelphia. We were told to take an evening train and to report to the pier at night. When we arrived, we were shown to our cabins and immediately got ready for bed. Early the next morning, the Serpa Pinta pulled out from the pier, sailing with full lights because she was a ship from a neutral country, Portugal.

When we came to the dining room for breakfast, we discovered that we were part of a contingent of thirty missionaries, many traveling with families. They were bound for many different countries by way of Portugal.

We enjoyed much good fellowship with these representatives from many different churches who, in spite of the rumblings of world War II, were courageously heading back to their fields of labor. On Sundays, we gathered in the lounge, and one of the pastors lead us in worship.

When we arrived at the port of Lisbon, we were surprised to find a crowd gathered there to meet us. Many were missionaries who were awaiting transportation the rest of the way to the U.S. Among them were some of my school friends, the Ericksons, who had worked in North Cameroon.

A Portuguese Protestant pastor came to welcome us and to give advice as to where we might find lodging while waiting to resume our voyage to Africa. There were several Augustana Lutheran missionaries in the group, headed for Tanganyika, East Africa. Leaving our freight baggage at the shipping company, we each took only our suitcase to use during our wait in Lisbon. Together with a couple of the Augustana girls, we got a taxi to take us to a rooming house. Tormented by fleas, tough, we found our way to a different place.

I had taken only one pair of shoes with me—not a very comfortable pair for the walking we found ourselves doing. So I went to a store to try to find comfortable walking shoes. Portuguese are small people, and the salesman couldn't find low-heeled shoes to fit me. Finally he was able to fit me with a pair of men's shoes!!

Having nothing to do while waiting for our embarkation for Africa, we spent much time exploring the beautiful city of Lisbon. At that time, automobiles in the U.S. were still quite large, and European companies had begun producing compact cars. In fact, one of the male American missionaries quipped: "You don't get into one of these taxies; you put it on!" But the charges were minimal, so we used them often. There was one cafe downtown where they served American-style ice cream. As one of the men cleaned his dish, he remarked: "That surely had a musty taste!" I said I thought it was delicious, to which he added: "I must have some more!"

Word got around that the travel bureau who had arranged our passage had overbooked, so there might be a possibility that we would be excluded, come sailing date. Laura insisted that we go to visit the agent and explain that there was no way that we could stay on in Lisbon to await the next boat. When we spoke to the agent (there were Americans at the agency, so we didn't have to struggle with the language), he was very vague about the possibility of our getting on that next boat. When the date for sailing came and our Augustana friends were all included, Laura said, "Pack up. We are going, too!"

When we arrived at the pier, the agent still shook his head, claiming that there was no place for us. But Laura was adamant. So he examined the list again. Coming back, he said, "I realize that you have paid for first class passage. But, as of now, I have only this possibility: there is a Portuguese lady in a second class, four-bed cabin who has paid for a berth for her baby. She has agreed to put the child in bed with her, so Miss Ramsey can have the berth reserved for the child. As for you, Miss Burton, we apologize for having to give you a space in third class. If you will bear with that for the first day out, when we get out to sea, the purser will try to make some better arrangements for you". Laura was glad to accept even that inferior accommodation in order to simply get on board! The agent did assure us that we would still have first class privileges: dining-room and lounge facilities. With good, tropical weather ahead, we were pretty sure we would not be spending much time in our cabins!

And, true to his word, the purser did arrange for Laura to move in to share a first class cabin with four Portuguese ladies, a cot having been added. She never complained about the crowded quarters.

The voyage down the west coast of Africa was pleasant. One of the first days out, we docked at the Madeira Islands. We could not go ashore, but people were allowed to come on board to sell their wares: beautiful, hand-embroidered linens. We did not have their kind of money, but they accepted good, used clothing in a barter system. I remember exchanging a hand-made, rust-colored, woolen suit for a set of beautiful doilies which made wonderful Christmas gifts after I returned to the States.

In the idyllic surroundings of our steamship, though it was certainly not a luxury-liner, we were completely oblivious to the horrors of the war going on not very far from us in the European and Asian theaters. We did not even get to hear newscasts!

Since we were on a Portuguese vessel sailing during wartime, with neutral status, we could not go in to the port at Douala, in Cameroon, which would have been the most convenient for Laura and me. We were booked to go onto Zaire, then known as Belgian Congo. The boat did not actually enter the port, however. They had to radio to a craft to meet us out in the ocean, which transported us to Banana, a tiny Portuguese port at the mouth of the Congo River. When the landing craft came alongside our ocean liner, we had to climb down a rope ladder. Our baggage was all swung over the edge in huge rope baskets. We were fifteen missionaries who disembarked there, mostly novice workers. Many of the rest were headed back north, mostly to Nigeria. I never did hear how they got to their destination. Our Augustana friends remained on the liner as well, headed for the end of the line, Mozambique. They would also have to find another way to their destination in Tanganyika.

Several hours later, we finally arrived on the coast of Africa!! As I expected, it was indeed tropical and primitive. We checked in at the hotel up the hill from the shore, and were served a good dinner. The men in our party were given sleeping accommodations at the hotel, but we women were conducted down to the shore, where an old hospital ship was tied up. Each of us got a narrow, iron bed. There was no bathroom, so we had to walk up to the hotel to use the facilities; we were, however, able to wash our hands and faces in the river.

Next morning, after an early breakfast, we boarded a speed boat. It took us all day to get to Matadi. There, the steamship line had arranged for rooms for us in a comfortable hotel. After three days there, we boarded another boat headed for Leopoldville, the capital of Belgian Congo (now Zaire). At one point, rapids in the stream made further travel by boat impossible. We boarded a narrow-gauge railroad train, powered by a steam-operated motor which burned wood. Ashes and live cinders often flew in the open windows. Each time we changed conveyance, all our baggage also had to be unloaded and reloaded, so we made a point of standing at a place where we could watch the operation and count it, to be sure that it was all included. By the time we arrived at our destination in Cameroon, I had lost count of the number of times those thirteen pieces of baggage were moved. In Africa, all the baggage, even large trunks, were carried on the heads or backs of black porters. Seldom did two men take something together!

In Leopoldville, we stayed at a hotel again; this time, it was Belgian-operated. Laura could communicate with the staff using French. In order to make arrangements for our boat trip to our next destination, we had to cross the river on a ferry to Brazzaville, which was French. There we paid passage on a river boat which would take us up the Congo River, branching onto the Oubangui-Chari, leading to Bangui, the capital of what is now the Central African Republic. We finally boarded the boat after spending three weeks in Leopoldville.

One day, while crossing the river on the ferry, we noticed a young man in an American army uniform. He had been in the military campaign in North Africa, but he did not explain why he was in the Congo. He was surprised to find us, two young American women in such a remote, to him, "god-forsaken" place. "Why would you leave the comforts of the U.S. to come here?" he asked.

I told him, "But Jesus left heaven for us!"

He responded, "Oh, but that was Jesus."

FOUR
Up the Rivers
"Under His Wings"

It was a good thing that our freight baggage was all well-boxed, as it had to be loaded and unloaded again, for the trip up river required three different boats. The first was quite commodious. Besides Laura and I, there were some fifteen French people who had decided to take vacations in South Africa due to the war going on in France. Among them was one young man from Syria. He spoke English, so he took it upon himself to spend time with me to help me learn more French. Again, we had plenty of time. The French people spent much of their time drinking. We often heard them bawling their orders to the African waiters: "Boy! Double whiskey!" They had an amazing capacity for liquor. I never saw any of them dead drunk. The waiter always brought the new order in another (clean?) glass which he had washed in the murky waters of the Congo River off the lower deck.

Laura and I shared a small cabin. One night, when I returned from the rest room, I asked her, "Have you seen those huge beetles out there?"

Laura laughed, "Haven't you seen cockroaches before?" I hadn't, but my African education was just beginning. I can't say cockroaches ever became my friends, but they surely did become acquaintances.

For the last day of the voyage, we were loaded onto a smaller boat which had no sleeping accommodations. The French people, aware that their vacations were about over, celebrated more wildly than ever, both men and women drinking and singing. Our Syrian friend remarked that they had undoubtedly drunk up all their savings on this trip.

Bangui!! Laura had never actually been in the capital city before, but now she felt as if she was nearly "home." Here, she could speak French to everyone, and she might even find someone who spoke Gbaya!

The Lord had a special surprise for us at the pier in Bangui. As we stood on the deck while the boat pulled in to the dock, we noticed a tall, white man watching the proceedings. He had "American" written all over him. When we got to him, he introduced himself as if he were an old friend. "I am from Mid-Missions, and I just came down to pick up the mail for my co-workers." The upshot of it was that he took us the five kilometers out to the mission. Nobody was home, as they were all on vacation, but he had keys for the mission houses. He opened the single ladies' house and invited us to spend the night there. He was already installed in the big house and had the cook include us in the tasty dinner which was prepared for him.

When he heard where we wanted to go, he said, "There is a new French transport company which has just opened service from Bangui to the seacoast, Douala. I will take you downtown to their office tomorrow, and we can make arrangements for them to bring you to your destination."

This company had, at strategic points along the road, built rest houses—a simple, concrete-block building with a thatched roof. Our baggage was (again) loaded onto a truck, along with African porters and a cook, camp-cots with thin mattresses, sheets, blankets, and mosquito nets, cooking utensils, and food supplies. Laura and I rode in an old, brown Chevrolet driven by a French chauffeur. Each day, he made a point to get to his destination by noon. Then the African porters would set up our camp-cots, and the cook would prepare meals. In the morning, he got us up very early. All of this was done in order to avoid driving during the heat of the day.

The second day, about noon, we arrived at the rest house on the hill west of the village of Baboua. Baboua, that felt like home to Laura. So when the chauffeur announced that he was going in to the village to ask the chief for a chicken for our dinner, she asked if we might ride along.

It wasn't every day that white people came to Baboua, especially white women! And then, more surprising yet, one of us addressed one of the more courageous boys in the Gbaya language. "Is Paul Sippison here?" she asked.

Someone responded, "He is out in his garden." So Laura asked him to get a message to Paul that we would be at the STOC rest house up on the hill, and we would like to see him.

In the meantime, the chauffeur had succeeded in getting a scrawny chicken from the chief, so we headed back to the rest house. While the cook was preparing our meal, we had time to get settled in our little room. It was still damp from the new concrete which had only recently been poured. We lay down on our camp-cots for a nap, and soon we heard voices outside, with the typical hand-clap and the call: "Dongwara!" which announces a visitor at the door. Sometimes a door is simply an opening in a wall, with nothing to close it but perhaps a flimsy mat, so there is nothing to knock on, hence the clap of the hands to announce one's arrival.

The message had reached Paul Sippison, who was our mission catechist at Baboua. He came with six of his students, teenagers who were interested in learning to read and to being trained in Christian doctrine. Several years later, when Lloyd and I came to work at Baboua, we recognized these boys who became leaders in the Church and attended Bible School. One of them had even become a pastor.

The rainy season had begun, and the night was chilly. Each of our narrow camp-cots was fitted with a thin mattress, sheets, and a cotton blanket. We were so cold that Laura actually crawled into bed with me to keep warm. It was a long night!

The next morning was Sunday, May 21, 1944, and our driver, as usual, got us up early. We were all surprised when, after only about an hour's drive, we arrived at our destination, Garoua-Boulai, our first stop in Cameroon. Had we known that Garoua-Boulai was so near, we should have gotten there in good time on Saturday afternoon—and had a comfortable night there in a good bed!

Our chauffeur brought us to the Arthur Anderson residence. It was still so early that they had not gone to church yet. Of course, there was great excitement and rejoicing that we had arrived. Though Laura had sent a telegram from Leopoldville at that time, we had been unable to predict our date of arrival.

That evening, Laura and I were guests when the Anderson family—Arthur, Bernice, Dawn, and Phyllis—had their evening devotions. Eight-year old Dawn was in charge. She prayed, in a very devout, preacher tone, saying, "Lawd, we thank you for bringing Auntie Lawwa and Auntie Beryl here safely. Thank you because you saved the boat!" Her parents had undoubtedly told the girls about the war going on, and that boats were occasionally destroyed.

FIVE
Orientation
"Teach Me To Pray, Lord; Teach Me To Pray!"

The missionary staff on the field at that time was very short-handed and weary. They had prayed for ten new workers. I was the first of the ten. It is a humbling experience to realize that you are the answer to people's prayers!

Laura had spent one term on the field, and now she had returned, bringing with her the first new worker. But, with so many needs to be filled, they had not been able to decide where we two women were needed most.

At that time, the mission owned one vehicle, a yellow, one-ton, GMC pick-up. At the time of our arrival, the Watne family had been using it to take a much-needed vacation. So, John brought the pick-up to Garoua-Boulai, and then he took Laura and me for a visit to Meiganga and M'Boula.

En route to Meiganga, we arrived at the Lom River. There was the new bridge! I couldn't see what they were so excited about: it was only a simple, one-lane, concrete structure! But Laura's recollection of the Lom River involved crossing on a fragile, native-made ferry, just a dug-out canoe, which necessitated several crossings in order to transport people and baggage. Now one could drive a truck across without hesitation!

M'Boula was the mission residence. It consisted of two large round huts with their conical roofs joined by a large living room. One of those houses held the huge cupboard which Mr. Gunderson had built of hand-hewn lumber, and which the missionaries called "All Your Needs." This was Ruth's room, which also served as her office. The other one, Pearl's room, held baby cribs wherever you looked. It served as the Orphanage, which included the Mbororo twins, Samuel and Lemuel. Was this what I came to Africa to do, to live and work in these conditions? God, spare me!

The missionaries held some consultations, and decided that since Alma Watne was not well, and John had been asked to do some building at the new station in Baboua before their departure for furlough, it would be wise for me to go there to help. The orphanage would be moved to Meiganga, where Laura would take charge of it in addition to running the dispensary. In the meantime, John would take Laura and me to Abba to visit with Madel for a while before her departure for furlough (with Pearl) by way of Leopoldville.

When John left us at Abba, he said, "Well, now you are stuck here!" Abba was beautiful, but it seemed to be a million miles from nowhere! I had never been anywhere where it was so quiet. Laura and Madel had known each other for years; however, since they had not seen each other for a long time, they had a lot of catching up to do. So they gave me a tiny room by myself. They did have the presence of mind to warn me about the owl who might perch on the roof at night and speak a weird, "Who? Who!" for no reason at all. Listening to the silence, I thought of the noise of the streetcars rounding the bend onto Seventh Street behind the Swedish Hospital dormitories.

There was a little verandah just outside the door of the room I slept in. Early the next morning, I was wakened by someone shaking the door. I thought I must have overslept, and the girls had sent someone to waken me. I opened the door, and was surprised to see an African standing there just as surprised to see me as I was to see him. Looking over at the (outside) kitchen, I saw the cook and house boy bending over, laughing. I didn't know why, but I just pushed my visitor out and shut the door in his face! The girls explained that my visitor was a harmless "simple-minded man" who had simply wandered to my door. Somehow, it didn't occur to me to be afraid of him.

Madel got her packing done. John returned for her with the pickup, taking her on the first leg of her journey for furlough, and bringing Laura to Meiganga, where she took over the orphanage during the time Pearl should be gone for furlough.

Alma turned out to be a great "big sister" and began to help me adjust to life in Abba. Though not a nurse, she had been doing simple medical work such as bandaging wounds, washing sore eyes, and administering aspirin and anti-malarial drugs. There was not much medicine to work with, but John remodeled the dispensary and even built me a primitive operating table, so that I would not have to bend over to do bandaging for patients lying on the dirt floor.

Besides all his other tasks, John took some time to give me a start in studying the Gbaya language. He called my attention to the fact that each language has its own melody. "You will learn this quickly," he said, "because you sing." John and Alma were singers, too, so we had much in common.

Their son, Joel was six years old, and since I had been a teacher before I took nurses' training, I tried to make up some basic elementary reading materials. At that stage in the mission's development, there was no school for the children of missionaries. Dawn had spent one school year at the Presbyterian School. She remembered it as a painful experience, having to be so far from home. I had thought to save Joel such an experience. Unfortunately, there were no books nor equipment to use in teaching, and I was becoming busier with my language study and medical work, so my good intentions to teach Joel sort of went down the drain. He turned out to become a lawyer anyway.

The missionary residences at Abba had been built, native style, though larger and more rectangular, constructed of poles and mud, with thatched grass roofs. When Madel left, I took over her house, but I had my meals with the Watnes because there was no cook stove in her house. At that time, each mission family provided their own furniture, which had to be moved when one was transferred to another station. Later that policy was changed, so the basic furnishings were owned by the mission.

When those houses were built, there was no cement available, so we had to be on a constant watch for termites. They were sneaky creatures, crawling up on the back side of furniture, and boring into things. One day, I returned from a walk to the garden, and, upon entering the house, I heard the tell-tale crunch, crunch of thousands of tiny teeth gnawing in unison. They had found a stack of my music on a shelf, and were making dinner out of it!

Then there were the driver ants, also called "army ants," who came in regiments that nothing could deter. The Gbayas have different names for each kind of insect; in their vocabulary, an ant isn't just an ant.

There was no electricity, but it didn't take long to become accustomed to kerosene lamps. I guess one did tend to go to bed earlier. I remembered kerosene lamps from my early childhood.

By this time, there was quite a number of believers, though not many had been baptized. They would gather in the chapel below the hill about six o'clock in the morning. It was good to hear them singing many familiar hymns, the words of which had been translated by earlier missionaries. Since few could read, it was necessary for them to gather in the church to have their morning devotions. At that time, very little of the Scriptures had been translated and printed. During the Sunday morning services it was customary for the missionaries to sit on the platform, facing the audience. Since I could not understand what was being said, my mind would wander. Soon I began to notice faces that seemed familiar, even though their skin was black: one tall, gangly young fellow looked like my own teen-aged brother, and another one like my uncle.

I wrote a lot of letters during that orientation period. A quote from one of my letters reads: "Now I must tell you about my cute little house. It was built of sun-dried blocks, known as "adobe" in the Southwestern States. It has three rooms, and a separate kitchen back of the dining-room. There is a verandah running all around the house,

and the roof of that connects with the roof of the kitchen, so when the table-waiter brings food from the kitchen, he won't get wet if it is raining. However, I am not using the kitchen and dining-room, as there is no stove for me, so the Watnes kindly invited me to take my meals with them."

One afternoon, as I was writing in the cool shade of the verandah, I looked out over the flower bed in front of my house. A tiny Christmas-colored bird was scolding me as he flitted from one huge, red canna blossom to another. He didn't seem to mind sharing their nectar with some large black butterflies with creamy polka-dot-bordered wings. On the trunk of a nearby tree was a shiny black-and-yellow lizard who seemed to be doing push-ups as he made his leisurely way down the trunk. By this time, I was already aware of the tiny gray-brown lizards who skittered up the walls in the house, especially up near the ceilings, where the mosquitoes were most apt to hang out.

Soon my teacher instinct was roused, and I wondered how I could help some of the children learn to read. (At that time, the government had not begun to set up schools in these villages.) I didn't know much of their language, but at least I could teach what I did know. John found some boards which he painted black, and he did find some chalk. We looked for usable paper: the few business letters we had received could be turned over and used for writing lessons. Previous missionaries had already constructed rough desks and benches, so school began, at least with reading, writing, and the singing of hymns. I remember taking some of those grimy little black hands, and guiding them in forming the letters on paper!

But why did the other boys not want to sit next to Buba? I investigated and soon learned that there were tapeworm segments on the bench where he had sat! Well, in the dispensary there was some powdered "male fern" which an African herbalist in M'Boula had made, and which cleaned out the worms, so I gave Buba some of it.

One day, I was called to see a young woman who was in labor—she had been for two days already! She not only needed a doctor, but she also needed a Cesarean section. We had no way to get her to a hospital, though—the nearest one was in the capital city of Bangui. Two nights later, we heard what soon became a familiar sound: the wails of bereavement when someone died!

Among the tropical diseases which plagued people in Abba was filariasis. A bite of the mango fly would inject a microscopic parasite into the blood stream. Some of these microfilaria simply floated around in the blood stream without doing any apparent harm. Eventually, though, if one had been bitten repeatedly, a person became aware of swellings here and there. John was troubled with them in his hands, which bothered him when he used a saw while doing carpentry. Some of these swellings became painful, like arthritis.

Occasionally, one of these microfilaria, for some reason, grew to be about an inch long, and as thick as a horse hair. They had a way of migrating to the eye. One day Alma called me to say that she had seen one of these worms in her eye, and would I take it out? "Who? Me?" She said I should just take a sewing needle, sterilize the tip of it, rip a tiny hole in the outer "sclerotic coat" of her eye, and remove the worm! Sounds easy, and that time, by the grace of God, it was! When I made a tiny hole, the worm poked his head out, and I grabbed him. Incidentally, one couldn't tell head from tail, so it was just luck—guidance—that lead my choice of the place to make his exit spot. Several years later, I was successful on an African patient, but, unfortunately, I also experienced failures.

SIX
My First Christmas In Africa
"Oh, Come, All Ye Faithful!"

As the Christmas season approached, my first in Africa, I wondered what it would be like. Alma managed a festive evening meal on Christmas Eve, after which we all went over to my house. Just then the courier came, bringing a big package of mail for us—a better Christmas gift could not have been imagined! We had decorated an artificial Christmas tree, and I had had a make-believe fireplace constructed. A flashlight wrapped in red tissue paper made a good hearth-fire. I had hung stockings on the mantle for the three Watne children, and there were other small gifts under the tree.

Early Christmas morning, we went with about fifteen of the mission boys to sing carols in the village. We sang in the court of the chief first. He was so pleased that he gave the boys money to buy meat for a feast that evening.

After breakfast, I biked out to the forest to pick flowers for decorating the chapel for our Christmas service that afternoon. The chief came with his whole retinue in great style, so the chapel was crowded, inside and out. Mr. Watne gave the message, and a Gbaya choir sang four songs.

Though World War II was raging in both Europe and Asia at that time, we were so isolated, and the surroundings so idyllic, that we were totally oblivious to the war. We did enjoy some benefits from it, however. Because of the U. S. Lendlease Act of 1941, enacted especially to help England with manufactured goods, some American products filtered through to us, arriving even in the tiny, tin-walled store at the market in Abba. To my surprise, I was able to buy two small, galvanized wash tubs in which my African helper did my laundry. This was an item not available in the U.S. at the time I was buying my equipment to take to Africa. This was actually a fortunate development, as they would have been very bulky to pack and transport.

Because it was wartime, the staples such as wheat flour and sugar were in short supply. The Africans had their own style of eating (which we had not adopted), so they didn't miss these items. To get our supplies of flour and sugar, we had to send a porter to a store in Bouar (remember, we did not have a vehicle). When the flour came, often it was thick with weevils, which had to be sifted out. Weevils eat the gluten out of the flour, so, when they had "done their thing," bread made with this flour did not rise well.

For a time, other food, too, was in short supply. Of course, no canned vegetables, fruits, or meat were available. The African butchers would have beef available in the market occasionally, though it was very tough. John usually had a good garden; he had even made an ingenious irrigation system, but he had not been able to get seeds. So, for some time, we lived on African sweet potatoes (white ones, which were not as sweet, fortunately, as the yellow ones we use at home). The leaves of these sweet potatoes were very tender, tasty, and nutritious, so they served as both a vegetable and a meat substitute. Needless to say, a diet of sweet potatoes and sweet potato leaves became quite monotonous! John did have a gun, and he was a good hunter, but a gun without bullets doesn't catch much game!

Though there was plenty of work to do, my life lacked structure. I did keep dispensary hours in the morning, and then, in the afternoon, taught the children, but there was nothing to occupy the long evening hours. The sun went down promptly at six or six thirty. After supper, (with the Watnes) I would light my kerosene lamp and sit down at the folding organ. Though the keyboard was small, I learned to play my favorite hymns and even some of my solo numbers. Singing helped to dispel some of the loneliness I was feeling. But I missed evening church activities, concerts, and the company of other young people. Alma was a good friend, but she was occupied with her three children (all born in Africa during this first term.)

So I remembered my dream of studying to be a doctor. When I was at school in Grand Forks, I had even written to the University for information on requirements for studying medicine, but it had just seemed to be too demanding! But to try to "do medicine" here, as the Gbayas said, with only a three-year course in nursing? I decided then that maybe after serving a couple of years in the mission field, I could go back to the U.S. and study medicine, after all.

SEVEN
Lloyd
"Oh, Promise Me"

But the Lord had a better plan for me.

Though there were so few missionaries on the field and communication was inadequate, they did make contacts when necessary. Alma Watne was not well; the family had been in Africa too long already. John had been asked to build a small house on the mission concession at Baboua, but he also had a number of believers who wanted to be baptized. John was painfully aware of his limitations because he was not an ordained pastor. So he asked if Pastor Sand, living then at Poli, in the northern part of the field, and who already knew the Gbaya language, could come to Abba to give the final, intensive instruction which these believers would need in order to be baptized.

So, one afternoon, to our great surprise, we heard the sound of an automobile. Soon, the yellow GMC rounded the bend and climbed the hill to the Watne's house. Pastor Anderson had brought Pastor Sand to Abba. These veteran missionaries all knew each other so well, and they were so excited to see one another that they forgot to introduce their newest co-worker to Pastor Sand. Finally, he approached me, saying, "Miss Ramsey, I presume."

Then Arthur woke up (!) and sort of apologetically said to me, "I intended to get him to you in time for Christmas!" What was that supposed to mean, I thought.

Arthur had brought his daughter, Dawn, along for the trip, so she spent the night with me. They left early the next morning, however, for their return trip to Meiganga.

A cot was set up for Lloyd in John's office, a lean-to on the north end of their house. Of course, we both took our meals at the Watnes' table. I had met Lloyd's parents and sisters in Minneapolis before leaving for Africa, so we did have some common ground. Besides the fact that we were both dedicated to serving the Lord in that part of Africa, we were both Lutherans, and also of full-blooded Norwegian stock! To top it all off, I found out soon after that, that he also had a good tenor voice.

January, the month of the dry season, was the Gbayas' time to go hunting. They would set fire to the dry grass which had grown tall during the rainy season. The fire would drive the wild animals out, and the men would be poised with their spears and poisoned arrows to attack them. The largest and fiercest of all the animals is the African buffalo, or bush cow, which is much smaller than the American bison, but also very fast. When one of these animals was wounded, it had an uncanny way of circling around to attack its enemy from behind. Its short, curved horns were sharp, and the huge head could gore a hunter, knock him down, and stomp him to death. The Gbayas thought these curved horns were placed on hinges, to be in the best position to gore the enemy.

One day, a hunter was carried into my dispensary, having been gored through his thigh. He had climbed up a tree, but had not succeeded in getting high enough, so the enraged animal had reached him with its horns. Evidently, his friends had rescued him before the beast could finish him off because there he was! They had undoubtedly cleaned off the blood while he was still out in the wilderness. Fortunately, the horn had only pierced the flesh, so his bone was not broken.

I had never been trained in suturing, but I knew I would have to manage. I had sulfa powder, so I poked as much of it as possible into the wound from each side. Then I ran back to my house and fetched a darning needle and some heavy white sewing thread. His skin was tough, but I managed to close both wounds, bandaged them, and sent him home.

About two weeks later, he came walking into the dispensary! When I examined his wounds, they had healed beautifully, but the one near the groin was swollen. I assumed that there must be pus in it, so I had him climb up on my operating table and proceeded to open what I thought was a pus pocket. There was no pus, but it began to bleed. Just then Lloyd walked in. I handed him a bunch of cotton-tipped applicators, saying, "Here!" expecting him to put pressure on the wound to stanch the bleeding. Suddenly, I realized that he just wasn't there. He had fainted!

The patient recovered (and so did Lloyd). I realized that, if these wounds had been sutured in a hospital, the doctor would have inserted a drain through the wound, so that fluid could have escaped from either wound. I had simply sewn it up too tight.

But, as so often happened during the years of my medical work, the Lord blessed my good intentions, and healed people in spite of me as a witness to His mercy and love. Because of this, people came to the Lord because we had helped them. My slogan: "Little is much, when God is in it!"

Now Alma had a new interest in life: she had decided to play Cupid! (with some help from John). When I was preparing to go to Africa, I had heard that Pastor Lloyd Sand was the only single male missionary in The Sudan Mission, in contrast with five very eligible, single ladies. So, I sort of concluded that he was immune to the charms of women. One afternoon, Alma came over to visit, especially to warn me that "rumor has it that Lloyd has a girl-friend awaiting him in the U.S." (seven years already!). But a day or two later, she revised that information: "I guess there wasn't anything to that. And, by the way, he is interested in you!" (John must have had some "man to man" talks with Lloyd.)

Now, how does one go about courting in Central Africa? Evidently, it is done by using the age-old system of matchmaking. So, a few days later, here was Alma again. "There should be a full moon tonight. I'll put the children to bed early, and we four will go for a walk."

Usually, we didn't dress for dinner, but that evening we did. Alma even found some candles to put on the table. Lloyd was seated across the table from me. There was something of a breeze which caused the flames on the candles to burn unevenly, so we found ourselves alternately rotating the candles to allow them to burn evenly. (Was it the reflection of the candle flames, or did he see stars in my eyes?)

Dinner over, of course the Gbaya hired house help cleared the table and washed the dishes, so we were free to go walking.

The motor road had been cut through a mahogany forest. Huge trees were left still standing as sentinels along the way, but they were not too thick to obscure the moon. Somehow, Alma and John walked faster, and they soon were ahead of us.

I remember telling Lloyd how very lonely I had been, to which he asked, "Couldn't I take care of that?"

I didn't realize that that was a proposal. So I answered, "It looks like the Lord may be leading that way." He took that as a positive response, embraced, and kissed me!

Just then Alma looked back, saw what happened, and said to John: "He kissed her!"

John said, "He must have asked her." So, as they rejoined us, Lloyd announced our engagement!

It so happened that, at that very time, Pastor and Mrs. Anderson and Laura Burton were on a business trip to Douala, Cameroon's seaport town. So a runner was hired to carry a telegram to the post in Baboua to be sent to the Andersons. It read: CUPID WON. SEEK TEN YARDS WHITE FOR DRESS, EIGHT FOR SLIP, SIX BLUE FOR LAURA. RINGS SIZES SOIXANTESIX MM AND SOIXANTE MM. DATE PENDING. CONFERENCE INVITED ABBA. (I still have a copy of that telegram!)

The telegram got through in record time; the cloth and rings were quickly purchased. The rings, forged of Cameroon gold, were obtained from a somewhat clandestine source which Pastor Anderson always preferred to keep a secret—with a twinkle in his eye!

Of course, we sent announcements to our respective families. Mom told me later that she wasn't really happy about it. They had contributed heavily to my supplies and travel expenses, and they were looking forward to hearing about my mission activities. Mom had the idea that, as a missionary wife, I would be relegated to just keeping house and raising a family. Actually, I never did give up my status as a full-fledged missionary. Our mission organization recognized the gifts and previous training of each person, and, down through the years, I was given assignments accordingly. Also, Lloyd was also very careful to encourage me to do whatever I could. I often said, "We were married to the work before we married each other."

Getting married in a foreign country is always complicated. As American citizens, we were guests of the French colonial system which required a civil marriage similar to that performed by a justice of the peace in the States. Lloyd contacted Dr. Jobson, superintendent of the mission in Bozoum, which was the nearest French government post where we could have this ceremony performed. It was arranged that, when all the required documents were completed, we would come to Bozoum and be the guests of the Jobsons. The Watnes had hoped that we could have the church wedding while they were still there, but their departure date arrived before our papers did, so they had to leave.

We were required to have copies of our birth certificates sent to the American Consul in Leopoldville; Lloyd needed an affidavit proving that he had no prison record, and that he was not subject to the draft for military service.

The fabric which we had asked the Andersons to buy in Douala arrived, and I proceeded to make my wedding dress. I had no suitable pattern, and the only mirror I had was about 10 by 12 inches, so, even though I had an abundance of material, the skirt turned out to be shorter than I had intended.

When the Watnes left for furlough, Lloyd moved to Baboua and took up residence in an African house. There, he supervised the continuation of the building of the mission house which John had started there, while also carrying on the regular mission work. He had no stove there; his meals were cooked, African style, over an open fire. So I had my cook bake bread for him, which I sent to him via a runner once a week.

Lloyd had his bicycle, so, on alternate weeks, he would come to see me. By this time, I was becoming quite familiar with the Gbaya language and some of their practices, so I wasn't too lonely. Also, of course, I knew my single state would not last too much longer.

I had inherited a well-trained cook from the Watnes who had learned his art from previous missionary ladies. He not only prepared my food, but he also did the marketing and the meal-planning. We had no refrigerator, so what was left over from one meal appeared on the table at the next meal. Of course, Alma had left her dishes and cooking utensils for me to use. The kitchen did not have cupboards as we know them, but tables and packing boxes served equally as well. When Matthew, the cook, had prepared a casserole for my dinner, instead of washing the empty dish right away, he would fill it with water to soak. There could be, at one time, five or six dishes soaking on the floor under the table. When there were no more available, he would then be forced to wash them!

EIGHT
Married Three Times!
"I Love You Truly"

Finally, all the required documents had arrived. But neither Lloyd nor I had a car, and the French official who would have to perform our civil marriage was a three-day journey away by car. Where there's a will, there's a way!

Lloyd knew a Frenchmen who operated a small gold-mining operation in a nearby village. M. Soulatsky made a practice of coming to Abba occasionally, and sometimes would be entertained for a meal at the mission. So a message was sent to him, asking if we might ride with him to Baboua on his next trip there. *We* meant not only Lloyd and me, but also two African helpers who would set up our camping equipment at the rather primitive rest houses along the way which were available for white people. When we went on such trips, we would always take camp-cots, bedding, mosquito nets, food, a supply of boiled drinking water, and cooking utensils.

In a matter of days, we received his positive reply. When we got to Baboua, we were deposited at the rest house where the government mail truck picked us up and took us to Bozoum.

The chauffeur kindly conducted us to the American Mission, where the Jobsons welcomed us. They were a bit limited for guest-room space, but they went the extra mile: Dr. Jobson gave up his twin bed, so I shared Mrs. Jobson's bedroom. He moved to the guest house, which he shared with Lloyd. Our African helpers were accepted by some of the Jobson's help in typical African hospitality.

During our dinner hour, Dr. Jobson explained that he had arranged to take us to the French official's office the next afternoon for our civil marriage. It was Thursday, August 31, 1945, when we appeared before a huge Frenchman in a white drill uniform. The ceremony was simple, and before we knew it, we were back at the mission.

But the Jobsons made no effort to change our housing arrangements. They explained that they, themselves, had begun their missionary careers as single workers and had also been married in Central Africa. But their senior missionaries had not considered the civil ceremony as a valid marriage, so they had been forced to wait until they could have the blessing of the Church at their subsequent mission conference. The situation was a bit embarrassing, but their fine Christian hospitality made up for that.

On Sunday, the mail truck was due to return and pick us up for our return trip to Baboua. We attended the Sunday morning church service with Dr. Jobson. Mrs. Jobson was not well that day. At that service, a young African couple who had already gone through their civil marriage were invited to stand before the congregation for a blessing of the Church upon their marriage. From our chairs on either side of the platform, Lloyd and I looked at each other, with identical thoughts: "Why not us?"

After the church service, with our baggage all ready for the return trip by truck, we ate dinner with Dr. Jobson. We had barely finished eating, when a messenger came to the door to notify us that the mail truck was "en panne" (incapacitated) so we would have to wait another week for our journey back to Baboua. Lloyd and I decided to ask Dr. Jobson if he would kindly perform a simple blessing of the Church upon the civil marriage which we had experienced on Thursday.

Dr. Jobson was only too glad to oblige, so he called in the two Africans who had come with us, Christians named Moise and Elie (Moses and Elijah), to serve as our witnesses. When the ceremony was over, they gave us the Honeymoon Cottage which we occupied for the week that we awaited the next mail truck.

But, you may ask, "What about that wedding dress you made?" Oh, that was waiting, because we were planning a church wedding at Meiganga, when all our missionary co-workers were gathered together. That ceremony actually took place on Lloyd's birthday, Sept. 28. And that's how it happened that we were married three times—to the same spouse!!

As per schedule, the mail truck picked us up, together with our two Gbaya helpers and all our baggage. The first night out, we spent at the rest house in Bouar. The next day, the truck took us to Baboua. They could take us no further as they were going onto Yaounde. But only a few minutes later, another truck pulled in carrying a load of lumber, destination Meiganga and north. So Lloyd arranged with the chauffeur, a Frenchman, to take us to Meiganga.

We rode in the cab with him. The load was overweight, and each time the truck traversed one of the flimsy wooden culverts, he laconically muttered in French: "casse!" (broken).

The mission staff at Meiganga, Rev. Arthur Anderson, his wife, Bernice, their two daughters, Dawn and Phyllis, and Laura Burton, welcomed us and put us up in the guest house—a building constructed of poles plastered with mud and painted with "yembe," a white clay found near some local river banks. The thatched grass roof kept the building cool and protected from the heavy rains. The Andersons invited us to eat with them.

Pastor Anderson promptly wired the Mathres at Poli to let them know that we had arrived. They replied that they would arrange for the first available bus or truck to bring them to Meiganga for a mission conference and our church wedding. They did not own an automobile, either.

Pastor Anderson performed the ceremony; Laura was my bridesmaid, Raymond Mathre was Lloyd's best man, Dawn Anderson Junior bridesmaid, and Phyllis Anderson was flower girl. As Bernice Anderson played nuptial music on her little portable organ, Lloyd and I marched in together. The church was packed with Africans who had come to see these two white people exchange their marriage vows. Pastor Mathre sang "O Perfect Love," and Lloyd and I sang "Together with Him." Lloyd choked up, however, and left me to sing most of it by myself!

Though we were only seven adult missionaries then on the field, we did hold a conference, and had good spiritual fellowship. Since we did not have a car, we had to hitchhike to Garoua-Boulai, and then eastward to Baboua. The conference had asked Lloyd and me to take care of the work both at the new station in Baboua, as well as the older, established work in Abba. John Watne had built a good-sized, three-room house of sun-dried adobe blocks, surrounded by a wide verandah, and Lloyd had (before our marriage) supervised the construction of the roof, made not of the usual thatched grass, but woven of the fronds of the palms which grew profusely near Baboua.

John's plan for the house included large windows and a wide front door. But, when we arrived there, the windows and doors were simply openings in the walls, with no woodwork, doors, nor window panes, so the cold, wet winds of the rainy season swept mercilessly through the house. We arrived there after dark and had quite a search to find a sheltered nook in which to set up our camp-cots! But we had each other, plus our two faithful Gbaya helpers from Abba, who helped us set up housekeeping at this new, not-so-welcoming building.

It was customary at that time to build one's kitchen separately. At this time, there was no kitchen, but there was an iron cook stove (I have no idea where it came from) which we set up right out in the open behind the house. By this time, the dry season had arrived, so, at least the open-air kitchen was not prone to daily showers! It was a rather comical sight, though; an iron range with a stove pipe sticking up right out in the open, belching out smoke. Obviously, it did not draw too well.

NINE
The Trygstads
"Come, Thou Fount Of Every Blessing"

On April 9, 1941, before the United States actually got into World War II, missionaries of many different churches bound for various mission fields gathered at the pier in Baltimore. They were there to board the rickety Egyptian ship, Zamzam, bound from New York to Alexandria via the Cape of Good Hope. One hundred and twenty intrepid American and Canadian missionaries put out to sea that chilly spring morning. Among them were two single ladies headed for The Sudan Mission in Cameroon and the Central African Republic. Sister Olette Berntsen and Alida Agrimson who had been there before.

But the ill-fated Zamzam did not make it to Africa. It was torpedoed and sunk. The passengers were transferred to other ships, and eventually they returned home. Alida, though, did make it to Africa a few years later.[1]

Pastor Gustav Trygstad had been a Lutheran missionary in China. His wife had died, and he was invalided home with tuberculosis. After treatment in a sanitarium, his health was restored, and he traveled in the US as an evangelist. He and Alida met and were married, and in 1944, they were accepted to go to Africa by Missionary Gunderson and the Board of The Sudan Mission. At the time, he had a handicapped son who they planned would accompany them, but the young man died before they left. The things they had packed for him were still in their baggage when they arrived at Baboua on Dec. 21, 1945. Alida had a good time giving away many of his things to her African friends.

One of the outstanding items which the Lord provided for them before they left was a Ford sedan, a gift from Nellie Ugland of

---

[1] For more information on the Zamzam see Eleanor Anderson, *Miracle At Sea* (Bolivar: Quiet Waters Publications, 2000). Ingrid Trobisch, *On Our Way Rejoicing* (Bolivar: Quiet Waters Publications, 2000).

Lake Mills. This was especially providential because, at that time, just after the war, it was impossible to buy a new car.

Pastor Trygstad, though already up in years, was a man of tremendous spiritual depth, dedication, and courage. He knew he would not be able to master a new language at that stage, but he did learn enough to minister, with Alida's help. Many Africans had come to faith during the early years of the mission, and he had the privilege of baptizing three hundred of them during his short tenure.

It was decided that the Trygstads should occupy the new (unfinished) house, so Pastor Trygstad hired men to make mats to hang at the windows and doors until proper closures could be produced. Lloyd and I moved into an African house with three rooms, and another small house was built for a dispensary, where I treated patients each day. I especially remember one teen-age girl who had a huge tropical ulcer on her leg. With daily treatment, it healed over well. Several years later, Ruth became the wife of Elie Barbou, the pastor in Baboua.

Early in 1946, Pastor Trygstad began to have serious health problems, so they decided to travel to the doctor at the Presbyterian hospital at Elat, in southern Cameroon. I was pregnant, so they agreed that we should accompany them to see the doctor, too. Since we did not then have a doctor on our field, having a baby there would be a bit complicated. So, since Lloyd had already been away from the States almost ten years, the missionaries decided that we should prepare to go home for the birth of our child, who was due in July. Actually, I had calculated my "due date" as July 22nd, and it never occurred to me that that baby could arrive before that time!

TEN
Our Race With The Stork!
"Step By Step"

So began a long, adventurous journey!!

To be sure we would make it back to Minneapolis on time, we left three months early, going by bus to Yaounde, and then by train to Douala. Since we were leaving so early, we thought we would have time to go by boat. But inquiries at the various shipping offices only gave us indefinite answers: "There should be a boat soon, but it will only be a freighter." After three weeks of that, we realized that time would run out on us. We had received a generous amount of monetary gifts as wedding presents, so we used that money to fly to Dakar, Senegal. There, we cabled relatives who gathered the money for our plane fares to New York. But since this was not long after the war was over, flight schedules were irregular, at best. We spent another three weeks there. Finally the American agent at the Pan American office had a flight for us.

After it was arranged, he inquired, "By the way, Mrs. Sand, when do you expect your baby?"

"In three weeks," I answered.

"Oh!" he paled. "I shouldn't be booking you!"

On Tuesday evening he took us out to the airport to check our flight. Returning to us after checking, he apologetically reported to Lloyd: "Leopoldville reports that there is only one available seat on this flight. But there will be another flight tomorrow evening. So I suggest that your wife go ahead on this flight, and then you will follow tomorrow." Fortunately, I still had my own passport.

So we bid each other good-bye, and the agent took Lloyd back to the hotel. Lloyd told me later that, on the way back to town, the agent had admitted that he was not entirely sure that there actually would be another flight the next evening! It was good I didn't know that.

Our first stop was Lisbon, Portugal, and who should meet me but the same Protestant pastor who had befriended our group of missionaries just two years before when Laura and I were there! Looking at the passenger list, he had found also an older single lady who had served as a volunteer with a mission in the Congo. So he invited the two of us to accompany him to his apartment to spend the long hours of waiting until our plane should take off again. He left us with his wife who spoke some English. At that time, the airport had no facilities for food or rest.

Besides his pastoral duties, he also had an office job. He did return to the apartment in time to take us back to the airport to make connections for our flight, though. His was a volunteer service "as unto the lord." Expecting that Lloyd would be tracing my steps in twenty-four hours, I left a note with him to give to Lloyd, introducing this friend who would be welcoming him, too.

So, on the next leg of our journey, I was in company with the American lady who had served on a temporary assignment with a mission in the Congo. The flight to Ireland, where we landed at Shannon Airport, was brief and uneventful.

When we were called for takeoff, we boarded the plane, and expected to be winging over the Atlantic in a matter of minutes. Of course, that was before the days of jet travel. The plane taxied to the end of the runway, and revved up, but did not take off. After some time, a voice came over the speaker and said: "There is some mechanical problem; passengers please return to the terminal." After several futile efforts to repair the problem, we were informed that the plane would not be taking off that evening. So all passengers headed for the U.S. would be taken to a hotel for the night.

For this, we were conducted to what looked like a school bus. It bounced along country roads for what seemed an interminable time. My companion who, by now, knew that my delivery date was imminent, became increasingly anxious. After a forty-mile trip, we stopped at a nice hotel. She immediately marched to the desk and addressed the clerk: "This lady (pointing at me) is pregnant, and needs to get to a room immediately!" So, of course, we got priority treatment. She ordered a hot bath for me in what turned out to be the biggest tub I had ever seen. Then, because it was quite cool even though it was the first of July, we were given each our big brown glass jar of warm water, called a pib, to heat up our beds.

The next morning, Sunday, the bus ride back to the airport was delightful. It took us through the famed Emerald Isle countryside, passing families en route to church, some of them actually in pony carts.

Back at the airport, announcements repeatedly spelled delay. But, of course, we did want the plane in the best condition for the long flight, so why complain? Finally, that evening, we were invited to board again. I thought of Lloyd, back in Dakar, probably boarding the plane about the time I was riding the bus to our overnight stay at the hotel. When we were airborne, I asked one of the flight attendants if the pilot had radio contact with other PanAm flights, explaining that I thought my husband might be on a plane following us shortly. Later, he returned and informed me: "Your husband is about two hours behind us now."

After crossing the Atlantic, we landed at Newfoundland and then took off again for New York. As we neared New York, we heard that there was fog, so we might have to go to Washington D.C. to land. Fortunately, that was not necessary.

So, when I got in to the airport in New York, I asked an attendant if I might wait somewhere, as I expected my husband to be arriving on the next flight. She kindly showed me to an upstairs room where I could rest. Imagine Lloyd's surprise when I met him as he walked off the plane two hours later! This delay worked out well for us, as we had arranged to take a taxi to the home in Brooklyn where our co-worker, Ruth Christiansen, was staying.

At that time, Lloyd's oldest brother, Alex, was living in Vermont. Lloyd telephoned him, and he invited us to come up to visit them. So, on the fourth of July, we took a train up there. There were so many travelers that day that we had to ride in an old passenger car which was not air-conditioned, and it was hot!! Alex and his wife, Vivian, met us and took us to their comfortable suburban home, Sandbakken. There was a picturesque ravine back of the house. His oldest son, Morton, and Morton's wife, Lynette, came to visit us there.

Perhaps because of the heat in the railroad car, I developed a bad cold. Because of the advanced stage of my pregnancy, Alex's wife took me to a doctor. He discouraged taking the long drive to Minnesota, so Vi offered to have us stay there for the delivery. But we had already come so far, so we knew we could trust the Lord to get us the rest of the way without any more problems. They had already revealed their own plans to drive to Minnesota, taking us along. Alex had been an officer in the U.S. army, so he had been able to buy a new car. This was a rare privilege at that time, so shortly after the war.

It took three days to make the trip, and we stopped to visit my parents in Iowa before going onto Minneapolis. As usual, the focal point there was Borghild's house, where Grandma and Grandpa Sand were still living. Lloyd's brother, Morris, and his wife, Verna, were spending the week at the Bible Camp at Medicine Lake, so they came and got us. On Sunday, the Sand clan congregated at

Minnehaha Park to welcome both Alex and Lloyd (and wives) whom they had not seen for ten years.

While the Sand clan members ate, visited, and reminisced, I began to realize that I was in labor! I told Verna, a nurse, about it. That evening, Morris had a speaking engagement, so he took Lloyd with him. Verna took me to Helen's house to sweat it out. The men returned from church, and, at about midnight, Verna decided it was time to go to the hospital. At 3:00 a.m., our beautiful baby girl was born. We called her Carole Dorothea.

We were very short of money, having just arrived from Africa. Sena K. Peterson, who had been Superintendent of Nurses when I was in training, was still there. She welcomed me, and arranged that, as a graduate of their school, I should be given a 25% discount on our hospital bill, and that we could be discharged on credit, promising to pay the bill later.

We stayed with Borghild for a while, but their space was limited, so she arranged for us to move in with their next door neighbor for a while. The Sands were members of Nokomis Heights Lutheran Church, which was involved in a building program at the time, so they were worshipping at the Nathan Hale elementary school auditorium. Carole was baptized in that auditorium by Pastor Ernest Larson, who had been a student at Augsburg with Lloyd.

ELEVEN
Our First Furlough
"In Times Like These"

July 1946; less than a year after the end of World War II. Soldiers were returning from service. Factories were being converted to peacetime activities. Housing was short. We could not stay with relatives indefinitely. Shortly after Carole was born, Verna introduced me to rummage sales. We needed so many things, and there wasn't much money. Second-hand stores stocked many nice items of clothing, but the idea was distasteful to me. I had never worn hand-me-downs. I was the first child in my mother's family, and my clothes were undoubtedly handed down, but there had never been any for me. Now I had to swallow my pride, and Verna was a good teacher in how to accomplish this. One of our best purchases was a used baby carriage. The bassinet part could be lifted out of the frame and set on the backseat of the car, where Carole often slept while Mom and Dad were giving mission programs.

But we needed a place to live. I had hoped that we could find a place near Swedish Hospital, so I could get a part-time nursing position, both for income, as well as for practice. We checked several places for possible housing. Again and again we met up with this ad: "Share housing in exchange for light housekeeping responsibilities." The address was 'way up north, and it meant living with an old couple and their single working son. Finally, we called the Husseys and went out to see them. Neil ran a hamburger joint, so he could buy food at wholesale prices. Grandpa sat in his big chair most of the time. Grandma had had a heart attack and was confined to her upstairs bedroom, but a public health nurse was supposed to be checking in on her regularly. Neil said he was giving her her necessary care at night, and he did take care of both of his parents when he was at home.

I wondered if the older couple would object to having a baby in the house, but they were delighted. So, we moved in. To start with, I didn't tell them I was a nurse, but when I observed that Grandma was not getting the care she needed, I made a deal with her son: "I will give her the care she needs in exchange for my board."

I would put Carole in her jumper-chair while I gave Grandma her bath, and whatever care she needed. In time, she gained strength, so she could get out of bed and walk around in her upstairs bedroom.

The house was old. The kitchen floor sagged at the north end. When I set Carole in her chair at the south end, and she jumped vigorously, before long, she wound up at the north end. Lloyd took classes in the Missions Course at the Lutheran Bible Institute, and he took occasional deputations, telling about the work we had been doing in Africa. During this time, we also began to make plans for a trip together, visiting churches to increase interest in the work of The Sudan Mission. In fact, this would be essential for us to gather funds for our return to Africa.

During the school year, all we received was needed for living expenses.

So we left the Husseys in April to go out on the road giving programs, showing some slides, speaking, and singing. Of course people were taken with our blue-eyed baby. Soon, it became evident to us that she was going to have a sister.

CANTON CONFERENCE

At this time, there were more of The Sudan Mission workers in the States than there were in Africa. Mr. Gunderson called us together for a conference at the Augustana Academy in Canton, S.D. Besides the Gundersons, there were Andrew and Margaret Okland with Korrine and Teddy, John and Alma Watne with Joel, Sylvia, and Janet, Ruth Christianson, Madel Nostbakken, Lloyd, Baby Carole, and I. At the conference, Korrine Okland and Sylvia Watne thought it was great fun to take care of Carole.

Pastor Conrad Jergenson and his fiancée, Marjory Shei, had been accepted, and after their marriage in August, they left for study in France. There they both attained the "Superiere" diploma needed to prepare for teaching duties upon arrival in Africa. We were encouraged to go back to Africa also, at that time, with the prospects of three other new couples to accompany us: Reubin and Mildred Johnson, Oscar and Martha Noss, and Sigurd and Florence Larson.

After the conference, Lloyd, Carole and I hit the road again, but soon it would be time to find a nest for our second little birdie. We found out that Lloyd's sister, Helen, and her family would be away for two weeks of vacation at just the right time so we stayed at their house. Linnea was also born at the Swedish Hospital, about midnight on August 16. While I was still in the hospital (two weeks that time), Lloyd took Carole down to stay with Grandma Ramsey. Carole had just started to walk, and even when she crawled, she was very investigative (Mom called her snuppy). Mom found that she had to tie the lower doors of her cupboards shut to keep Carole from depositing all their contents on the kitchen or dining-room floor.

Linnea was baptized at Bethel Lutheran Brethren church by Pastor Reisem.

Our mission did not provide housing, and rental housing was still very scarce. Finally, our friends near Joice found an un-occupied farm house for us. They also rounded up the furniture we would need, with the understanding that, when we were ready to leave for Africa again, each family would retrieve their contribution. This worked well for us, as we would not have to dispose of it then. This was a huge house, but fortunately, rooms we did not need were fitted with big doors which we could close off, so, when the weather got cold, we did not need to heat it all. In the ceiling above the kitchen stove was a vent, so the bedroom above it got the heat which rose from that stove.

After about three months there, the owner wanted to rent that house, but our friends found us another one: smaller, but colder!! We had gotten a crib for each of the girls. Carole's was big enough so she used it also as a play-pen because the floor was too cold for her to play there.

Having two babies just thirteen months apart was definitely not my choice! At that time, Lloyd had many invitations to travel and speak for the mission, which was also our source of income. This left me at home along with my babies much of the time, though. We had electricity, a wood-burning stove (two of them, counting the heater stove in the living-room), and running cold water. When I washed clothes, however, there was no drain for the dirty water, so I had to carry the water out. I really felt sorry for myself! One day my cousin, Lois, came to visit. She had had her first two babies close together as well. She made a statement of her philosophy at that trying time: "This, too, will pass!" It did! By the grace of God.

TWELVE
Back to Africa
"He Leadeth Me"

With another spring approaching, we definitely set our eyes toward Africa. We had made numerous purchases of needed supplies, but the greatest need was for a vehicle. We decided that we wanted to buy an enclosed vehicle instead of a pick-up, so our children would not have to ride in the open. We had hoped to get a carry-all, but they were not in production yet, so we settled for a panel delivery truck. Lloyd hitch-hiked to Dearborn, Michigan to buy it at the International factory, and then he drove the shiny maroon-colored vehicle back to Iowa.

Many years later, someone told me that he had asked my Dad how he got the money to finance the purchase of that truck for us. "Oh," he replied in his quiet way, "I just took a load of pigs to market and gave Lloyd the money." ($1800 at that time.)

Homemakers were converting their kitchens to gas or electric stoves, so wood-burning stoves were inexpensive. We found a good, used one at the hardware store in Joice. Lynn and Leroy Tweed bolted it to the floor of the truck, just behind the bucket seats, so it wouldn't slide around. When everything else was packed, we spread a crib mattress on top of the stove, and the girls took turns resting on it when we traveled.

Another item in our load was a massive oaken desk which Lloyd had found at a rummage sale in someone's basement for three dollars. We packed all the drawers full of things we would need during our next five year term in Africa. Baggage which did not fit into the truck was sent on by rail to the shipping point in Norfolk, Va.

Our first stop along the way to the East Coast was the home of Odin and Jewel Erickson, veteran Lutheran Brethren missionaries who had worked in north Cameroon, who were now serving the church in Ottawa, Illinois.

In the morning, as we were preparing to leave, for some reason there was a wire coat-hanger suspended on the back of a chair in the kitchen. As Carole toddled by, it somehow got caught in the corner of one of her eyes, and she tugged at it. It did not take her long to detach it, but we were afraid that there might be damage to her eye, so the Ericksons telephoned a doctor, and we brought her in. As he flushed her eye, I saw what I feared to be a scratch on her cornea, but that turned out to be only a mucous shred, and there was no damage. Praise the Lord!

At that time there were few motels, but Tourist Homes, the equivalent of modern bed-and-breakfast were available and inexpensive. When we arrived in Norfolk, we found a Bible School situated in a beautiful, old Southern mansion. The fourth floor had rooms for rent, so we got a place to stay there. A number of young Navy wives were also occupying rooms there.

Lloyd had the address of the steamship company, so he went to check on arrangements. Our freight items had arrived and were already on board, but he was told to wait to put the car on board until the day of sailing. When that day came, March 4, 1948, it turned out that the captain and the first mate had failed to communicate, so there was no longer any space available for the car in the hold. So, they did the next best thing, they lashed the car to the deck, so it stood right outside our little cabin. In fact, we strung a clothesline from our cabin window frame to one of the hinges on the car door, so we could hang clothes there to dry. With two babies in diapers, there were numerous items to wash and hang out daily. I had brought a good supply of cloth diapers, but on that trip, we only used a few of them, choosing rather to wash daily. (Nobody had disposable diapers at that time!)

To wash! That was something else again! The laundry was a pair of tubs in a room five flights down into the hold, where sailors were moving forth and back in various stages of undress. So Lloyd chose to do the washing rather than to have me down there in such circumstances.

Our first stop was at Dakar, Senegal, where they unloaded 5,000 tons of flour and cornmeal. We were there for ten days.

The freighter had a great deal of cargo to discharge at Port Bouet, Ivory Coast. The city of Abidjan lay on the north side of the lagoon, which was closed by a strip of land. Work was being done to cut a canal through that strip of land, so ocean liners could pass through and pull up to the docks. But at that time, the steamships had to drop anchor out in the bay and unload onto small boats called "lighters." These were in short supply, so it took a long time to unload. It was fascinating—and scary—to watch heavy equipment such as big trucks, caterpillars, and road-building equipment being unloaded and transported on those small boats.

This was complicated, also, by the fact that many different freighters called at that port. If a banana boat came for a load of the fruit which had been prepared for them, they had priority" because of the perishable nature of the cargo. If an oil tanker came in, or a passenger boat, they also had priority over a freighter. So it turned out that our boat was held up at that point for three weeks, and it was hot! We could not go ashore, but we really didn't get bored, because we had the two children to care for—and to wash clothes for!! Also, the food was good. The ship's cook made delicious bread.

The captain took a liking to Carole, and one day he ordered the ship's carpenter to make a sandbox for her on the top deck. He arranged for a load of sand to be brought from the beach, and then she had a nice place to play. The Captain also had a little white dog who spent some time with Carole in the sand box.

On this freighter, there were only a few passenger cabins. Besides us, there were two single girls going to Nigeria, and a young, just-married couple headed for Spanish Guinea. We missionaries enjoyed good fellowship together. One Sunday evening, I put the girls to bed, Linnea lying on the top bunk. After we had had our devotions, I decided to go down to our cabin to check on the children—it was so pleasant to sit on the deck in the cool evening breeze. As I neared the door of our room, I heard Linnea crying, and even before I opened the door, I could tell that she was on the floor. I picked her up and dashed up the stairs to the group on top deck, wondering if she was all right. Obviously, she had fallen off the top bunk. But there was no sign of injury, so we praised the Lord again.

Freighters have their prearranged routes; we passengers were just along for the ride—they obviously didn't make any money on us. I'm sure we consumed as much in food as we had paid in fares. So we couldn't complain when they sailed past Douala, Cameroon, and went on south to Angola to unload the cargo slated for that country. Then they turned back north again, and put in at Douala. There, our freight baggage, including our car, a kerosene refrigerator for us and one for the Oklands, was all unloaded. When we had loaded our International panel delivery truck on the boat in Norfolk, they had not removed the freight items that filled it. So, when the customs men checked it all through, they did not charge for anything that was inside the truck.

As we had to wait for the other freight items to clear customs, we went to the headquarters of the Presbyterian Mission, where we were made welcome to stay while we waited. The missionary whose

job it was to take freight through customs also arranged for our
freight items to be sent by truck to Meiganga, so we only needed to
take our personal items in the panel as we drove up-country. The
road from Douala to Yaounde had not been improved yet, and it
was rainy season, so I remember our vehicle climbing the muddy
hills sideways. By the grace of God, we never slipped off the road,
nor did we get stuck in the mud, but it was tough going, often in
super low gear.

The year was 1948, and someone we met along the way made the
prediction: "The white man has ten more years to work in Africa!"
There were rumblings of agitation for independence from the rule
of the colonial Europeans, which erupted in bloodshed later in the
former Belgian Congo. Forward-looking government and mission
leaders began to train some Africans for leadership, but not nearly
enough. Looking back now, we realize that much more should
have been done.

THIRTEEN
Second Term
"Take the Name Of Jesus With You"

The mission conference had chosen Lloyd to be Mission Superintendent which meant that we would live in Meiganga. In the past, the superintendent had also been treasurer, and his wife acted as bookkeeper. This had never been my strong point, so I was not too happy about that placement.

When we arrived in Douala, we received letters from several of our fellow missionaries, saying that there was a tremendous need over in the A.E.F. (now Central African Republic). A number of them felt we should go to Abba. Also, we had our re-entry permit, which could be hard to get. Ruth Christiansen had been appointed Treasurer and was doing well, so they felt that such paperwork as the Superintendent would need to take care of might be done at Abba as well as at Meiganga. Word came from the Mathres that they might come down in June, so we could have a short conference. Trusting that the Lord was planning to send a new couple to work with them in Poli, Raymond had built a nice, new house. The house was later occupied by the Reubin Johnsons.

We arrived at Garoua-Boulai on May 14th. On Sunday afternoon, May 16th, we drove over to Baboua. Selmer and Esther Myklejord and their daughter, Marilyn, had joined the Trygstads there during our two-year absence. It was thrilling to see the many improvements they had made during that time.

Living at Baboua, the Trygstads were also responsible for the work at the Abba station, so Lloyd took them down there to check on the work. Then we went back to Meiganga to await the gathering of the other missionaries. Marilyn Myklejord went with us to take care of our children—she was lonesome at Baboua, and enjoyed having something to do.

In the meantime, Oscar and Martha Noss and their two little boys, Philip and James, had arrived at Meiganga (James spoke of it as "Daddy's ganga"), so Lloyd took Oscar with him on a trip to one of the outstations connected with the Meiganga station. Several of those villages are off the motor road, so the men had to walk.

Laura had left an African nurse in charge of the dispensary, under Pearl's supervision. Since Pearl had so much to do with the orphanage, I volunteered to take over the dispensary as long as we were there. The little house where we were staying did not have kitchen facilities, so we took our meals with Pearl and Ruth, as did also the Nosses. I tended to fret about being a bother to other missionaries. It would be great to be by ourselves eventually.

Carole enjoyed playing with some of the orphan children who even had a pet monkey. Her dolls were in the baggage that was still on the way, but she managed to find something to be a pretend baby. Ruth Christianson called her "Lille Mor," Norwegian for "Little Mother." Carole was especially fond of the orphaned Mbororo twins, Benny and Lemmy, particularly Benny, whom she called Binny, just like the Gbayas did. One rainy afternoon, she brought the twins, another five-year old, and the monkey into our house. What a rumpus they made, the monkey leading the chase!

Ruth told us about a Gbaya lady, Paulina, who had been the wife of a catechist, but he had rejected her. She had had a little girl, whom she had given good care, always keeping the child neat and clean. (I don't know what she died from. Infant mortality is high here.) So Ruth and Pearl were hoping Paulina might be interested in serving us as a nanny, even if we should go to Abba. She was interested.

FOURTEEN
Mission Growth
"Leaning On the Everlasting Arms"

From a letter written July 23, 1948:

We have just recently welcomed seven new missionaries to our field. Three more are coming. Naturally it will cost much more to run the mission, but God, who has sent them, is also able to provide. Of course that means many more houses. At least four new stations should be opened soon, as there are thousands of people in these areas who have never heard the Gospel. That means building churches and schools. Two of the new missionaries have been farmers, and are handy with tools, so they will be building, starting gardens, planting trees, etc. Fruit trees do not grow wild, but do well when planted.

The newest additions to our mission personnel arrived just in time for the conference. Reubin and Millie Johnson were assigned to the station at Poli, along with the Mathres, and Ruth Eleanor Hanson was sent to Abba with us.

The conference decided that, when we got settled at Abba, we were to call in the catechists for a short course. They had had very little previous training—some can scarcely read—but they had a burning desire to share what they did have with their people. They were definitely Spirit taught. At that time, they had only the Gospels and Acts and a few of the shorter epistles translated into the Gbaya language, mostly in mimeographed form.

As we were about ready to leave for Abba, one of the Christians in the Meiganga church came to ask Lloyd to perform a Christian marriage for his eldest daughter on Sunday afternoon. She was the first one, baptized there as a baby to be given in marriage at the Meiganga church. I dug through my things, found a fairly good, used sheet, and made her a white wedding gown. Up to the present (1995), the marriage is still going strong and has endured for 47 years. They went through Bible School and seminary together, and he has been a pastor for many years.

In looking through carbon copies of letters sent in 1948, I found this copy of an article sent for publication at home:

About 4:30 on Saturday afternoon, July 31st, we drove in to Abba station after an absence of over two years. Soon a crowd of old friends gathered about us. Carole and Linnea were the source of greatest interest. The Gbayas had heard about the "two gifts" God had granted us while in our homeland, and they were all eager to see them. After we finally got in the house, we heard a song of praise from the group gathered outside. One after another lifted voices in prayer, thanking God for sending us back safely, and especially thanking Him for our two little girls. Finally, we had to ask them to leave, so we could get settled for the night, but we would see them all at the Sunday service.

The Trygstads have been making more or less regular trips to supervise the work, but since they had not been able to stay long at a time, we expected the place to be a bit run down. But they had encouraged the Gbayas to make it look nice for our return, and they surely had! Of course the spiritual development of the people with no regular pastor was our chief concern. But God had watched over His work and prospered it. Whereas during the first fifteen years of the mission work here, only a few had been baptized, now the number has grown to about 200. "I sowed; Apollos watered; but it is God who has given the increase," Paul said. It is especially interesting to see many of the older people coming now. Before, they seemed so steeped in old heathen ideas that we thought they might never be won. Job Bea, a witch doctor, threw away his medicine (witchcraft), believed, and was baptized. Whereas he had before been in ill health, after his baptism, the Lord raised him up. Now he goes hunting like a young man, to the amazement of his friends. This has been such a testimony that other older people are also coming to hear for themselves, and not a few have asked to be taught the Way of Salvation and to be baptized.

Last week Lloyd made a trip out to a plantation where a Frenchman, who came out as a gold miner, now produces nice potatoes and other vegetables to sell to the growing numbers of white people who come long distances to buy from him. While on this trip—over a hundred miles in all—Lloyd also visited seven out-stations where we have catechists and baptized Christians. Four of these places are gold-mining camps where there are large numbers of laborers thus reached with the Gospel. The white men in charge are not Christians, but they realize the stabilizing effect of the Gospel. So they have encouraged the work, some of them building chapels for worship and homes for the catechists. In these out-stations there seems to be a growing openness to the Gospel.

Chief Abba, who formerly attended services regularly, and when the Andersons were here, came for instruction, learning to read, has in recent years become too busy to come. When we have gone to preach at his court, he has always received us kindly. Recently he told Daniel Yongoro, our catechist, that he wants to come up some time and have Lloyd explain to him the dif-

ferences between Islam and Christianity. Many of the "big men" of the village are practicing Moslems, and the chief goes to the Moslem prayer house which is conveniently located just next to his court. But we thank God that His Spirit is still working in the heart of the chief. What an influence he could exert for the Church if he would confess Him openly. One of his sons, who had five wives, was converted, sent away four of them, and is now a witnessing Christian, taking the name of Solomon.

When we returned from our furlough, we brought a kerosene-operated refrigerator, but we could not always use it, for lack of kerosene. Since we used powdered milk, we would only mix as much as we needed so it wouldn't spoil. But one day, the chief sent word that his pigs were doing so much damage in the fields, that he was going to butcher some of them, so he asked if we wanted one. We decided to buy one, so we started the refrigerator. Though the pig was full grown, it was not large, with very little fat. We gave the head, feet, tail, kidneys, and innards to our help. All the rest went into the refrigerator, with plenty of room left for other food.

From my letter of September 22, 1948:

It is very humbling to realize that one is the answer to someone's prayers. The Christians here are still thanking God for sending us back, with the added blessing of our two dear little girls! Our Carole and Linnea are a daily source of interest to all who come and go. Yesterday afternoon a crowd gathered to watch Linnea take her first toddling steps! They were as thrilled as I was when she put one chubby foot ahead of the other and to hear her squeals of delight when she was successful. In fact, I was one of the onlookers, for it was one of our "nannies" who was teaching her. Sometimes I am envious of the help, as I have so little time with the girls these days. But, when bedtime comes, I send the help away, wash off the dust of the day's play, and tuck my toddlers into bed. "Mommie, pray," reminds two-year-old Carole.

The fact that so many of our believers cannot read, weighed so heavily on my heart that I felt I must do something to help them. There are almost a hundred, both men and women. We have no books, so I make up lessons, draw some little illustrations, and then Ruth Eleanor types copies. Some of the students are learning quickly, but others seem to be hopeless. I remind them that "with God nothing is impossible," and that they should pray for the enlightenment of the Spirit for learning.

We haven't been here two months yet, and my dispensary hasn't been repaired and set up for medical work. But so many have been coming for help. I haven't the heart to turn them away, but neither can I have them sit around on our porch with their sores and inflamed eyes. Lloyd went to the coast to pick up two American church representatives who were coming to visit our mission. I had told him that I wouldn't try to start medical work while he was gone, but seeing so many patients in need, I gave orders for workmen to get the dispensary ready. It is below the hill from our house, and Joseph Bakisa, who helped me before, is here, and he can do a lot of the routine work. When we have regular hours, we can also have a short introductory Gospel service each morning. We can then reach many who would never come to school or church.

I have a baby in the house, too—a black one. When he was about two weeks old, his mother developed pneumonia, and her milk stopped. I couldn't bear to see the baby starve, so I asked the parents if I might take him until she regains her strength. He is a fairly good baby, but the last few nights he has kept me awake quite a bit. The mother is getting stronger, so I trust she'll be able to take him back soon.

I am so thankful to our friends who rolled bandages and sent old sheets, pillow-cases, and cloth feed sacks, white and colored. Besides serving for medical purposes, one sheet served as a shroud for the body of a Christian whose family could not afford cloth to wrap his body. I have made simple dresses for the girls who take turns helping care for my children, and some of the white feed sacks are serving as aprons for my house help.

One set of colored ones made up into curtains for the office, which has served as guest room on occasion.

And, oh, how thankful we are to friends who contribute funds for running our car. As our work grows, Lloyd needs to get out to visit and encourage the believers in more villages.

We have a wonderful garden now, and last week we got a good shipment of powdered milk and kerosene, so we can run our refrigerator. Yesterday Pastor and Mrs. Trygstad came to spend a month with us. Our men will have a Bible Short course for the church leaders. Alida went out with her gun and came in with a nice guinea hen. Tomorrow morning she promised to go out with the boys and try to shoot a monkey for them. We don't eat monkey, but they will enjoy it.

From a letter written November 11, 1948:

Have I told you that our oranges and grapefruit are getting ripe now? We also have a lot of papaya, a fruit which grows on trees, but tastes like muskmelon. It feels good to be able to share fruit with others. Yesterday a French miner who had gotten fruit from us sent us a dish-pan full of meat, which he knows is hard to get here.

From a letter to the Watnes (in the U.S.) written December 4, 1948:

Did you know there is now a motor road out from the "back" of Abba out Pokorta way to Bouar? Early this week, five military men in two jeeps came. I was fortunate in having lots of eggs, so they had a good American breakfast of toast and fried eggs. They gave us a wild rabbit they had shot en route from Baboua. At noon we had a married couple and a young man who are now at Michel's place. There is a Frenchman in charge of a mine at Babaza now. He has a lot of chickens, so he sends us eggs, as well as beef, whenever he butchers, so we share fruit with him.

FIFTEEN
Medical Emergencies
"The Great Physician Now Is Near"

January 1949

One day, a young woman was brought in on a stretcher from a distant village where her husband was working for a miner. Meat is scarce there, so when she found some caterpillars in a tree, she prepared them as food for herself, her husband, and a brother. She knew that people have become seriously ill, temporarily insane, or have even died from eating this kind of caterpillars, but, like so many people, she took a chance. When she was brought to me, she was delirious, and I could not get her to swallow anything. They took her to her father's house in the village. Later that day they notified me that she had taken a little water, so they wanted me to come and give her a strong laxative! I gave both her and her husband big doses of castor oil, and the next day they were better. When we went to visit them, we explained that we had no power over this poison, but if God would see fit to bless our medicine, they would recover. They did!

A few days later, I was called to see the wife of one of our believers. The women had been in labor two nights and a day. The poor girl was frightened and exhausted, and badly needed a Caesarian section. As I walked home in the beautiful tropical moonlight, my heart was heavy for the many deaths which could be prevented if we had a hospital and doctors.

The next day, shortly after noon, we heard the death wails in the village, so we went to speak to the crowd gathered around the corpse. All were quiet except the one using a pick-ax on the hard ground, digging her grave. They had placed her body in a half-reclining position on a low, slanting chair. She was dressed in what must have been her Christmas dress, and friends had put small coins on each cheek, and stuck paper money under her head-kerchief. This money would later be used to buy food for the mourners.

It was dry season, and hunters would set fire to the tall grass in a given area. When the fire drove the wild animals out, the hunters would stand with their spears poised for the kill. But one man got excited, and his leg came between the hunter and the animal, so the spear pierced his leg. Fortunately, the spearhead did not break either bones or tendons, and the bleeding had been stanched by the time his friends got him to the dispensary. My needles wouldn't puncture his tough skin, so I closed the wound with sterile adhesive, and he healed up without incident.

I tried to keep regular hours for medical work, but sometimes in the afternoon, when I was trying to write letters or get caught up on sewing, patients would come to our porch and wait for me. Sometimes, three-year-old Carole would come in to tell me that someone wanted to see me. Often, she could relate exactly what the patient's complaint was, and if I didn't leave what I was doing quickly, she would reprove me. Sometimes, I would let her hand a pill and a glass of water to the patient. Linnea soon wanted to get in on the act, too. But she liked to tease: when the patient would reach for the medication, she would hide it behind her back with a twinkle in her big, blue eyes. Since the girls heard us talking Gbaya all the time, they learned it before they learned English. In fact, I found myself augmenting my own vocabulary with their help. But there were also people who enjoyed "enriching" their vocabularies with vulgarities that we did not understand. One day, my cook enlightened me about some of these.

SIXTEEN
Watnes Return
"We've a Story to Tell to the Nations"

John and Alma Watne, and their children Joel, Sylvia, and Janet had been in the States almost four years. John had realized his life's dream of taking seminary training in St. Paul. Since housing was less expensive in the country, the family lived in a farmhouse near Lake Mills, Iowa.

They would find changes: young people who had not even begun to show interest in the Gospel were now leaders in the growing Church. We didn't have a Bible School yet, so believers were sent out as catechists shortly after their own baptism. The government had built roads, so all villages in this territory were accessible by car, with a lot of wear-and-tear on the car! The long, narrow house with its crooked walls and picturesque grass roof, which had been the Watnes' home for the seven years of their first term, was so undermined by termites that the Tryg-stads had had it taken down, so John would have to replace it.

So, for Lloyd and me, it was back to Baboua. Baboua was a larger town than Abba, really four villages clustered around the French government post with a French family in charge, a customs office, and gendarmes (French militia). Not too long before two Frenchmen had opened a garage, but they didn't sell gasoline, so we would still have to order our bulk supply from the coast.

Since Baboua was situated on the "main highway" from Douala to Bangui, the capital of French Equatorial Africa, we got some interesting visitors. Marybelle Taylor, a nurse at the Presbyterian Mission down south, brought a lady doctor who taught at the Illinois University School of Medicine. She wanted to get some first-hand information about tropical diseases. We plied her with questions until almost midnight. She was disappointed that missionaries did not wear trousers, boots, and long sleeves to protect us against insect bites. She said some didn't even boil their drinking-water, nor sleep under mosquito nets. We did. We didn't have cats or a dog, but we did have a pet chick! We had three nice, big hens, and a great big Leghorn rooster, from French stock. One day a man who worked on our yard brought his mother hen and three chicks and put them in our little chicken house without permission. In the morning, the mother hen was dead—some animal had bitten her on the head. We kept the chicks, but two of them died. The survivor slept in a box in the kitchen, behind the stove. Carole and Linnea enjoyed letting him crawl up their arms and snuggle underneath, where he would chirp most contentedly. But one day, when he was out in the yard, a hawk swooped down and plucked him up right in front of us all. I acquired four hens after that, three as gifts, and one in payment for medicine.

SEVENTEEN
Jergensons
"Give of Your Best to the Master"

November 1949

New neighbors! Conrad and Marj Jergenson had worked hard studying French in France, and now they had arrived to take up the work to which the Lord had called them. Pastor Okland had driven the big mission truck down to Douala, the seaport, to transport their baggage and supplies for the mission. Now they were busy unpacking, and Conrad was making furniture out of their packing boxes as fast as they were being emptied. Madel Nostbakken, who was working on the Gbaya translation of the Gospels and Acts with Lloyd and some of the African leaders, spent some time each day in giving them a start on the study of Gbaya. John and Lloyd called in most of the church leaders for a Bible short course, and Connie did some teaching in French.

While they were getting settled, they took their meals with us, and Carole and Linnea enjoyed getting acquainted. Marj was surprised to hear them talking Gbaya, which seemed so formidable to her.

One day, Linnea developed some itchy spots on her skin, which the Gbayas thought were due to the bites of small spiders. So I prepared a warm soda water bath in the big wash tub. Carole thought that looked like fun, so she began to complain of itching, too. There was room for her in the tub, too, so she was glad to climb in with her sister!

Some time ago, Reuben Massa, one of our Christians from Abba, and his wife and three children went to Meiganga seeking medical care for the baby. He had a low hernia, which, of course, could only be treated by surgery. There was definitely something wrong with him, for, though he was very fat at seven months, he could still not hold his head up nor sit up. After their return from Meiganga, he was fretful—I thought it might be malaria, so I treated him accordingly. Then he broke out with some gray spots in his throat over the tonsil area. That went away, but there was evidently something else wrong with him. One day, his mother said she thought he was better, but I noticed that his "soft spot" was indented. That evening, I suggested that maybe we should try to get him to a missionary doctor, but that night, he died. This was a blow to the family, but I think they realized that he would evidently not have been normal.

He, his two brothers, and his mother had been baptized on Pentecost Sunday at Abba.

A few days later, we decided to drive out to some of our outstations to check up on several patients. Reuben Massa and his family rode along, en route to their catechist post, Zaramie, to resume work.

At Garga we found two children with pathetically ulcerated toes (one was an orphan). Since they walked barefooted all the time, jiggers had gotten into the skin near the toenails, and if the mother did not remove them promptly, the poor children suffered terribly. One boy, about ten years old, came back with us for more prolonged treatment. He looked like a bright boy. I told my dispensary helper to teach him to do some little jobs, and help him learn to read.

Even though we always wore shoes, and we insisted that our children wear them, at times a jigger (the Gbayas call them sibati) would sneak in and build a nest next to a toe-nail. The insect would surround itself with a sort of capsule. Some of our help were expert in removing them: using a large needle, they would painstakingly push back the skin all around the capsule, and then, hopefully, lift it out intact. It was a good thing to remove it intact, because that capsule was full of eggs, and, if it ruptured, could proliferate under the skin again. Michel, my dispensary helper, could do this without drawing any blood, so our girls became accustomed to his operation being virtually painless, too.

We were in contact with many ladies' groups in American churches, and they were faithful in mailing us boxes of rolled bandages, as well as left-over pieces of soft cloth which I would sterilize in my pressure-cooker. They knew I could not go to a supermarket and pick up groceries, so, one precious farm-wife, who evidently used a lot of Karo syrup in feeding her family, made a practice of stuffing two cake-mixes into an empty gallon can, and filling the spaces with chewing gum and suckers for the children. For a long time, when we ate her cakes, I wondered why every cake had a "spearmint" flavor! Usually the packages (22 lbs, limit) would take several months to reach us. The cake mixes were all right in those tin cans, but Jell-o usually became a solid lump which didn't jell very well, but made delicious jelly-beans. In fact, when we came back to the U.S., our girls wondered why Jell-o was powder!

Some of the ladies who packed boxes of bandages and old sheets wondered if it was worth the postage to mail this old, worn out cloth. But those items, of no commercial value, were worth their weight in gold for our medical work. Eventually, postage rates became prohibitive, but now these equally necessary items are packed in the immense containers which are shipped to mission hospitals and then dispensed to the medical workers in rural areas.

We usually lived in one of the more remote stations, so mail, especially packages, was a real morale-builder. I made a point to write a personal letter to everyone who sent a gift, but I was also aided by friends who kindly typed, mimeographed, and mailed out our circular letters. So, our letters were read and prayed over by many faithful friends whose names never became known to us. I like to think that, when rewards are being handed out in Glory some day, many of these friends will share in them, as those "who stayed by the stuff." (I Samuel 30:24).

A former Bible School classmate wrote: "It must be wonderful to be able to spend your whole time in spiritual pursuits." Well, Martin Luther is quoted as saying that the lowliest scullery maid is doing work that is just as sacred as that of a theology professor. So, when my husband returned from a bush trip, bringing the panel truck half full of miserable patients and the relatives who needed to come along to provide for their daily needs, that was spiritual pursuits. Often these people would, in response, begin to follow the Lord, the Great Physician, whom we served.

EIGHTEEN
Witchcraft
"Safe Am I" or "Under His Wings, I Am Safely Abiding"

The Gbaya tribe are considered animists; that is, they worship the spirits of their ancestors. When a person dies, he/she is buried right outside his house, so every village is also a cemetery. Back of a heathen home, there was a worship-place consisting of three stones, like a regular cooking place, where the oldest son of the diseased would put food in a pot for the spirits. (The young people would say that they knew the dogs came and ate that food.) Certain trees and certain large rocks were believed to be inhabited by spirits. An enemy could prepare "medicine"—and put a hex on someone he wanted to harm or get even with. So there was much fear, suspicion, and animosity among the people.

Foh was one of the larger villages which Lloyd visited often in his ministry in the Baboua District. Pierre Kaparang, one of our Christians, was sent there as a catechist, but it was a tough place to work. The chief made the work there especially hard, because he forced the Christians to work for him on Sunday. Once he actually announced: "There is no Sunday!" The Christians were given grace to be obedient, and this made a profound impression on him.

One day, the witchdoctor/sorcerer came to the catechist, trembling, evidently in great fear. "What kind of magic are you using?" he asked. "We have been doing all the 'hocus pocus' we know, the most powerful medicine, but it has done you no harm! I must know what it is that has been protecting you. I want some of your 'magic'" So Pierre gladly explained how, as followers of the True God, we are under His protection: "under His wings we are safely abiding."

In every village of any size, there usually were Moslem teachers who would spend a lot of time visiting with the chief and the leading men of the town. These Moslem "lay evangelists" had a diabolical influence. They had a way of making money. They would usually construct a simple mosque where they observed their five-times-a-day prayers, offered in the "sacred" Arabic language. Some of them could not even read, much less understand, the Arabic, but they memorized the prayers, and taught them, by rote, to the little boys who were sent to their schools. So a certain competition developed between the Moslem mallum and the Christian catechist, who was the Christian lay preacher who was also establishing a church in the village.

At one of our district conferences, a Gbaya man stood up to tell us how he had come to be a Christian. "My wife and I had been doing the rote prayers for some time, but one day I asked her: 'Are you getting anything out of this ritual? Our friends who gather with the catechist tell us about answers to their prayers. I think we should go and hear more about their faith.' So we did, and we found that, as we learned to pray in the Name of Jesus, good things began to happen in our lives. We experienced answers to our prayers. Now we are learning to read, and we are preparing to be baptized."

The chiefs in these villages couldn't help noticing the difference in the lives of the people who had become Christians, so some of them also asked to be baptized, and they became leaders in the Church. One young man, who was attending our Bible School, later was called back to his village by the death of his father, the chief. The leaders of the village chose him to succeed his father. The Moslem teachers in the village exerted tremendous pressure on him to join their faith, but he held firm, and the local Church leaders were supportive.

NINETEEN
Rei Bouba Trip
"My Faith Looks Up To Thee"

The mission conference in February 1950 received pleas from people in four different areas for stations to be opened. Lloyd and I were chosen to go to check on possibilities for work in the Rei Bouba area, which was a large, non-evangelized territory ruled by a despotic Moslem king. During World War I, he had befriended the French government forces, so they had assured him that they would not interfere with his rule. When the old king died, it was told that, when they tried to dig his grave, the ground was too hard. The people said he was so wicked that the very earth refused to receive him! Now that his son had taken over, the French government was placing a Commandant there. He had not yet even accepted an application for permission for our mission to work there, but he did permit our missionaries to make visits among the people, and even to the king. Our planned strategy at that time was to request permission to establish a station at a neighboring center, Adoumri, with the hope that we might work in to Rei Bouba from there.

It was decided that Andrew Okland would lead the expedition and that Ruth Christianson, who had made several trips to Rei Bouba and was an expert in the use of the Fulani language, should accompany us.

Sisters Olette Berntson and Magda Peterson at Garoua-Boulai offered to keep Carole and Linnea while we made the trip. I had never been separated from them before, so it was very hard to leave them. To make those "aunties'" home more familiar to our girls, we brought their cribs and high chairs along. I found out that they adjusted very well to this adventure away from mama, the first of many such separations.

The men had arranged that we should stop off first at the mission station in Poli, where Pastor Mathre was putting a new roof on their house. Pastor Okland brought a load of sawed rafters from Meiganga to supplement the ones that Mathre was cutting in Poli, using a small saw which he ran with a gasoline engine. Missionaries Okland, Sand, and Reubin Johnson put on sunglasses and helped him nail the gleaming sheets of aluminum roofing onto the rafters.

With that project completed, we drove on north to Garoua, where the men talked to the French government representative and got his permission to visit the Lamido (king) at Adoumri, and then to go onto Rei Bouba.

At Garoua, we stayed at the Lutheran Brethren Mission, where we were guests of the Philip Sunwalls, whom I had known at school in Grand Forks.

Early the next morning, we started down the dusty road, crossing the dry beds of several rivers. During the dry season, the people in that area get their water by digging holes in the sandy river bottom and dipping out the water which seeps into the holes. Even for this, they often have to walk many miles. Indeed, it is a "dry and thirsty land."

The Adoumri area was ruled by the Lamido in Bibimi, a young man who was very friendly. He was very proud of his shiny, new automobile, so he took Ruth and me for a ride in it to the guest house. In the afternoon, he dressed up in a lovely white satin robe. He had some slaves parade three beautiful dappled gray horses before us. Then he called in some forty of his leading men and two elderly Moslem priests. They squatted on the ground while Ruth Christiansen and Pastor Mathre gave them Gospel messages in Fulani.

The next morning, we set out for Rei Bouba. The sun was beating down in dry-season fury as we stopped before the huge gate to the city of Rei Bouba. The village is much like any other African village, but it has a wall around it. The gate is a big, red clay house with a door on each side big enough for a truck to pass through— or be locked up inside it, for that matter. A guard came to determine our mission and how many we were. When we came to the guest house, a tall Moslem in the usual flowing garb came to greet Ruth. He remembered her from previous trips she had made, as he had been the official interpreter for the old Lamido Rei Bouba.

Slaves of the king brought baskets of rice, jars of peanut oil and honey, and big dishes of food for our boys—also live chickens and eggs for us to prepare for our meals. We were notified that the king would see us at five o'clock so we fixed dinner, and had a short rest. It was Thursday evening, the beginning of the Moslem sabbath, so as we approached the king's court, his royal musicians were playing the fierce, wild rhythm which we would hardly call music. We were led through a long hallway lined with native soldiers holding long spears. As the huge wooden door to the throne room of the king swung open, we saw Lamido Rei standing to greet us. He was a huge man, and he stood on a sort of mattress covered by a brightly colored rug. Behind him was a big, old-fashioned iron bed with a figured blanket on it. The floor was covered with deep sand, which had been smoothed to perfection before we entered. After we had all shaken hands with him, we sat down in the nice armchairs provided for us, and Ruth began to converse with him in Fulani.

First she visited with him, mostly about his father, who had received her very kindly on her previous visits. Then she spoke to him from the Word. She reminded him how, in Moslem Scripture, the truth of the second coming of Christ is presented. She spoke of their belief that, when He comes, God, whom they call Allah, the One True God, will give Christ the position as Judge over all men. So she asked him, "Who can be greater than that?" He agreed, and asked when He is coming. She had a chance then, to challenge him with the truth that He might be coming very soon, so it behooved all to repent and prepare to meet Him. It is hard to tell just what was going on in the heart of such a man, but we prayed that the Implanted Word might bear fruit. We did not have a chance to preach to any of his people. Only the interpreter was present when we spoke to the king.

The next morning, we left again, returning to Adoumri by 8:30 a.m. The Lamido who had promised to meet us there had gone to Garoua to have his car repaired, so we went walking around, looking for a place which we thought would be suitable for building a mission station. The scenery there was different from the rest of our field. There were more small hills, but off in the distance one could see mountains. The place we chose was not far from a river which was all dry, except for a few holes where people dug into the sand to get drinking water. They said that, during the rainy season, it was a rushing stream.

Later, a formal demand was submitted for permission to build there, but that was turned down, which was evidently of the Lord because we did eventually get the permission we had been waiting for, to open work in the Rei Bouba territory itself.

Life in that part of Africa was still very primitive, but the regime of the Lamido did exhibit a certain degree of pomp. His citizens were subsistence farmers, cultivating their tiny farms with a short-handled hoe. A levy of a certain percentage of their crops was exacted by the "dogaries," emissaries of the King, who had absolute power over their lives.

There were not many trees in the Rei Bouba territory, so the people built their houses of a mixture of soil with water. As they erected the walls of this mud-mixture, small rocks were imbedded in the walls. When the wall got to be about two feet high, it had to stand and set a while before the next layer was added. A conical roof structure was constructed on the ground, so that, when the wall was finished being built, the roof framework was raised up and set upon it. Then the thatched grass, woven in long strips, was arranged on the framework of roof poles, with a cone-shaped cap placed over it all.

Even the king's house was built in the same style, though much larger. His compound was surrounded by a wall, and at the entrance was a large structure open to the street.

The return trip was uneventful, and, as we approached Garoua-Boulai, we wondered how Carole and Linnea would greet us. We had heard that they had announced that Mommie and Daddy could go back to Baboua, but they would stay on at G.B. We arrived as they were eating their noon meal. Linnea stretched her arms out to me first, and then Carole reached for Lloyd. Somebody asked them if we should go away and leave them there. Carole began to sob, and, flinging her arms around her Daddy's neck, clung to him.

It was great to be home together, again!

TWENTY
Prenatal Care
"In the Service Of the King"

As Lutherans, the Word of God is an integral part of our faith and the propagation of our theology.

Many of our missionaries had graduated from, or at least attended, the Lutheran Bible Institute in Minneapolis. Our first LUTHERAN BIBLE SCHOOL was in session in a very primitive, three-sided building which had been built as a garage for our car. The car was moved out and the carpenter, Nathaniel Nguile, made crude benches and desks for the students and installed a blackboard.

Marge Jergenson writes in a letter on May 4, 1950: "We're meeting in one end of the carpenter shop...there are no windows, and the walls are mud, as is the floor. The only light comes in from the open end. My flannel-graph easel is set up in front, and on it hangs a world map as well as a blackboard. The most essential isn't quality equipment, but quality students who mean business with the Lord. (She then lists the names of the twelve students, several of whom later became pastors. All had already had experience as catechists in Gbaya villages.) These students have the level of our grade school children, scholastically. The curriculum for this first class is: Gospel of John, Catechism, Romans, Genesis, and the Epistle of James."

The students arrived with their wives and numerous children and constructed their own simple, native-style houses south of the mission concession. They were mature Christians, couples who had already served the Church as catechists for several years and had weathered many of the storms which buffet Christians in a pioneer setting. Also, they received little or no financial support from their home churches, so they eventually started gardens to produce their own food. But manioc, their staple food, takes a whole year before it is ready to eat, so, in the meantime, we had to buy food for them in the villages around Baboua.

Carrying on school work in a primitive setting was difficult: no textbooks, no library, not even a Bible in their mother-tongue. We only had the catechism and a few copies of some of the Gospels. Some of the students were hardly able to read; the teachers lectured, but found the students unable to take notes. Pastor Jergenson tried to learn the Gbaya language, but resorted to teaching in French, which the students didn't really understand that well.

So, in late August, it was decided that the school should take a break. The students would spend two weeks on preaching trips out in the villages to share what they had been learning.

This gave us missionaries a chance to get away for combined business, health, and vacation trips. The Jergensons went west and north, heading for our mission station at Meiganga. They also visited the Norwegian mission at N'Gaoundere. There they had physical examinations by the Norwegian doctor, and even bought a milk cow from a French cattle buyer.

We headed east to visit friends of the United Brethren Mission who had visited us from time to time, as well as to have physical examinations by Dr. Taber. In addition, we wanted to observe the work he and his able nurse-assistant, Miss Tyson, were doing.

This was the height of the rainy season, and the roads were heavy with mud, rutted, washed out, or slippery, depending on the soil in the area. The trip to Yaloke could be made in one day when the roads were good. At Bouar, we were told that there was a new road, a short cut to Bozoum. We had told the Beaver family that we planned to reach their place on the 28th.

Late that afternoon, while yet a long way from their station, we came to a deep trench which rushing water had cut diagonally across the road all the way down a long hill. As we stood, wondering what to do, an African told us that a Frenchman who ran a tanning establishment out there, half-way between Bouar and Bozoum, lived just off the road. Soon someone went to tell him of our predicament, and he and his brother-in-law came out to help. When it was evident that we should not be able to get across before dark, they kindly offered us lodging. "And it came to pass, that before ye call, I will answer..." That was the only white man's home on that whole road, and that was where we needed help. Though we were perfect strangers, the man, his wife, two children, and her brother, welcomed us and supplied us with food and lodging. As we waited for the evening meal, we heard African boys chasing a scrawny rooster 'round and 'round the house. He appeared on the dinner table! And in the morning, they set a crew of workmen to get the car across the bad spot—all without remuneration. Furthermore, after we had crossed the wash-out, the car refused to run, so one of the Frenchmen worked several hours seeking the source of the trouble and getting it started.

The next handicap was a stretch of road about two blocks long which was covered with water. After Lloyd and a couple of our African helpers had waded across and found no soft spots or holes, Lloyd decided to try driving through it. But he asked me to wade across first, and our helpers carried the children over. The motor died twice in the crossing, but at last the car was on dry ground again. In a couple of hours, we were received by our kind missionary friends who had expected us the day before. Incidentally, we called on the Jobsons, where, exactly five years before, we had been guests when we went to Bozoum for our civil marriage. Mr. Jobson was now Field Director of their mission, and in his travels, he had visited our home often. Mr. Beaver was in charge of their Bible School, training young men in the deep things of God, and in Christian leadership. The Beavers had three children much the age of our two, so Carole and Linnea wanted to stay longer. Lloyd was much interested in the Multigraph, a duplicating machine which they had taught an African to operate, and with which they had economically solved their problem of printing smaller pieces of Christian literature and teaching materials. This was a crying need in our mission—to get the Word into the hands of the people NOW, when they were awakening to their need of something better than their old, heathen ideas.

The next morning, while driving the three-and-a-half miles from the Beavers to where the Jobsons lived, we had a blow-out, and then we came to a bridge where the rain of the night had washed a sharp hole. Workmen were at hand to fill it with rocks, but after that, each time we came down a hill toward a bridge, Carole would insist that we pray. We had need for much more prayer that day before we reached our destination.

About half-way, with no towns in view, the car sputtered to a stop again. (Missionaries need to be trained mechanics!) Often, the gasoline we bought was dirty, so the carburetor and/or the gas line would clog. Lloyd cleaned everything he could see to be cleaned, and finally, after much prayer for guidance, he got the car to run again. Fortunately, it wasn't raining! In the ditch beside the road, a lot of clean, white sand had accumulated, so the girls had fun playing in it while he worked. We arrived at the Tabers about nine that evening, had a refreshing lunch, and went to bed. Being missionaries, they were not surprised to have their guests arrive at such an inconvenient hour, so they welcomed us with uncomplaining, Christian hospitality.

They had a guest house equipped for housekeeping, and we had some of our African helpers with us, so we could make our own meals. We spent several days at Yaloke. Besides being an ordained Brethren minister, Mr. Taber was a medical doctor. So he gave us all check-ups and confirmed the fact that I was two months pregnant.

Their facilities were much like ours; for bathing, we brought a galvanized wash tub into the bedroom and took our turns bathing in the nice, warm, spring water. On Sunday morning it was quite cool, so I had dressed the girls in their warm, corduroy overalls. The tub of bath water was still standing in the room, and suddenly Linnea fell backwards into the (now) cold water. Of course she had to have a complete change of clothes! But we all had a good laugh.

Then there was the trip home again!! We had another blow-out and had to spend time out at a French army camp for repairs. Then we had another change of tires after dark, with rain threatening, but finally we limped into a station of the Swedish Baptists at Doaka at eleven p.m., and the just-repaired tire "expired" just as we stopped. That left us with no spare tire, but the kindly Swedish brethren lent us a spare to make the rest of the homeward journey to Baboua.

We drove up the hill to our home at eight p.m. Yes, there were lights on. But what a surprise to find that it was the lights of Jergensons' car, as they had just driven in ahead of us. Each had thought that the other family had returned two or three days earlier, so there would be bread and boiled water available at the other house for supper. Fortunately, Mrs. Andrew Okland had given the Jergensons a half loaf of fresh bread and a quart of milk as they left Garoua-Boulai "just in case the Sands shouldn't have returned yet, either." So, as we shared pot-luck at our table, we recounted our experiences on our respective trips. It turned out that the Jergensons were expecting, too.

TWENTY-ONE
Tick Fever

From a letter written July 12, 1950:

On Saturday morning, July 1st, Linnea seemed unusually warm, so I gave her an extra dose of quinine, thinking perhaps she had malaria. About ten a.m., as she lay on the bed, I discovered that one of her ears was red, swollen, and painful. It was the exact spot where I had taken out a tick a week before. Thinking the fever was from the tick, I read up on tick fevers and determined what to give her. But I lacked the medication named in the book, so I consulted the African trained nurse who was running the government dispensary in the village. On Monday, she was worse, and Lloyd thought we should go somewhere to see a doctor. We didn't have gas, but we thought we could borrow some. It would have taken from one to four days to get to a doctor, so I feared that the very trip would be too hard on her. So Monday forenoon, we invited the Jergensons and the Bible School students to come in for a prayer session with us.

I was especially broken that morning, because, before breakfast, while I was trying to give medicine to a sick Gbaya child of about two, the child died! Words cannot express the helplessness which overcame me as I poured the medicine out on the ground and went back to my own sick child! The prayer session was a real blessing to all of us. One of the verses read (1 Peter 3:8) was: "The eyes of the Lord are upon the righteous, and His ears are open to their cry." For a while, Linnea had a fever of 104, but by Sunday it was normal again.

One night, while Linnea was sick, Carole woke up at 4:00 a.m., having had a bad dream. She asked me, "Why did Linnea die? Who will put a new Linnea in her bed?" I had to pick Carole up and show her that Linnea was there, sleeping peacefully.

TWENTY-TWO
Another Christmas In Africa
"Joy To The World!"

From a letter written January 1, 1951:

The American School at Garoua-Boulai always puts on a good Christmas program. The Watnes, who live at Abba, have their three children in school there, so John and Alma came to Baboua in their pick-up and we all piled in (Conrad and Marj Jergenson, Lloyd, Carole, Linnea, and I). It is ordinarily an hour's drive from Baboua to Garoua-Boulai (thirty-five miles).

How Carole and Linnea enjoyed the program! They got each their little chair and pulled up close to the stage (made of planks) and just drank it in. They didn't even go to sleep until we were in the truck going home again. The Watnes had their camp-cots along, so they slept here (cots all over our living-room) and went on home to Abba the next day. Carole and Linnea are always so glad when Sylvia and Janet come to play.

We had our Christmas program for the Africans here on Christmas morning. Though the program was announced for nine a.m., the church was packed by eight. The children did very well on their parts: songs, drills, and recitations.

We had our own "family" gathering over at the Jergensons. The gifts sent by our family in the U.S. did not arrive in time, but Marj's mother had sent some little things for Carole and Linnea in an earlier package. I had saved out some things from another gift box, too, so we had gifts for everyone. Marj had improvised Christmas stockings on the side of a table, and the girls had a lot of fun pulling chewing gum, candy bars, and some little plastic toys out of the socks. I was so thankful that Mom had sent those darling light blue dresses for the girls, so they had them new for Christmas. Your Christmas box came on New Year's Day, but the one from Sears has not come yet. We have heard that the Sands sent a box about the same time, and some other friends have sent things, too, so we will have Christmas several times yet. Last year we got the last package in March. So we can't say, "Christmas comes but once a year!"

As I read through the carbon copies of the letters I wrote during the year of 1950, I was impressed with the number of packages that relatives and friends had sent. My mother and Mrs. Ose, a farmer's wife from Thief River Falls,

became especially adept at packing and wrapping, so that things arrived in-
tact. The weight limit at that time was 22 lbs., so Mrs. Ose said she would
go to the store, get a sturdy cardboard box, set it on a scale, and keep putting
things in until the limit was reached. Then she would wrap a cotton sugar
sack around it, stitch it together, label it, and send it off with a prayer!

When we think of the number of times those packages were loaded and
unloaded, it is amazing that they ever arrived intact. When they came to
Douala, by boat, they were sent to the customs shed, where they could be
stuck for three months. Evidently the customs people were obliged to do house
cleaning about every three months, so then those long-awaited packaged would
be on their way again. Then they were put on the train to Yaounde, which
was the end of the line, where they were loaded on a truck along with x-
number of passengers. If it was rainy season and there had been a heavy rain,
the trucks would have to stop at every rain barrier until eight hours had
elapsed since the rain abated. Sometimes rain was almost non-stop, so their
wait could be a very long one.

In another letter I wrote:

Two of our missionaries came from Meiganga, bringing mail, including the
contents of your package. The wrappings had completely disintegrated; the la-
bel must have been intact, so postal workers had salvaged most of the contents
into a bag.

TWENTY-THREE
Wanda
"Glorious Things Of Thee Are Spoken!"

With doctors few and far between, medical facilities rare, and roads bad, preparations for childbirth had to be planned well in advance. Since we had traveled to the Mid-Missions doctor for my (one) prenatal exam, we had thought we would go there for the delivery. But Dr. Tabor's nurse was going on furlough, and Laura was taking over the orphanage in Meiganga, so she could not accompany us. The Jergenson's baby, Allen, was born in N'Gaoundere, but the Norwegian Doctor Bjaanes thought he would be away at their annual conference in March when our baby was due. Then, fortunately for us, the date of their conference was changed, so they thought there would be a chance that they would be back home in time after all.

We missionary families, though we were usually miles apart geographically, managed to get together from time to time. All the children called the adult missionaries "Aunt" or "Uncle," and usually, they felt closer to them than to blood relatives. So, when the Watnes heard that we would have to take the rigorous trip to N'Gaoundere for the birth of our third child, they offered to take Carole and Linnea to stay with them during our absence.

So, when Lloyd and I went to N'Garoundere, as usual, we took our house help with us and moved into the Endersons' house, while they were away at a conference. It was a relaxing time. We had time for long walks, reading, and just resting. Lloyd had been very busy, so it was good to have some time off. One evening, as we enjoyed a restful walk, he remarked: "I feel as if my soul is now having a chance to catch up with my body!"

We went to visit the French doctor who was in charge of the government hospital to make his acquaintance, just in case I should go into labor before Dr. Bjaanes' return from conference. He was very congenial, and we were confident that he would be able to meet the need, should it arise.

During this waiting time, we also did a lot of research on possible names for this, our third little Sand. In my family, we were two girls and then two boys, so I somehow believed that this one would be a boy. In the Endreson's library were many books which provided ideas for names. If it should be a boy, we settled on Dwight Orloue, and for a girl, we decided to honor my "Little Sister" from nurse's training, Wanda Stime, W also being the initial of my mother's name, Wilma. We settled on a second name, Aileen, to also fit my mother's second name, as well as Lloyd's mother's second name: Alexandra.

Our baby graciously awaited the return of the Norwegian missionaries from their conference, and on the second morning after Dr. Bjaanes' return, my labor began. He came over to the Endreson's house and prepared a single, hospital bed as a delivery table. The hospital was still small; it had not grown beyond the original foundation stones. Lloyd had set up a camp-cot in the room, since he preferred to stay at my side. Reubin and Millie Johnson, with their 17-month-old Amy, were in the next bedroom, having come from Poli to begin their trip back to the U.S. for their first furlough. Harriet Stovner, also stationed at Poli, had accompanied them, planning to return to Poli after seeing them off. Harriet is a practical nurse so she was put to work assisting in the delivery and subsequent care.

At 3:00 a.m. on March 22, 1951, Wanda was ushered into the world, a beautiful, healthy girl.

Having seen his third daughter safely into the world, Lloyd took off with Andrew Okland on a trip into the Rei-Bouba territory to stake out a concession for a mission station in Tchollire. Reubin Johnson had an errand to Baboua, so he carried the news of our baby's birth that far. The Sigurd Larson family was there, en route to Abba, so they brought word to the Watnes, and to Carole and Linnea.

TWENTY-FOUR
1951 Conference
"We Gather Together To Ask the Lord's Blessings"

Packing; moving; traveling! So much of a missionary's life is made up of that. So, with our new baby, we drove down to our main station, Meiganga, where we met with all the missionaries who had come from their respective stations for a conference. Of course, the Watnes brought Carole and Linnea to be reunited with our family again. It was good that we had not known all that had transpired during those two months of separation. Alma reported that, shortly after the girls arrived in Abba, Carole had come down with a severe attack of malaria. At one time when Alma went in to check on her, Carole was lying so quietly that Alma thought she was dead! They actually contemplated bringing her to us at N'Gaoundere which would have been a long, difficult ride, but the next day she began to improve.

Then both the girls developed boils in their hair! What a mess that must have been: painful for them, and painful for their loving Aunt Alma. They evidently lacked vitamins, and, of course, they had no antibiotics for treatment.

When all of us missionaries converged on the Meiganga station for conference, all possible room arrangements were improvised. The French elementary school was suspended for the duration of the conference, so that dormitory and classrooms could be converted to temporary living quarters and meeting rooms for the missionaries. A small, two-room building had been constructed for the "Moyen Cour" (Middle School) out of the red, laterite rock so abundant in the Meiganga area. Our family was assigned to one of those rooms, and there we set up our four camp-cots with mosquito nets, the baby crib, a wash stand, an arrangement for hanging clothes, etc. There was no plumbing at that time, so Africans were hired to carry water from the spring, and everybody knew where the outhouses were.

For meals, Arthur and Bernice Anderson entertained all the children. "Uncle" Arthur had a special gift for this, and he actually enjoyed it. Ingrid Hult led sessions for the children, and "Aunt Alma" trained them in singing, so that, near the end of the conference, they sang for us. Ingrid also coached them as they worked out skits, imitating the adults in various activities which they had observed. The most entertaining one was their imitation of "Uncle" Oscar and the G.M.C., the old, yellow mission truck. They used pots and pans for the wheels—and, of course there was a blow-out! They also imitated a conference session where they discussed and planned the construction of a chicken coop at the Poli station: "I move that...motion seconded...passed).

But there were some very serious events at that conference: word had come that our founder and executive secretary in the U.S. was seriously ill. Then, before the conference concluded, a cablegram announced that Mr. Gunderson had died. The older Gbaya believers, who remembered the Gundersons' first years in the area, called him "Massa." One of these older men came to Ruth Christiansen after the news spread among them, remarking, "When I heard that Massa had died, I knew the conference would last a long time."

During the annual conference the previous year (1950), we had carried on some very serious discussions regarding the future of our faith Mission. It was obvious that Mr. Gunderson would not be able to handle all of the home base work alone. The Sudan Mission Committee seemed to have become either inactive or impotent. Our mission work was growing rapidly. Support had been coming in well for our missionary living allowances, but we lacked funds for buildings and institutions, such as schools and medical work. So we had done a great deal of soul searching and had come up with some proposals which we sent to Mr. Gunderson. At that time, our missionary personnel represented several different synods. In one of his prayers, Lloyd made the request: "Lord, forgive us our synods!" But nothing had come of those proposals, so, now that he had died, we knew we needed a different arrangement. Most of our missionaries were members of the [then] ELC, so what eventually developed was that Dr. Syrdal, the Mission Secretary, came out to assess the situation, with the result that the ELC did actually take over the work.

After the conference closed, we stayed on in Meiganga a few days so that Lloyd, as Mission Superintendent, could finish up some mission correspondence.

In one of those letters, Lloyd wrote:

> *On getting back from the conference, I'll be taking a few trips to the cate-*
> *chists' posts, helping them with their problems and administering communion*
> *and baptism. Conrad and Marj (Jergenson) will be doing all of the teaching*

at the Bible School for a while. Then in about three weeks I'll be going to Abba, as Miss Nostbakken and I were delegated to go over the Gbaya translation of Acts in view of getting it ready for printing at the British and Foreign Bible Society. The four Gospels will be sent in also so that we'll have them and the Acts printed in one volume. Please pray for these different projects, and especially for Beryl and the children, that the Lord will bless them and make them a blessing on the home front at Baboua.

TWENTY-FIVE
Molding

"Mold me and make me
After thy will
While I am waiting,
Yielded and still."

All during our missionary career we employed African help: cooks, a laundry-man, wood and water carriers, people for child-care. Early on, Pastor Anderson told me once: "Don't do anything yourself which an African could do because there are so many things they cannot do. So you need to give yourself as wholly as possible to those things." Much of the time, we would gather our house-help for morning devotions. Eventually, many of these men went onto attend Bible School, and some became catechists and pastors. We always employed men because the women were busy with their own families, cooking and carrying wood and water. Also, working for us became a man's career, and there was actually a certain amount of prestige connected with this domestic employment.

When we moved to Baboua at the beginning of our second term, we were accompanied by our cook, Garga, and his wife and two daughters. Now, after our conference, Garga announced that he had decided to remain in Meiganga. So, getting home to Baboua with a new baby, I was devoid of my experienced cook and had to hire and train a new one.

When Carole and Linnea were little, being bottle-fed, I could put them down with a bottle, propping it for them. But Wanda did not take to that. She wanted to be held while being fed. So I took to setting a book at a convenient angle on the desk, so I could read while feeding her. One of the books I read was E. Stanley Jones' "Christ and Human Suffering." The Holy Spirit was showing me many of my weaknesses and short-comings by directing me to this book, so I prayed: "Lord, cleanse me and mold me, whatever it may take."

During my pregnancy, and also after Wanda's birth, I was troubled with itching on the skin of my whole right thigh. In one of the letters I wrote while at Meiganga after the conference, I mentioned having an infected hangnail. I had several of these from time to time (undoubtedly due to a vitamin deficiency), and since I could not keep from itching the skin of my thigh, it was not surprising that I developed a humdinger of a boil (a furuncle). Using hot packs on it, I finally got it drained, and I seemed to be getting over it. But the infection went up into my hip in what became an extremely painful condition. Lloyd was at Abba doing translation work, so I had to be taking care of the children. Finally, I could bear it no longer. I sent a message to him: "You will have to choose between your wife and your work. I can't handle this alone any longer!"

We had no doctor on our field, and the nearest doctor at a neighboring mission was too far away: I couldn't bear to travel to see a doctor. We sent a letter to the French government doctor in Bouar, asking if he could come to see me, but he did not respond. Finally, Lloyd wired the missionaries in Bouar who had been sent by a Baptist mission in Sweden, asking if he might bring me to their mission in hopes of getting treatment by the government doctor. The Swedes did not have a doctor, either.

In the meantime, I spiked a temperature of 104, and had to stay in bed. Pastor Jergenson drove to Abba to get Frances Sterner, a new missionary nurse who was studying Gbaya with Madel. She agreed to go to Bouar with us, as the Swedish missionaries did not have a nurse in Bouar, either.

Lloyd set up a camp-cot in our panel truck, and I was carried out and placed on the cot for the 75-mile trip to Bouar. Word had gotten around among the Gbayas that Mrs. Sand was seriously ill and was being taken to Bouar. So, as I was carried out, the yard was full of weeping friends. I am sure they thought I was as good as dead! Our three little girls were left in the care of Marj Jergenson, and a few days later the Watnes came and took baby Wanda to stay with them.

We knew it would be a painful ride because the roads were bad. So Lloyd asked the French government official if the local "infirmier"—African nurse—could give me an injection of morphine. He (the nurse) not only gave me the shot, but he also went along.

The road was so bad that it took five hours for the trip, and the morphine wore off about half way. So I got the idea to sing. I sang hymns all the way, which somehow relieved the pain and served as quite a testimony to those in the car.

When we got to the mission in Bouar, I was carried in and laid on a camp-cot in the mission guest house. In tears, I asked, "Don't you have a bed?" In a short time, a native-made bed was brought, and I used that throughout my hospitalization there. (I have reason to believe that Mrs. Erickson, my hostess, gave up her own bed for my use.) The Ericksons, I learned later, were very short of funds at that time because he was building a beautiful church out of cut granite, and the money allotted him by the mission had run out. Not wanting to give up the project, he was using his private funds to pay the workmen.

After getting me settled at the mission in Bouar (with Franny as my nurse), Lloyd returned home and took care of Carole and Linnea.

When the French doctor at Bouar had examined me, he diagnosed my condition as osteomyelitis, and said I must take the first plane to Bangui, where there is a hospital with X-ray and surgical equipment. At first, we thought we would try to do that, but arrangements would have to be made, so we needed time to think and pray about it.

About a week later, Lloyd came to visit me. It was Sunday evening, and the Swedish missionaries at Doaka, the station about 20 miles from Bouar, came in for fellowship. Thankfully, they all spoke English. They chose to meet in my room, so that I could be included and we asked them to pray for my healing. They were men and women of faith, and they believed strongly in prayer for healing. So they prayed. During the prayer session, I experienced an itching sensation in the infected hip. Telling the group about this, I explained that the feeling was similar to what one feels when a wound is healing. We took that as a sign from the Lord that the healing process had begun. I think the Swedish missionaries were disappointed that I did not jump up and walk out, healed, but I accepted that small sign as an indication that the healing process had begun. Actually, it took a long time to accomplish a complete recovery, but it did come.

So the French doctor came, examined me, and prescribed a shot of penicillin daily. This penicillin was available at the local pharmacy, but no syringes nor needles were for sale. The Ericksons sent word to their colleagues at Doaka, and they sent one syringe with one large needle. Each day Franny gave me a shot of the penicillin, washing and sterilizing the syringe and needle. No disposables there! Finally, the needle got so dull that it just bent over, and that was the end of that! (Now, why did I not have Lloyd bring me syringes and needles from my supply at the dispensary in Baboua?

The French doctor also prescribed sulfathiazole tablets, one each hour! Finally, I began to hallucinate: I saw a spear come at me which just glanced off my shoulder. I also had nightmares: I dreamed that I murdered one of my best friends. So the doctor discontinued that medication. He felt frustrated, because he wanted to send me to the hospital in Bangui, the capital of the colony, but we had no money to make the trip. Also, didn't we believe that God was healing me?

At one time, the doctor told us that the abscess would have to be opened and drained. Franny and I were very apprehensive about that, but we agreed. He said he would come to do it the next afternoon. Come the designated time, he did not show! The next day when he came, he had a lame excuse that his car was not running. But Franny and I fully believed that God had hindered him. To this day, I am convinced that, if he had opened that hip, the condition would have become much more serious!

In the French colonies at that time, there were very few white people. Besides the colonial government officials, there were some Greek, Lebanese, and Portuguese business people, usually men with their families who kept small stores where they sold an amazing variety of goods: canned food items, yard goods, pots and pans, fish-hooks, building materials, etc. Of course, the French people had to have their cheese and wine. Once, we got some canned horse meat. It was delicious! There was an interesting bond among these white people. We were all classed as Europeans because Americans were in the minority. They all spoke French, some no better than I did. I remember a Portuguese businessman who came to see me while I was sick, bringing me one big, juicy apple. Apples don't grow in that part of Africa, so this had been imported, and was worth its weight in gold.

The Bible verse which the Lord gave me at that time was I Peter 5:10: "But may the God of all grace, who called us to His eternal glory by Christ Jesus, after you have suffered a while, perfect, establish, strengthen, and settle you." This was what I had asked for, so my convalescence period was a time of rich blessing. At that time, I had no pain, but I had become terribly weak and could not walk. I did a lot of reading, sitting up in bed. I remember Franny persuading me to inch my way to the end of the bed, to sit up and dangle, little by little, to increase my strength.

One day, when Lloyd came to see me, he brought Carole along. I asked why Linnea didn't come. She had said, "No, I can't go; somebody has to stay home."

TWENTY-SIX
Convalescence
"Great God Of Wonders"

After a month at the Swedish mission, with Franny Sterner doing 24-hour nursing duty in caring for me, the doctor said that I could return to our home in Baboua. How our friends, black and white, praised the Lord for my recovery! I still was extremely weak; when I was finally able to stand on the scale I weighed 122 pounds. My normal weight at that time was around 145 pounds. I could not walk from the bedroom into the dining-room, so our little girls and I worked out a system: getting out of bed, I would slide onto a chair. They would place another chair next to that, and I would slide onto it. They kept exchanging the chairs until I was situated next to the table. Fortunately, we had good house-help, so I wasn't required to clean house and cook, or supervise them. A wheelchair would have been helpful, though!

Since Mr. Gunderson, our Executive Director, had died earlier that year, and we had requested the ELC to take over our work, their Executive Director, Dr. Syrdal, came out to survey the field. So a special conference was called to meet in Meiganga. I was unable to attend the sessions, so the children and I stayed in Garoua-Boulai where we had a room at the mission station, and my meals were brought to me. Ingrid Hult had recently arrived in Cameroon and was getting established as the teacher at the American School. (It was during that school year that she became engaged—by correspondence—to Pastor Walter Trobisch, who was then in Germany. After school was out, she got a leave of absence and went to Germany to marry Walter. Her book, "On Our Way Rejoicing," tells of her experiences at that time, as well as what occurred during the subsequent years of the couple's missionary work.)[2]

In a letter to my mother written December 3, 1951:

---

[2] Ingrid Trobisch, *On Our Way Rejoicing* (Bolivar: Quiet Waters Publications, 2000).

I believe I wrote you of the Watnes' generous offer to take us to Elat (the Presbyterian Mission station where they have a good hospital) for the X-ray of my hip. (We could not drive our car at that time, because our tires were worn out.) Well, as the time drew nearer, I felt less and less like going, because my hip was so much better.

The Watnes came about 1:30 Monday afternoon, Nov. 26th. They were glad to hear that I was so much better, and were not sorry to give up the trip. They brought our Wanda baby back to us. She is just about the sweetest little thing I have ever seen! You know I didn't care to play with dolls when I was little, but now I enjoy my "real doll". She is nice and chubby now, very solid. She sits alone, but doesn't try to pull herself up yet. I'm glad as long as she doesn't, as there are so many more dangers when they get to that stage. She didn't know me when she came back, and the first evening she kept looking for Alma. But the next morning she was happier, and soon she began to play with her sisters. I'm afraid Alma and John thought their house pretty empty when they came home without her. John called her "Pebble," a take-off on Sand. They have a little orphan baby they are taking care of now, and Alma does dispensary work, too, so she will be too busy to be lonesome very long. (Their three children are at school at Garoua-Boulai, living in the dorm.)

TWENTY-SEVEN
Tchollire—Rei Bouba
"All Hail the Power Of Jesus' Name!"

For years, our mission had been praying for an opening to work in the great territory of the Moslem king, Rei Bouba. Again in 1952, it was decided that our family should go up there, camp at Tchollire, where the French government official had recently established a post. Hopefully, we could make contacts which would lead to opening a mission station there.

There were very few white people in Cameroon at that time— especially in the northern part of the country. But there were occasional tourists who came through, especially hunters, so the government had constructed guest houses, similar to those we had stayed in during previous trips in Africa.

At that time, we still had the maroon-colored International delivery truck that my Dad had provided for us in 1948, and Lloyd became an expert at packing all our travel equipment, as well as our family and our help into it. He had made a preliminary visit in April, when he obtained permission from the administrator to bring the family for a stay of about two months. He warned Lloyd that we must come before May 15th. The rivers in that area dry up during the rainless months of November to March. During those months, large mats are stretched across the sandy beds of the rivers so trucks can cross. But when the heavy rains come, usually by the middle of May, these "bridges" wash away, and transportation is cut off. He said that, when we had unloaded our camping equipment at the guest house in Tchollire, we should have to drive the car back across the river and leave it there until we should be ready to leave again. He told us that, after the water gets high, they expect to bring a ferry down from Garoua, so that should be our mode of exit. That never came about, so we crossed the river in dug-out canoes, having hitched a ride to the river with a French contractor who kept one truck on each side of the river. He did this so he could travel to Garoua for building supplies, which were then ferried across the river to be loaded on the second truck to haul to Tchollire.

The citizens of Tchollire, which in Fulani means "city of birds," were from several different ethnic groups, but all spoke some Fulani, which was the official market language. Lloyd had learned Fulani when he worked at Poli, so he handled it pretty well. He found a contingent of laborers who had migrated from the neighboring area of the Laka people. Many of them were Christians from the Baptist or Brethren Missions. They spoke the Sango language, which our Gbaya help from Baboua also understood, so they found friends there.

At one time, Lloyd made a contact with a Moslem leader who permitted us to join their worship on their holy day, which is Friday. Lloyd was invited to speak briefly, after which he led in prayer. They were very reverent, and, as he prayed, each man extended his two hands, as if he were expecting to receive something from God, whom they call Allah. It was very impressive to me. Five times every day, they go through their worship routine of a ceremonial washing with water which they carry around in a small tea-kettle. Then they bow down on a mat, facing Mecca, and pray in the Arabic language, prayers which they have memorized, and which many of them do not even understand.

Since I was neither doing medical work nor teaching during that visit to Tchollire, I was able to spend the time with my little girls: Carole almost six, Linnea, almost five, and Wanda, 11 months, just beginning to walk.

After this preliminary, exploratory visit to Tchollire, we returned to our home in Baboua.

TWENTY-EIGHT
Building the Bible School
"God's Word Is Our Great Heritage...."

The Bible School students and teachers had to work in very primitive conditions. Since this only made it more difficult to teach and to learn, we decided to make some improvements.

On June 29, 1950, Marge Jergenson wrote:

We are going to start building two or three months from now: a permanent Bible School. We must make kiln-dried bricks ... " (Connie made the 4-brick molds; the bricks laid out in the sun to dry, and then stacked in a kiln to be fired.)

Thinking back on this project almost 50 years later, I marvel to think of Conrad, a pastor who had grown up on a farm in Minnesota, being able to make and carry out such a project with no previous study or experience. It seems that he must have been inspired something like the various writers of Scripture were.

On September 13, 1951, he wrote:

Margie put out a workbook on the Gospel of John of over 100 pages. She has also produced Colossians, the first printing of that book in the mission (in Gbaya) which was translated by Madel Nostbakken. I (Conrad) am working on a workbook teaching the students how to write. Very few know how...and many can hardly read. I am also making a book for the recording of offerings in the native chapels in the out-stations, which will be the first of its kind; also another book for the listing of catechumens (those studying for baptism). I have been teaching every morning from 9 to 12, besides directing all the workmen on the station and supervising the building of the school. When we see the bricks for the Bible School, burned and awaiting construction, we thank God for the future we see in this kiln of bricks...This will give them a school like the Lutheran Bible Institute, at which God so blessed our own souls.

Marge's letter continues:

I have just finished typing the manuscript for the Catechism. The Africans are so hungry for anything in their own language. They were fighting in the kitchen over the discarded sheets on which I had made some errors, and which I had thrown in the waste basket.

Marge wrote in another letter of November 1952:

During this school year we have been doing the big task of earth moving to landscape the site. Our "earthmovers" are 4 Baboua Brand wheelbarrows which Connie made that have given excellent service on interchangeable mahogany axles. On Dec. 1 we break ground for the foundation. Most of the foundation rock has been dug and much of it sized. (Connie had to get permission from the government to dig and haul out the amount of rock which he would need for the foundation, as well as for the logs he would cut and haul out of the forest for lumber for the structure.) The building will contain one large classroom, two smaller classrooms, a library/ study room, and a small office for an African assistant. (One of the small side rooms eventually became a mimeograph room.)

To get the necessary logs from the forest, a road had to be cut and smoothed (somewhat) so the felled logs could be carried out. Africans have a wonderful system of carrying together. A leader called out: "eer-ya-ya" and the group respond, and then they lift together. They carried most of the logs out of the forest like that. The sawyers then dug a deep trench, and one ten-meter log was laid over it. Then, one man stood down in the trench, and the other above. Finally, synchronizing their movements, they would work through those immense logs, producing the hand-hewn lumber needed for the rafters, joists, and window frames. Some of the logs were hauled on the faithful, old mission truck to Garoua-Boulai, where they were cut into lumber for the building.

In February of 1953, Marge made this poignant entry:

Connie couldn't be with me for the birth of Stevie at Batouri, the Presbyterian Mission, because he needed to supervise the building of the Bible School...."(There was no doctor on our mission yet.) "Connie read books about how to build a fireplace, so that is coming along fine in the main classroom, and will be appreciated in the chilly wet season. Because of the brevity of time before we leave on furlough in May, Sig Larsen and Reubin Johnson will come to help with the roof construction by nailing down the aluminum sheets before the rains start.

Sand had to be hauled and sifted before the floors could be laid. All the cement had to be mixed by hand. Two weeks ago Connie was able to contact the Brethren Mission in Bozoum and hire their trained mason to lay the concrete floor and brick walls. He was the only skilled laborer we had. A trucker failed his promise to haul the cement up from the coast. If the French commandant hadn't given us from his own supply, the work would be at a standstill.

HOME-SCHOOLING

Today there is much talk (and controversy) over home schooling or private schools as alternatives to public school for one's children. Missionaries, as well as government and/or employees of corporations who work in foreign countries often had to resort to the education of their children in their homes. In fact, the Calvert System had long been the choice for mothers who may not have had education degrees, but wanted their children to get an American education while living abroad.

Carole was six years old; our mission had had a school for missionaries' children, but that year, there was no teacher available. So I ordered kindergarten and beginning materials for first grade and hoped that, having had experience in teaching, I should be able to home-school my two older girls.

But I was "Madame Doctah" and had a reputation for meeting the medical needs of young and old alike. So it turned out that, sure as I would sit down to try to teach my girls, someone would come to my back porch with a sick baby.

It was the feeling of our co-workers that we should take our furlough soon, and then, upon our return, start the work in the Rei Bouba territory, so there was the hope that our girls would then be able to get started in school in the U.S.

TCHOLLIRE AGAIN

Early in 1953, Lloyd went to Tchollire alone, hoping to build a simple dwelling where we, or some other missionary, could live.

The French government official designated an area well outside the city limits where the Mission should begin. (Years later, when we visited there, one of the African church leaders asked us why the mission was established so far from the center of the town.)

Lloyd appealed to the local chief to assign him some laborers to do the building. It would have to be done according to the traditional style: walls of mud reinforced with some rocks and capped with a grass roof.

But either the local Africans were suspicious of this new white man, or they were just not interested in work, so it took a long time to get a labor force to even get started. With everything being done by hand, many workers were needed. Finally, Lloyd was able to contact some expatriate laborers who had come from the neighboring Laka tribe in French Equatorial Africa (now known as the Central African Republic). He had met some of them when we visited there the year before.

In North Cameroon, house construction is done during the dry season when work will not be interrupted by rain. In Tchollire it was HOT at that time. The mission site was far from the guest house, so Lloyd set up his living quarters in the open, nearer to the site. Several years later, one of our co-workers, Mrs. Mathre, told us that the local Africans had decided that the reason Lloyd could sleep out in the open that way and not be in danger from lions, was that "the angels carried him away at night and brought him back in the morning!"

When the main house and kitchen were ready (openings in the walls served as windows—no frames, and of course, no glass), he left the construction of the second house to his work crew and started back to Baboua for his family. So we packed up again, with a better idea of what lay before us. We also had planned to leave from there for our furlough.

Included in our standard equipment were our mosquito nets, hung from the rafters, on supporting poles, over each bed. In this house, however, the nets not only kept out the mosquitoes, but also the numerous bats who had taken residence in the underside of our grass roof. And what about the open windows? At nightfall, two or three bundles of roof grass were leaned in front of each open-space window to provide privacy.

But the greatest problem we had was that of water. Here in the U.S., where we can simply turn on a faucet and have clean, safe, drinking water, we don't realize that many people in the world lack this very basic element. Because this is a vital health need, the government had hired men to dig wells in each part of the village. These wells were still open, about five or six feet in diameter, and twelve to fifteen feet deep. But the water level must have been very low because only a small amount of water would seep into the bottom of the well. Our water carriers would try to get to a well early in the morning to dip out for us what little had trickled in. As it was, they would walk from one well to another, and come back with only a bucket of very murky water.

I had prepared for this by buying filter candles, a cylindrical, plaster-like device with a length of red tubing extending from it. This filter was dropped into the very dirty water in a large clay pot. The tubing would then siphon the clean water into a bottle. But even after that, we would boil the water for drinking. For a while, we thought we could get by with using the unfiltered water for washing, but Linnea developed a skin rash from it, so we ended up filtering all the water. I had five of those filter candles, and I found myself spending much of my time cleaning them because after they had been in the murky water for a while, they became covered by thick, brown sludge which clogged the pores, so they no longer functioned.

We had brought our faithful Gbaya cook and house-boy with us, together with their wives and two daughters. How did we ever get all these people and baggage into our panel truck? They were indispensable, though, and Lloyd had become a "master packer," so we managed.

TWENTY-NINE
The Trobisches
"Jesus, I My Cross Have Taken"

When Ingrid Hult first came to Cameroon, she was stationed at Poli with Harriet Stovner and began to study the Fulani language. But then the mission needed her to teach the children of the missionaries at the American School in Garoua-Boulai, so her language study was interrupted.

After her marriage to Walter Trobisch in Germany, and after he was accepted by the ELC for missionary service in the Cameroon, they were notified that the mission wanted them to take up work at the recently opened station at Tchollire, in the Rei Bouba territory. They had hoped to spend some time in Meiganga for Fulani language study, but since we and our family were due for furlough, they were notified that they would have to study Fulani "on the job."

In her book "On Our Way Rejoicing," Ingrid gives a dramatic account of their arrival in Tchollire "after dark, and very tired, thirsty, and disillusioned."

Pastor Sand and his wife, a missionary couple who had come to get things ready for us, appeared out of the darkness. They had not expected us until morning. When we explained that our water canteens had been emptied during our journey, he produced a small pail of boiled water and offered it to us. It had a strange, smoky taste, but we gulped it greedily. At least it slaked our thirst. Lloyd told us we would be able to get water in the future from a water hole about half a mile from the village. But we would have to be careful not only to boil the water, but to filter it first ...

After only a few days with the Trobisches, we packed up to leave for furlough. Our French builder friend kindly conveyed us, our baggage, and our Gbaya helpers to the river. When we had crossed, Lloyd went to start our red International delivery truck which he had left on the Garoua side. But, to his dismay, he found that children had been playing around the truck, removing the cover of the gas tank and running sand into it. So, several hours were lost while Lloyd and the others cleaned that out. There must have been a supply of clean gasoline available because he eventually got the car started, and we were on our way.

Down the highway, just a graveled road, we came to Gode, where Pastor Mathre was waiting for us. This meant another long delay, as the two men evidently had many weighty matters to discuss. Finally, we were on our way again, but when we arrived at the Benoue River, across from Garoua, it was pitch dark, and the ferry was not available. Lloyd and his Gbaya helpers walked along the bank until they found some fishermen. One of them agreed to take us all across the river in one of their canoes. Lloyd rented a bicycle from an African and rode up to the Lutheran Brethren Mission. I remember lying on the warm sand, suffering from a severe headache while we awaited his return. Finally, Lloyd returned with a young Frenchman whom he had found at the mission. None of the missionaries were at home, but the visitor had his truck, and he kindly transported all of us across town to the Mission. Fortunately, he had a key to the guest house, where we practically fell into the beds and were off to sleep in no time flat! Of course we had our cook with us, so the fact that our hosts were absent did not constitute a problem.

We had a couple days of rest while we waited for the weekly departure of the plane for Europe. Our Gbaya friends had never seen a plane up close, so it was a great day for them when they actually got to see the inside of the one which flew us out. We gave them money to take the bus back to Meiganga after we had left.

THIRTY
Furlough In Moorhead
"Savior, Like A Shepherd Lead Us"

Arriving in Minneapolis, as usual, we went to Lloyd's sister, Borghild's house. One of the first items of business was to find an inexpensive but reliable used car. Then, we drove down to visit my family in Iowa. We had been assigned to spend our furlough in the mission residence in Moorhead, Minnesota, so that was our next stop.

Soon it was time to register Carole and Linnea for school, and though they were both in first grade, they were assigned to different rooms, which we felt was wise. There were many things for our children to learn besides the 3 R's. Linnea's teacher told me once that, as she was reading to the children, the story included something about being in the basement. Linnea asked, "A basement, that is what?"

Wanda was at home with Mommy. One day, a neighbor lady came to ask if I would open our home to a Child Evangelism meeting. Several preschool children congregated with Wanda and me. During that time, she memorized John 8:12, which she stored up in her "memory bank."

During that fall, I heard about a one month's course in Tropical Nursing which was available at the College of Medical Evangelists in Loma Linda, CA. I had felt very inadequate for the work I was doing in the dispensary which I operated at every station where we worked. So, I contacted the Mission Board of the ELC and got their permission to take that course with all expenses paid. Lloyd agreed to stay home with the girls during the time I should be traveling and taking the course.

The most valuable training I received during that time was the use of a microscope. When we returned to Africa, Dr. Eastwold gave me one, which made it possible for me to diagnose the many intestinal parasites which are so prevalent among the rural African population.

Easter fell on the weekend when I was half-way through that course. Lloyd's brother, Morris, and his wife were living in Hollywood at that time, so I took a bus in to visit them. They took me to the Easter sunrise service at the Hollywood Bowl when the Waldorf Choir sang there.

When I returned after completing my course to the Minneapolis-St. Paul airport on May 1st, it was snowing!! I took a bus back to Moorhead, arriving there in the middle of the night. I tried to telephone Lloyd from the bus depot, but got no answer, so, when the cab driver brought me to our house, I asked him to wait to see that I got in. We had a hard time rousing Lloyd to open the door!

Some time during that furlough, we met Oscar Noss' older sister, Bertha, who lived in St. Paul. Bertha was an excellent seamstress, and she was inspired to do advance sewing for our girls. She made many cotton dresses in different sizes, which the girls eventually grew into. She also had a contact with some company where she got bias tape seconds, good quality tape, but with flaws. She gave me a good-sized box of that tape, as well as decorative rickrack. There was so much in the box that I had tape for a long time. Later, I got the idea to use tape for making letters on banners. Today, when women make banners, they cut the letters out of felt and glue them onto the background. I drew my letters on the background first, then stitched the tape on to form the letters, using my sewing machine. In the little Hausa stores, one could usually buy plain blue or green wash-fast cotton yard-goods which I used for the background of banners.

During that furlough in Moorhead, a letter came from Laura Burton in Meiganga, informing us that "our beloved Paul Sippison, the very dedicated catechist at Baboua, who had been chosen to study with Pastor Trobisch in Tchollire, with the goal of ordination into the ministry, had been suddenly killed by lightning in the village of Zusami, near Meiganga." It seems that he was supposed to have met up with Andre Garba in Meiganga, and the two of them were to have gone to take training to become pastors. As it turned out, Andre Garba did eventually get some training, and he was the first man to be ordained in the Church in our mission. As the Gbayas are extremely superstitious about lightning, there was a great deal of suspicion and hard feeling following this tragic death.

THIRTY-ONE
Our International Travelall
"Children Of the Heavenly Father"

Back when I was preparing to go to Africa the first time, Pastor Reisem of the Lutheran Brethren Church, rural Joice, had informed the editor of the periodical THE MORNING GLORY of my plans and preparations to go to Africa with the Gunderson Mission. An elderly reader in Salem, Oregon noticed this, and responded by sending me a gift of $100. I had since kept in touch with him, and from time to time he would send money. He had been a tailor, but had moved into a nursing home. About the time we were preparing to return to Africa in 1954, Mr. Anderson died, and we learned that he had bequeathed the remainder of his savings, $4000, to us to be used for a car to take back to Cameroon. The Home where he had lived contested the will, but we were awarded the money. We contacted a dealer in New Brighton who gave us a good deal on the purchase of a green International Travelall for $4000!

Putting a luggage rack on the top, we loaded all of our baggage, and drove to the East Coast, where we boarded the S.S. African Dawn, which brought us to Douala. We drove up-country, arriving at our old home in Baboua in the Central African Republic.

There were still many African children who had no access to school, so, again I worked out a teaching system, using flash cards set in grooves on a board which our African carpenter constructed for me. Joseph Moury, one of our catechists, took over most of the teaching of reading with some supervision and encouragement from me.

The Jergensons had received a large shipment of mill-end paper from our publisher friend, Gordon Aasgaard, in Lake Mills, Iowa, and they shared some of it with me for this project. Marj used much of the mill-end paper for mimeographing little booklets—the strips of paper were not all the same size, so it took some ingenuity on her part to find enough of one size to put out an edition of booklets.

Carole and Linnea went to Garoua-Boulai, to enter second grade at the American School there. It did not bother them at all to go away to school and stay in the dormitory because they got to be with other American children. They did enjoy playing with African children at our station, but school was more interesting.

Miss Ruth Johnson, sister of Reubin Johnson, who taught the American School in Garoua-Boulai for two years, writes in a form letter for Christmas, 1953:

> My first Christmas away from home was spent in Africa. Seems hard to believe, but I'm forced to reality when we hear the screams of and see the tracks of leopards. For snowy hills we substitute burning grass fires to offset our horizon. We decorate palm trees instead of pine. Of course we know that the true spirit and joy of Christmas is found not in snow, Christmas trees, etc., but the glad realization that Jesus, God's Son, came to the world ... Christmas will have more meaning for me this year as we join the natives in singing "Joy to the World, the Lord has come!" Life in Africa is so interesting, and every day brings new adventures. My first Monday morning we were interrupted by the announcement that a leopard had been trapped and the natives were outside with it, doing their victory dance around the body that was tied to a pole. Its mouth and right paw were covered with leaves, because they believe that the evil spirit dwells there and they fear he may still cause harm.

About her school house she wrote:

> We consider our school house very modern in an African sort of way...John Watne made lovely desks. The mission board sent out blackboards, wall maps and athletic equipment...We have six grades with a span from first through ninth, which, of course, keeps us going at quite a busy pace all day long. We begin classes at eight o'clock each morning and have a siesta at noon. We dismiss around five o'clock. We spend the next hour in walking or bicycling, but we dare not venture too far from home, since total darkness falls around six. Out here you live very close to nature. The crickets seem to sing louder, the moon and stars seem brighter, and the sunset so much more beautiful. The climate here is perfect, with very cool mornings and evenings. The average day time temperature is between 70 and 80 degrees, perhaps slightly warmer in the direct sunlight. Of course, we always have the danger of snakes, and we never venture out after dark without our flash-lights. It is good to know that we are constantly under the Lord's protecting care.

About her trip coming to Africa she wrote:

> It was like taking an imaginary trip in a geography book. Only it became real when the plane started rocking over the Atlantic Ocean. It took me about a week from the time I left Minneapolis, until I reached N'Gaoundere, the nearest airport. Included in that week is five days in Paris seeing Versailles, Eiffel Tower, the Arch of Triumph, and hundreds of other historical monuments. You know there is something interesting about the old and the

past, but I think I prefer the present and the future. It doesn't have that musty smell!! Traveling has made me thankful that I am an American. After boarding the plane in Paris, we were soon swooping our way across France, stopping at Marseille. Crossing the Mediterranean Sea, we stopped in hot, humid Tripoli for refueling. It was wonderful to arrive safely in N'Gaoundere and see my brother Reubin and family again. I plan to spend Christmas vacation with them at their new station, Doumba ...

I can't begin to tell you all about life here. Guess I've left out things like the wildcat's nest we found a few feet from the schoolhouse, and other happenings. We solicit your prayers for our school and the mission work here. We know that no good thing is accomplished outside of His grace and will.

During the months of April and May, 1955, Lloyd and I substituted as house-parents at the American School while the Michelsons were in N'Gaoundere for the birth of their baby. Back in the Baboua district, we assisted the Jergensons with district conferences, a sort of refresher course for the catechists in charge of the little congregations throughout the district. I participated in some of these conferences by giving health/hygiene lectures. We had discovered that, among the carry-over ideas which plagued the Gbaya Christians was their superstitious fear of death. They had no concept of diseases being caused by germs, poor sanitation, infections carried by flies, and the very prevalent intestinal parasites. So I gave some illustrated lectures at conferences, as well as at the Bible School. Paul Darman, one of the earliest pastors, who later became the Church President, and in that capacity traveled to Europe and the U.S., told me that my health talks were so liberating, because now the people could refer to the fly, for instance, as the "widua" (the goat, or evil spirit) who caused illness and death, instead of trying to determine which human enemy might have caused it.

THE HUNTER WITHOUT A GUN

From an article written for publication at home:

Lloyd was Mission Superintendent for ten years: 1948-1958, but that did not mean that we lived at a central point. If there was a vacancy at one of the stations, we moved. During one 5-year term, we moved five times. Also, those were years of great expansion in our mission, so he and the "building committee" took many trips to select and survey concessions to apply for government permission to establish a station.

During those years also, the mission extended from Cameroon into the western part of the Central African Republic, because the Gbaya people had not been limited to artificial geographical borders.

So Lloyd tried to get home as often as possible. One night, driving along a dirt road with high grass on both sides, the lights of his International Trave-lall fell upon a deer with her fawn, standing right in the middle of the road, obviously blinded by the lights. Some of his passengers saw them, too, so they shouted: "Step on it, Pastor! Get them." So he did, and when he backed up, he realized that he had killed them both. The next day, when the help butchered the doe, they discovered that she also was carrying young, so he had actually gotten three animals.

Our kerosene-operated refrigerator had a fairly large freezing compartment, but we always shared the kill.

Many of the animals who roamed the country roads at night were of the cat family, which we did not eat, but the Gbayas appreciated any source of protein. It happened so often that Lloyd would just swerve a bit to run over an animal that the Gbayas dubbed him "the hunter without a gun." And of course he never traveled alone, so his passengers got the benefit of his success.

At Baboua, there were no other missionaries' children, so our little girls played with the Gbaya children, especially our cook's daughters and those of the resident catechist. Some of the village children would come to play, too. One day, I found that they had taken our big, native-made cane chairs out on the veranda, tipped them end-to-end, covered them with blankets, and made cozy houses of them. Then, on the edge of the concrete porch, they lined up the children for "school." One day, I discovered that Carole had taken our Egermeier's Bible Story book out there, found a story with a picture, and was telling the story in Gbaya, perfectly. And I had been discouraged because they seemed so squirmy and inattentive during our family devotions!

When they were little, I made a practice of singing them to sleep with the hymn: "Children of the Heavenly Father."

THIRTY-TWO
Fulani Language Study
"On Eagles' Wings"

At our mission conference early in 1955, it was decided that Lloyd and I should move to Poli to work there, though he would continue to serve as Mission Superintendent. In the Poli district, many different languages are spoken, but Fulani is the lingua franca, understood more or less, in the simple form used in the market, by most of the people. Lloyd had already learned Fulani and used it when he worked in Poli before our marriage, so I felt that I needed to learn it, too. So, because several new missionaries would be coming, some of whom would be stationed in the North where Fulani is used, it was decided that Ruth Christiansen should give me lessons in Fulani.

For this reason, we moved from Baboua, in the Central African Republic, to Meiganga: our three girls, our white (French) dog, Toplette, and a little black kitten, Toutnoir (all black).

I have never gotten settled in a new home so quickly, as I needed to help welcome the new missionaries who were coming from France. Also, there were several other veteran workers returning from furlough in the U.S., coming by way of France. Among the new missionaries were Ted and Dorothy Ellingboe.

Dorothy was Ruth Christiansen's niece. They, and the other eleven new missionaries, had been studying in France. Ted had written that he had arranged plane passage for the whole group from Paris to Garoua. When I heard that they all planned to come on the same plane, I objected, and we wrote to him: "You should not all come on the same plane. What if it goes down, and we lose all of you?" But he wrote back, saying that the booking was final and not to worry.

Several of us had this same premonition, and we prayed much for God's protection over this precious group of missionaries.

Later, Dorothy wrote about the experience, entitled "Miracle at Fort Lamy, Africa." Here is an excerpt:

I thoroughly enjoyed the plane ride, and the good fellow-ship of the other missionaries. The day and night passed so quickly, I could hardly believe it when Ted said, "Brace your feet, honey, we'll be landing soon." The only problem then seemed to be that at that moment there was a storm swirling around our plane, with rain and wind pounding the windows. We continued to descend, downward toward the runway. As I looked out, instead of seeing the runway, all I could see through the rain was a native village and Africans running helter-skelter from their grass-roofed houses. Yes, we were so close to the ground, we could see their faces as they ran, full of terror. At the time, we were not aware that the fierce storm had taken our plane like a toy and was about to deposit us right in the middle of the village. Suddenly, the plane shook violently, and, as the plane's motors roared, things were becoming in disarray inside the plane. It had been losing oxygen, and the hostesses were running back and forth with oxygen, especially for babies, and other hostesses were busy supplying passengers with throw-up bags.

After shaking for some 'long' minutes, the plane which was (to quote the captain later) "about to crash", was suddenly beginning to gain altitude again. We all know that this Scripture was the answer: Deuteronomy 33:17: "The eternal God is your refuge, and underneath are the EVERLAST-ING ARMS; He will thrust out the enemy from before you, and He will say: ... DESTROY!"

Yes, the plane soared upward, and soon we were above the turbu-lence...About two hours later the plane arrived at the Garoua airport, down country, closer to our mission. As the plane gave up its weary passengers, we looked like quite a motley group of travelers. We were all praising the Lord. Even our pilot learned about our powerful God, as he said, "I've never come so close to crashing in my many years as a pilot...IT MUST HAVE BEEN SOME KIND OF A MIRACLE!"

At 6:00 a.m. that same morning, at the very time we were going through this storm, my aunt Ruth Christiansen, at Meiganga, awoke with a heavy burden to pray for that plane. Getting out of bed, she immediately knelt and cried out to the Lord: "Lord, I know there is something wrong with that plane; I don't know what it is, but I know that you do, and I trust you to deal with whatever it is, and bring them all here safely." Yes, Satan would have loved to have destroyed that plane and all the missionaries on board, but P.T.L.,(Praise the Lord!) his best plans were as nothing against the great power of our God!

For our Fulani lessons, Ruth was assisted by the Fulani teacher, Modibo Abbo, who was also helping her with her translation of the Bible into the Fulani language.

Carole and Linnea were back in school at Garoua-Boulai, and Wanda was having a good time playing big sister to the many or-phan babies who were under Aunt Pearl's care. Since I had learned to use the microscope, I helped Laura with her dispensary work by doing lab work in the afternoons. She was treating about a hundred patients a day, with four African assistants. I especially remember one patient who came from Djohong, and had been to N'Gaoundere to seek treatment. The medical workers there had not found the cause of his problem. Shaking hands with him, I had noticed how cold and clammy his palms were. I checked his stool specimen several times, and finally substantiated my suspicion that he was suffering from schistosomiasis (also called bilharzia), a parasitic infestation acquired by bathing in water infected by the larvae a this particular kind of worms.

Laura had the medication he needed: injections which were very painful and must be taken three times a week for six weeks. Though unpleasant, the treatment is generally successful. (Then, of course, one has to be careful not to become re-infected.)

During our stay in Meiganga, Dorothy and I both discovered that we were pregnant; her daughter Beth was born a short time after the birth of our son Mark.

THIRTY-THREE
Poli
"Lead, Kindly Light"

Coming to live in Poli brought back many memories for Lloyd. After having worked in the Gbaya area for about five years and gaining a good command of the language. He and Andrew Okland had written a Gbaya version of Luther's Small Catechism, which became almost a Miniature Bible for the Gbayas because they included so many Bible verses which had not yet been printed. Then, when Rudolph Stephenson came to the field, the missionaries decided that Lloyd should move to Poli to live and work with him. So, the two of them set about learning the Fulani language. They had been most successful in reaching a group of teen-age boys from the Namdji tribe The missionaries later learned that those tribes people preferred to be called Dowayo, as Namdji was a derogatory title conferred on them by the ruling Fulani. Namdji means "grinders." In preparation for Christmas festivities in 1942, the missionaries translated Bible verses about light and taught them to these boys.

The Dowayo were animistic and superstitious, living in fear of the numerous spirits whom they thought lived in certain large trees and/or rocks. Unaware of this, the men cut down a large tree which the people thought was the abode of an especially powerful evil spirit. So they were filled with fear when the witch doctor announced that the spirits would retaliate by taking the life of someone. Shortly after that, Ahnru, one of the boys, became seriously ill. As he was dying, he looked upward with ecstasy, crying out: "Take me to the CITY OF LIGHTS!"

Some time later both the missionaries went to Meiganga, the main station farther south, to attend the mission conference. After the conference, Pastor Sand was asked to stay on to work with Andrew Okland on a translation project. But Pastor Steffenson felt constrained to return to the work at Poli. Not long after, the missionaries at Meiganga received a telegram from the French government official saying that Pastor Steffenson had been taken seriously ill and had been transported to the government hospital in Garoua. At that time, the hospital was poorly equipped; there was no electricity. Pastor Steffenson's African attendant spent the night sitting beside him in his room because of this. In the middle of the night, Pastor Steffenson spoke to him: "Dawson, did you not blow out the light?" Dawson said he had. "But I see a bright light—children playing and singing in the streets!" Then he died. The French administrator in Garoua arranged for a funeral. There were no missionaries present there then, but there was an African church leader at the Lutheran Brethren mission who conducted the service.

Upon our arrival to work there, Lloyd found that the situation had changed a great deal; the church had grown. We joined our new missionaries, Pastor Bob and Joyce Martinson. Joyce was a nurse, and she had already begun to do dispensary work. When they were anticipating departure for their first furlough, Joyce was worried about having to do speaking in churches while on deputation. She was a nurse, not a pastor!

I told her not to worry: "You have something to say!"

While we lived at Poli and Lloyd was still Field Superintendent, he was away from home most of the time. Wanda was our only child at home, so she went about with me a great deal when I went to visit patients in their villages. I used to call her "my little shadow."

One warm day, the two of us went for a walk down to a little stream near the mission. It looked so clean and cool, so I let Wanda wade a while. Then my eyes lit on some small black snails on a rock. Schistosoma!! The snails are vectors for the larvae, the intermediate phase in the metamorphosis of the bilharzie. When a person wades in the water, these tiny larvae penetrate the skin and get into the blood-stream which takes them (usually) to the intestines. When mature, they pass eggs—microscopic, but with a telltale thorn on one side which, when passed in the feces, will show up under the microscope. The bilharzie worms lay hundreds of eggs. The thorns on these eggs pierce the insides of the intestines, so the infected patient will pass stools that have a characteristic fresh blood stain on them. I got Wanda out of the water as quickly as possible, but the damage had been done.

Almost two years later, after we moved to Djohong, I noticed blood in her stools, so I checked with the microscope and was horrified to find the very distinctive eggs, with a thorn on the side which were an indication that she had the parasites. When we brought her to Garoua-Boulai to start school, and I told the doctor what I had found. He said, "Take her home and give her the treatment yourself. It would be too hard on her to have another nurse give her those painful injections." Also, it would have been very hard for the nurse to do it.

THIRTY-FOUR
Baby Boy Born!
"O Master, Let Me Walk With Thee"

Because of road conditions in our part of Africa, doctors advised pregnant women to come to the hospital two or three weeks before the due date. I had jokingly told the doctor: "I have such long, slow labor that I think I can stay home until the first contraction." I really did not intend to do that though. We were planning to leave Poli two weeks before Mark was due, but about four o'clock that morning, I was wakened by unmistakable discomfort. I sent Lloyd to tell Joyce, who came to check on me. She kindly made all the last minute preparations for the journey. It was time for Carole and Linnea to go back to Garoua-Boulai to school, so we had been getting all their things lined up for that trip, too.

We got on our way in good time, and, all the way from Poli to N'Gaoundere, I was having contractions every ten minutes, but they were not hard. We arrived there late afternoon, and I reported to Dr. Eastwold. Lloyd and the girls set up in the guestroom where we were to stay. I stayed at the hospital that night, but, as nothing was happening, I walked back to the doctor's house and spent the day relaxing there. After supper, it was evident that things were happening in earnest, so we went to the hospital again. Mrs. Eastwold had special ability in coaching a mother in breathing during a delivery, known as the Lamaze system, so she took up her position there. Laura happened to be there, too, as well as Myrtle Noss, the regular nurse at the hospital, so there was quite a welcoming committee. At eleven o'clock that Saturday night, Aug. 18, 1956, Mark backed into the world and promptly sprayed the ceiling!

Everything went well. The girls got to see their brother before they went back to school, so everyone was happy. On his eighth day, we walked to the Norwegian church where Mark was baptized by Pastor Endreson, with our co-workers, Oscar and Martha Noss, as sponsors.

One of our co-workers had an errand to Baboua a day or two after Mark was born, so the folks there got the news. Accordingly,

Marge Jergenson fashion, we received a telegram: BUBBLING BECAUSE BABY BOY BORN...BABOUAITES!

In his capacity as Field Superintendent, Lloyd was always available to both Gbaya and Fulani-speaking people. So, the day we were preparing to return to Poli, we didn't get off until late afternoon. We had wired the Martensons that we planned to come. Darkness fell when we were still on the main road, and we were going at a fairly good clip, when, coming over a hill, we ran smack into some deep ruts in the road. The jolt sent a piece of baggage flying over our heads to hit the rearview mirror on the windshield. No doubt about it: we were there to stay the rest of the night!

It was rainy season, and hot, so we soon found ourselves surrounded by mosquitoes. Wanda was lying in the crib which was just behind Lloyd's seat, but she was restless, so she would not keep the mosquito net over her. I was holding baby Mark, and Lloyd used his hat to fan the swarms of mosquitoes away from him. It was a long night! As to be expected, Wanda came down with a bout of malaria about a week later. Mark did not.

In the morning, Lloyd found an African who consented to walk cross-country to Poli to notify Bob Martenson of our plight. In the meantime, Lloyd walked on ahead, around a slight curve, and found about a dozen trucks mired in. Finally a crew of friendly Africans dug our car out of the mud and helped Lloyd drive it up on the bank and around the trucks that were stuck there. We finally got home about noon that day. The runner Lloyd had paid to bring the message to the Martensons had not arrived, so they were surprised but pleased at our arrival.

THIRTY-FIVE
Christmas At Poli, 1956
Lee Caps
"Hark The Herald Angels Sing!"

Grandma Ramsey was wonderful about buying and mailing gifts to us, especially for Christmas. Usually, the packages took a long time to reach us, but one year it came early. She had found a carton labeled LEE CAPS into which she packed her gifts. It must have come in November, because it seemed that the girls had to wait a dreadfully long time to open it. I set the package on top of a tall cupboard, and often they would read that caption: LEE CAPS!

I don't remember their begging to open the package early. When Christmas finally arrived, we discovered that the box held a beautiful doll for each of the girls. Grandma had sewn underwear, slips, dresses, and dark red coats and caps for each doll. In fact, Mom so hated to see naked dolls that she had stitched the underwear securely onto each doll's body, so it would be almost impossible to remove! Those dolls moved about with us wherever we went as long as we lived in Africa. They did eventually get the underwear off, for I have pictures of them giving those dolls baths, and Wanda, later, wearing her replica uniform of a Swedish Hospital student nurse, giving her doll a hypo, with Allen looking on with a pained expression on his face! Later, we ordered buggies for Carole and Linnea's dolls. At one time when I visited them in their dorm room, the buggies were full of the clean underwear which they had failed to put away in their clothes closets.

From a letter written to my parents on January 12,1957:

Our Poli Christmas began on Dec. 15, as the Martensons and the African school teachers here had trained the children to give a simple Christmas pageant. (They LOVE to do anything dramatic!) They enjoyed the costumes Joyce improvised out of bathrobes, old curtains, towels, and old sheets. They took their presentation to several of the nearby villages and gave the program of Bible readings, pantomime, and singing.

On Tuesday, Dec. 18th, we Sands (Lloyd, Beryl, Wanda and Mark) left Poli about four p.m., reaching N'Gaoundere about ten that night. We were given lodging at the Eastvold home. The next morning the doctor performed two surgical operations and numerous other routine tasks, and that afternoon, after establishing their two little girls at the home of one of the Norwegian missionaries, they accompanied us on our trip to Garoua-Boulai to be present at the annual Christmas program presented by the American School. This is not only a time of great joy for the children, but the one time, outside of our annual conference, when most of us count on seeing almost all the rest of the missionary family.

The programs presented by the children are always good, always a bit different from that of the year before, even though the theme is the same ageless Christmas story. This year, besides the ten children from our own mission, we also have three boys and a girl from the Lutheran Brethren Mission farther north in Cameroon. In true Erickson tradition, they all have good singing voices, so they were a real asset to the program. We thought our two-day trip was tiring, but they (the Ericksons) had to travel four long days each way, taking their children home for the holidays, and then bringing them back again when school began. The Ernest Ericksons came down for them, and the Bennet Ericksons brought them back after vacation.

For us, one of the high-lights of the program was the trio sung by our three blondes. Wanda carried the melody without a fault; Carole took the alto, and Linnea the high tenor. Their voices blended so well that everyone tried in vain to figure out who was singing each part. Wanda is eagerly awaiting the time when she will be a regular member of the school chorus.

Back at Poli, we had our family Christmas on Monday evening, and then the church program on the twenty-fifth. The next day the Ernest Johnsons from Tchollire brought the Ellingboes and Harriet Stovner over for a visit. The day after, Lloyd, Ted Ellingboe, Ernest Johnson, and Harriet Stovner, left for a meeting at N'Gaoundere. Helen Johnson and Dorothy Ellingboe and Baby Betty Ann stayed on with us. When Lloyd returned from the meeting at N'Gaoundere, he brought the Eastwold family—all seven—for a week's vacation. We surely enjoyed having them. That same day, Dec. 31st, the Tchollire folks left, as they expected the Nosses to visit them on New Year's Day. Nosses came here on the 2nd, and the next day we took them out to the Faro River for a picnic. There is a game reserve there, and often one sees deer, wild pigs, hippo, and many kinds of monkeys and birds.

On Sunday afternoon, Jan. 6th, Lloyd took the Eastwolds back to N'Gaoundere, and the next day went on to Garoua-Boulai, bringing Carole, Linnea, Conrad and Barbara Eastwold back to school.

Obviously, our car got a lot of mileage put on it. At one time, while we were at Poli, Lloyd got a telegram from Dr. Eastwold saying something to this effect: "Get your brakes repaired without delay!" The road north of N'Gaoundere included several miles of rapidly descending hairpin turns where good brakes were essential!

Our second year at Poli was one of firsts for Mark: his first step, his first tooth, his first haircut—events to photograph and remember. Our house help at that time spoke several different languages, so Mark was hearing and learning smatterings of Namdji, Fulani, Gbaya, Sango, and, of course, English. Like all missionary children, he was quick to recognize people from these varying ethnic backgrounds, and to give the appropriate greeting when they came to our door.

As usual, wherever we lived, I kept a dispensary. One day a Fulani-speaking man brought his poor little donkey. A hyena had eaten off a big hunk of its rump. How could I bandage that? I dusted the open wound with a lot of sulpha powder and tried to protect it from the ever-present flies. What happened? I never saw it again.

When Don and Grace Flaten joined us at Poli, I was asked to teach them the Fulani language. Of course they went onto surpass me in becoming experts in the use of Fulani, but at least I gave them their start.

One day, when both of our husbands were away, a man came from a village some twenty miles away, asking me to come to get his mother who had such a bad sore she could not walk in to Poli. Since our car was gone, Grace kindly agreed to take me and the supplicant to his town. She drove their English Land Rover.

When we arrived at the village, a sorry sight met our eyes. Not only was this one woman afflicted with a bad sore, but most of the population was sitting around in various stages of pain. Their village was situated on the banks of a river from which they drew their water supply. The problem? A small water flea, which they could even have strained out of their water, using a piece of cloth. This flea, when swallowed, goes through a·metamorphosis in the stomach, turning into larvae, then into a worm which finds its way in the blood stream. Usually it would lodge in one of the capillaries in a foot, or maybe a hand, or, worse yet—and quite often—into the eyes, causing what is known as "river blindness" because it happens to people who live along a river. This Guinea worm, then, produces a swelling in the flesh which eventually pops open, and the head emerges. The people know that they cannot remove the worm immediately. They will attach it to a small piece of bamboo, and, as it emerges, they wind it onto the stick. If the worm breaks off, the part which is left in the flesh causes an infection and a painful ulcer. Some of those people in that village had several of these ulcers in various parts of their bodies.

What a miserable lot! I tried to tell them that the solution to the problem was simple sanitation. Boiling the water would be the best. This condition is fairly common in remote areas in Africa. Fortunately, in some places, aid groups have come in and dug wells for these people.

THIRTY-SIX
Move Again—To Djohong
"For Those Tears I Died"

Conference time always got to be fruit-basket upset time.

As our terms were for five years, with one year of furlough between, when we were leaving, another family would be moved in to
replace us. As Lloyd and I could speak either Gbaya or Fulani, we
were available to work at any one of our stations. Consequently,
during this one five-year term, we moved five times.

We had packed up, and were about to move to Djohong, when,
early that morning, before we got up, a Frenchman came to our
door with the message: "Mr. Johnson (Ernie) at Tchollire, asked
me to come to tell you that Mrs. Johnson just died." Of course we
thought such a sudden death had to be a heart attack, but we found
out later that it was a ruptured ectopic pregnancy. The message was
also relayed to Don and Grace Flaten, so they went immediately to
Tchollire, where Don performed the funeral. Later a memorial dispensary was built next to Nurse Helen's grave.

In his distress and grief, Ernie just jumped into his pick-up truck
and followed us to Djohong. He helped us unload and do some
unpacking there, and then went on to visit some of the other missionaries. He finally returned to his lonely house in Tchollire,
where the Lord brought him comfort, and where he gave himself
to his ministry of teaching young African men to serve the Lord by
way of auto mechanics and carpentry at the Industrial School
which he built there in response to the dictates of Lamido Rei
Bouba, whose agreement to the establishment of a mission station
was contingent upon our mission providing that kind of training
for some of his subjects. Later, as these young men went back to
their villages, ostensibly as mechanics, they also unofficially shared
their Christian faith, so that, in time, over 100 villages in the Rei
Bouba territory became Christian. They also learned that the Christian life was not easy. Many of the church buildings were burned by
rabid Moslem soldiers in the service of the King. In time, however,

the Constitution of Cameroon declared religious liberty, so further persecution of that nature was prohibited.

Later, Ernie married Evelyn Jolson, who had spent the first part of her missionary career teaching at the American School in Garoua-Boulai.

FROM DJOHONG to GAROUA-BOULAI

Though we moved into the Johnson house and got into the work at the Doumba station, our stay there was to last only four months. At the mission conference, Ted Ellingboe was elected Field Superintendent to replace Lloyd. The Michelsons, who had been in Garoua-Boulai, were sent to replace us in Djohong, and we just exchanged houses with them, moving into their residence in Garoua-Boulai. Being freed from the constant travel which Field Superintendent had required, Lloyd was now, at last, in full-time translation work. Mr. Gunderson, the founder of our mission, had originally reduced the Gbaya language to writing. Several books of the Bible had been translated and most of them had been run off on the trusty(?) old ABDick mimeograph that Arthur and Bernice Anderson had struggled to keep going, usually with a minimal supply of paper. Several small editions had been printed in the U.S., paid for by friends of the missionaries. In order to work with Lloyd on this project, Madel Nostbakken and her Gbaya assistant, Solomon Mamadou, moved from Abba to concentrate on preparing the manuscript of the Four Gospels and Acts to be printed.

Working in Garoua-Boulai meant that our children could live with us while going to school. We were quite a group of missionaries on the station at that time, so we had good fellowship, especially at our Sunday evening gatherings when we, of course, used English—in contrast with the church services which were all in Gbaya or French.

I decided to have all the missionaries over to our house for Christmas dinner. Having read in old English stories of the delicacy, a suckling pig, roasted and served with an apple in its mouth, I decided to try that. I had bought a young pig from an African in town, but wondered what kind of a roaster would accommodate that? I had our cook build a fire in the backyard, and I found a wash boiler in which I roasted it. I got quite a sunburn myself, checking on my roast in the bright, dry-season sun and over the open fire.

It looked good, but what a strange flavor it had! It did not taste like any pork I had ever eaten on the farm in Iowa. We didn't get much pork in Africa because the Moslems, who ran the meat market, do not use pork. The missionaries were polite. They ate the other food, but most of the meat was left. Even our African help refused it. Some time later, one of our lady missionaries, Alida Trygstad, discretely asked me: "Didn't you grow up on a farm? You should have known that a male pig that has not been castrated is not fit to eat!" No, I did not know that, but I remembered how my Dad and Uncle would be doing something in the pig yard that made the pigs squeal, but I, being a girl, was forbidden to see the operation, nor was it ever explained to me. Now I understood the squealing!

THIRTY-SEVEN
Furlough 1959-1960
"It Is Well With My Soul"

With our precious manuscript of the Four Gospels and Acts in Lloyd's briefcase, we flew to London, where we presented it to the British and Foreign Bible Society to be printed. While we were in London, we stayed at a mission hostel which was home to a number of young people from European countries who were studying the English language in preparation for missionary service in one of the English colonies.

We had very little time or money for sight-seeing, but it was a restful time, and the children enjoyed the beautiful garden back of the hostel building. I was also able to hang clothes on the line in the garden, clothes which I had washed out in the communal bath tub down at the end of the hall.

With our mission in London completed, we boarded the S.S. Queen Mary for the trip to the U.S. There was a nursery on the ship, and Mark enjoyed playing with the other children and the many toys. I did notice that there was one little boy who did not look well. Sure enough, when we arrived in Iowa, Mark came down with the measles. Before we realized what was going on, though, he was extremely irritable. My mother, our hostess, exasperated with him, exclaimed: "Can't that child say anything but 'No?'"

When we arrived in New York, Ruth Christianson's two nieces came to the pier to meet us, helped us through customs, and brought us to visit at the Haroldson's suburban home. A couple days later they also brought us to the airport for our flight to Minneapolis.

Mom and Dad had retired from the farm and moved to Joice. Dad wasn't really ready to retire, though, so they had moved back to their second farm and were having a good time cleaning out the grove and remodeling the old house. Dad had recently traded in his Packard on a new car, but when he realized that we would need a reliable vehicle for the year we would be on furlough, he went to the dealer, bought the Packard back, and gave it to us.

This time, the housing that was arranged for us was a duplex on Como Avenue in St. Paul, not far from Luther Seminary, so we moved in there and the girls enrolled in school in St. Anthony Park. It was great to be so close to most of Lloyd's family in Minneapolis, as well as many missionaries who occupied the other houses provided by the Mission Board. These houses were completely furnished, down to the last dish towel, and even a few groceries in the kitchen, for starters.

After a short time for getting settled, Lloyd took assignments for deputation work. Occasionally, on week-ends, the family went along. We were going to a church in SW Minnesota. for Thanksgiving Day, so Lloyd took the car to be washed. It was cold, so the trunk lid froze shut. We had to put all our luggage in the backseat with the children—a bit crowded!

Our old friends, Reidar and Mrs. Brockman, who had been faithful supporters, invited us for dinner one evening. She had called to set up the date a couple weeks in advance, and when the time came, I completely forgot about it. While we were eating our supper at home, the telephone rang: "Did you forget that you were to eat with us this evening?" I had, but we got up from the table and went. On the way, I told the children, "If she serves us ham and whole-kernel corn, please don't tell her that we just ate that at home." She did; and they didn't.

Carole had just become a teen-ager, and she was experiencing some of the rebellious feelings of adolescence. One Sunday afternoon when the family was invited out, she begged off, wanting to stay home alone. When we returned, she shame-facedly related what had happened. For some reason, she had stepped out on the little back porch, and the door locked behind her. It was cold. Assessing the situation, she decided maybe the window of the upstairs bedroom, just above that porch, might not be locked. So she climbed up one of the porch poles, got onto the roof, and checked the window. It was locked, so, in desperation, she broke the window and let herself in.

We had expected to have a full year of furlough, and the time went fast. But, in May, we got word from the mission office that, due to some new regulation about our visa, we would have to leave three weeks early. We had only started to pack our barrels, so we worked hard. There was a ruling about occupying a mission house: "Leave it as clean and neat as you found it!" Wava and Palmer were living in Minneapolis, so I called Wava and made a deal with her: "If you will clean up the house after we leave, you may have all the groceries that I am leaving." She told Mom later that the groceries she found there were ample payment for the work she did cleaning up after us!

Before we came home for that furlough, I had set my heart on buying an electric organ to bring back to Africa with us. To pay for it, I got a job working nights at Midway Hospital in St. Paul. I made contact with the Wurlitzer Company in North Tonawanda, New York, and put in an order for the organ. I wrote a check on our account, sent it off, and expected the organ to be included in our freight shipment to go out from New York. After having been back in Cameroon for a couple months, we received a statement from our bank, indicating that the check had not been cashed. In response to my letter to the agent at Wurlitzer, I heard that he had never received the check. So I made out a new order, and the organ finally arrived.

Mom and Dad had given us money to purchase an Onan 1000 watt gasoline-powered generator, which we bought from a company in St. Paul. They packed it and shipped it to New York. It did make connections with our freight shipment.

We had corresponded with some of Lloyd's relatives in Norway and made plans to visit them on our way back to Africa. So we took a Scandinavian Airlines plane to Denmark, where we did a little sightseeing in Copenhagen, including the world-famous Tivoli Gardens. We boarded a night train which ran onto a ferry boat that brought us to Oslo by morning. Lloyd's cousin, Oydis, met us at the pier and took us to visit at her apartment and to see something of the capital city.

We rented a car and drove the seven Norwegian miles (about 40 American) to Randsfjord to visit the Sand farmstead and Lloyd's cousin Olga. Both farmhouses were huge. In the past, when it was easy to get house help who lived in, big houses were the style. But now they were impractical, so Olga and her husband had had a wing of their house torn down. Olga's husband took us up on the mountain back of their house to see the artificial lake which his grandfather had constructed. The water running down the mountain from this lake provided power for their private generator—more than enough electricity for their needs.

We also visited Lloyd's cousin, Helge, who served as mission secretary for the Norwegian Mission Fellowship. Later, his son, Aage, a medical doctor, spent several years serving in Cameroon, and the second son, Sven, worked there as a "diakon," doing laboratory and X-ray work, plus many other odd jobs, similar to our paramedics.

After that pleasant three-day visit in Norway, we retraced our steps to Denmark, flew to Paris, and then onto Africa.

THIRTY-EIGHT
Africa—Djohong Again
"There Shall Be Showers Of Blessing"

It was good to be back in the familiar sights, sounds, and smells of Africa again. It took a while to get our last-term car in running order, still minus a starter and headlights, and to get our household goods (pots, pans, and yellowed linens) out of the Mandsager's attic and on a truck for Djohong, where we had spent part of last term. Djohong was the highest, coldest, rainiest, and windiest station on our field, but I loved it!

A nice, roomy, new house was being built for us, but in the meantime, we occupied the tiny house just vacated by Harriet Stovner. There were only screens on the windows, and we really felt like staying in bed with the covers up over our ears. But there was work to do, so out we came!

That house consisted of one large bedroom and a living-dining-room combination. From there, one descended by four concrete steps to the kitchen. At one time, we had a mother cat who gave us four cute little Tabbie kittens. They had a habit of climbing those steps, hoping to get into the dining-room. One night, in semi-darkness, as I groped down those stairs, I stepped on one of the kittens. What an awful feeling! Of course we had to finish it off.

En route back to Africa, when we were in Copenhagen, we had watched the changing of the guards at the palace—young men wearing natty uniforms and tall, plumed caps. At Djohong, we had a spring-wound Victorola on which we played John Philip Sousa band recordings. Mark liked to march around the table in time with the music, saying he was a "marcher man" like the guards.

We used kerosene lamps since our generator had not yet arrived, and one evening the lighted lamp was standing next to the window, and the curtain blew over it and ignited. Carole grabbed the wash-basin and doused the fire. The grass roof was only a matter of inches below that flaming curtain. This was a close call.

That grass roof was damp and musty, and Lloyd was subject to asthma attacks. One night, just home from an evangelistic trip, he gasped: "Get me the inhaler that Chief Meiganga gave me." It took me a while to understand that, on his last visit to that Chief, Lloyd had shared with him that he was subject to asthma attacks. The Chief said he was, too, and that the French doctor in N'Gaoundere had issued him two of these very effective inhalers. So the Chief had given Lloyd one of them, which he used often, with great relief!

Almost a month had passed since Miss Stovner, who was a practical nurse, had left for furlough, so it seemed that there was a back-log of sickness awaiting treatment. I took a week to get settled, then got out my old uniforms and went to work. Fortunately I was able to get the same faithful (if not the neatest) cook I had had last term. So I was happy to leave the kitchen to him, while I worked at the dispensary, visited patients in their homes (we have no hospital facilities here) and conducted classes.

On August 19th we went to our annual mission conference at Garoua-Boulai, where our American School is located. We then had two full-time teachers for the 23 children, teaching grade school plus 9th and 11th grade of high school. Carole and Linnea were in 8th grade then, and Wanda was in 4th. They wrote that they were very happy to be back at school and to live in the new dormitory.

During conference, Mark came down with a light case of infectious hepatitis, and Wanda had it after him. Though somewhat contagious (it was endemic out there at the time), it had not spread wildly. It seems that adults get it harder than children. When Wanda had it at school, she wrote a tearful letter, wishing that her own nurse-Mommie could come to take care of her, but adding that Aunt Florence, the House Mother, was doing a good job of substituting.

From my letter written October 10, 1960:

Puff! Puff! I just pumped up our kerosene pressure lantern so I can see to pound out a few letters, as mail goes out tomorrow (a once-a-week affair). My 4-year old Mark is enjoying a tub bath (a wash tub, I mean) in front of the fire-place in the new, unfinished house, into which we moved recently.

Mark surely enjoys our new house. Though unfinished, it is very roomy. We don't use the 'master bedroom' yet, as it is on the windiest side of the house, and the window panes have not come yet. Lloyd got screens on the living-room, kitchen, and the little bedroom today, so the mosquitoes won't be so bad. Also, when the strong winds blow, the mats hanging outside the windows can't blow 'way into the room, as the screens will hold them back, and then the rain will not be able to blow in so badly. We are thankful that we have doors, anyway. It is pretty chilly when the wind blows, but of course it never freezes here.

About a week ago, Lloyd finished translating the Constitution for the new Church from French into Gbaya (the constituting convention will be held in December) and he went down to Garoua-Boulai to check it over with Andrew Okland. He took the bus this time, so the car is here, but last week I notified the people at Fada that I would not be coming for my weekly medical trip, as I didn't have the courage to drive the car by myself. I used to go out alone last term, but we are using the same old car, and not only does the starter not work (we have a new battery) but something else is wrong, so sometimes it has to be pushed and PUSHED and PUSHED to get it started. It is only 17 miles to Fada, but the road is such that it takes 40 to 60 minutes to drive out there, so it isn't exactly a 'joy-ride.' Fada is a town larger than Djohong, and is populated chiefly by Mbororo people. Also, it is the market center for many more who live in the country with their herds of cattle. These people, being nomadic, have been very hard to reach with the Gospel. They are looked down upon by the Gbayas in whose territory they roam, and whose fields their cattle often damage. (The cattle tramp through our garden from time to time, too). But now the Fada people have asked us to make weekly medical trips on market day, when people come in from the out-lying areas. Treating 40 to 50 people in three hours does not make for very thorough medical care, nor do we have an opportunity to preach, as a rule. But we hope to make friends with them this way, and then get them interested in the Gospel, too. Here at the station, I have found a number of them very open and glad to hear our short devotional messages at the dispensary, and sometimes I read to the women on our back porch (in Fulani) after I have bought their milk, butter, and/or eggs.

Dahyo, an elderly Mbororo grandmother, has become a special friend. After I have measured out the milk I am buying from her, I have been making a practice of reading to her from the Fulani New Testament. Though my diction isn't too good, she seems to understand. Some time later she told me that she was praying in the name of Jesus. (The Mbororos are mostly Moslems, who believe in God—Allah—but they do not accept Jesus. They ask: "How could God have a Son?")

At one time Dahyo introduced me to a daughter, grand-daughter, and a great-granddaughter. I got a picture of the four of them. In the fall, when the rains have ceased, the Mbororos must move their herds to areas where there is water and grass for them. (They don't know how to make hay.)

One day Ardo Djahy, Dahyo's husband, came to our back porch and asked to talk with me. He said, "We are leaving soon, and during the dry season we have to move around many times. So I want to ask you if I may store some of my things in your attic." I agreed, and on the next market day he brought a metal trunk, his umbrella, and a heavy, brass teakettle, the kind the Moslems use for their ritual ablutions. Though it was blackened from being heated over an open fire, I could see that it was inscribed with Arabic writing, done in a very artistic style. The next time Dahyo came in, I remarked to her about the teapot. I asked her if she thought he would accept a trade: I would buy him an aluminum one that I had seen in the market in Meiganga. She said, "Oh, I am sure he will. He doesn't actually like this one. It is too heavy. A friend of his who had been to Mecca gave it to him when he returned from his pilgrimage." We did make the trade. He was happy with a shiny new teapot, and I got his heavy brass one. I used cleansing powder to clean it up, and had a treasured souvenir to take to the U.S. when we retired. (In 1984, when out house burned down, the teapot was ruined, along with all our other African souvenirs.)

Another memory that I associate with Mbororos at Djohong was the one where a woman came to ask me to go to help her co-wife, who had been in labor a long time. We started out on the long walk to their camp, but when we had gone about half way, another women from their clan came to meet us. She said, "Oh, Patuma became impatient. She started out walking to meet you. Then she had her baby right out on the path, just like a cow!!"

One day, two Mbororo women came to my back porch. In a piece of cloth one of them had her earlobe which she wanted me to re-attach. They were married to the same man, had been fighting, and the other woman had grabbed hold of a couple of the huge rings which hung from her "enemy's" ear and yanked the lobe off with it. I had no way of re-attaching the piece of flesh. Some time later, I noticed another woman whose earlobe was missing. "Yes," she replied when I asked about it, "I was fighting with my co-wife, and she yanked it off."

One day, a Mbororo woman brought her baby, who had an extra finger on each hand. One of these fingers was dead—it had been bumped too many times, so it hung limp. The mother asked me to cut it off, so I did. Then she suggested that I remove the extra digit on the other hand, too. That one was very much alive, and when I cut it off, a stream of blood spurted out and hit the opposite wall. I had forgotten that I should have tied it off before cutting it. But it soon quit bleeding, and the child was none the worse for the experience! Dahyo had been telling me about one of their customs, the ritual celebration they called "Indere," simply "Naming" a new baby. I asked her to let me know when there would be one, as I wanted to come out to observe. Some time later, she did invite me to go out with her. She said: "It isn't far." I took a Bible picture roll along, hoping that I would be permitted to speak to the crowd. We walked, and walked, and walked, climbing hills and descending them, crossing the streams which coursed between the hills—something like seven of them. Finally, we arrived at the camp. A meal was being prepared, but the naming ceremony had already taken place. I saw Ardo Djahy and asked for permission to speak to the crowd. He invited me into a house—only elderly men were gathered. I did show them a Bible picture and spoke briefly, but I didn't feel that they were very receptive. Maybe my use of the Fulani language was so poor that I wasn't getting the message across.

Wherever we lived during our missionary career, we usually kept a cat. The one we had in Djohong had an interesting habit of jumping up on our bed and then crawling up under the bedspread. When I noticed that she was pregnant, I thought: "Oh, no. I bet that is where she will have her kittens!" She did, but she did such a good job of cleaning up after the birth that there was no mess on the quilt!

I don't have so much time for evangelistic work, or medical work, either now, as we have a new missionary couple, Pastor Rod and Joan Ellertson, their two pre-school children, and a single girl, Donna Simonson, here for language school. I try to spend 5-6 hours a day with them, because the mission conference only allowed them three months for language study. But I have a fairly reliable medical assistant who takes care of the dispensary. He has no theoretical training, but he can recognize the common ailments and treat them. He is good about consulting me on things he doesn't understand. This means that my Gbaya language classes are interrupted frequently, but that provides variety and sources of conversation (orientation). Our new co-workers take their meals with us, so we get some opportunities for discussion during mealtimes, too, depending on the behavior of their two little ones and our 4-year old.

Their Sammy and Mark play so nicely together. Mark will really miss him when they move to the Woumbou station about Christmas time.

One day I had to take time out from our language lesson to remove an inch-and-a-half long filaria worm from the eyeball of one of our catechumens. Her husband, a Moslem, one of the important members of the Village Council, sent me his profound thanks the next day.

Another day I was called to a Fulani home where a woman was in labor. She had delivered the baby feet first, and the head was caught. I was unable to extricate it. I'm sure it was dead already. So I went home, very sad. The next day I called on them. The dead baby had somehow been delivered, and the family simply stated: "It was the will of Allah!" They have an entirely different way of mourning than the Gbayas do, who scream and cry with a great deal of emotion.

THIRTY-NINE
Travel Trials
"Amazing Grace"

After the new dorm in Garoua-Boulai was completed, we had a good place for our annual missionary conferences. Sometimes we met at the end of the school year, in late May, when we would be coming to bring our children home for their summer vacation. At other times, we met when the children were due to return to start a new school year in late August.

After school was out in 1961, Lloyd was asked to attend a seminar for translators which was being held at Ebolowa, one of the stations of the Presbyterian mission. He rode with another missionary, and they took a couple of Gbayas along. They had some excellent sessions with Dr. Bratcher from England, and Dr. Nida, from the American Bible Society, besides translators from several other missions.

So it was up to me to drive our ailing Green Beetle home to Djohong. We had mislaid the ignition keys, so Lloyd showed me how to jump-start the motor by raising the hood, using a huge screwdriver, and making an electrical contact which would start the motor. (Now, 35 years later, I don't remember what I did. I guess this is one of the tricks car thieves are good at.)

The Travelall was, as usual, packed to the gills—our four children, our baggage, our house help, and other Africans who had found it absolutely necessary to get a ride NOW!

The floor of the Travelall which, during the dry season, seemed to suck in the red African dust, also admitted much exhaust fumes from the motor. On this trip, it had rained recently, so we were not bothered by dust, but we were plagued by exhaust fumes. Carole, sitting in the front seat, had her window open, so she got fresh air. But the exhaust fumes seeped in and became thicker toward the back of the vehicle where Linnea was sitting. When we arrived at our station, and I opened the back door, Linnea literally fell out on the ground. Everyone was sick except Carole, so nobody cared to eat any supper that evening.

When our children were home for Christmas or summer vacations, they played with the children of our African pastor and the catechists. On moonlight nights, especially, the Gbayas like to sit around a camp fire out in the "begara," the open space in front of their houses. They would tell folk stories which included singing and sometimes dancing.

One year, during the Christmas vacation, which was in the dry season, we decided to take a trip to the northern part of Cameroon where there is a game reserve and much interesting scenery. Knowing that our car admitted so much dust, I made masks for all of us, like the surgical masks we used in the hospital. On the way to the game reserve, we stopped at several mission stations. We were quite the curiosity, covered as we were by the red road dust. Even in spite of the masks, we inhaled a lot of dust. For some time after we got home from that trip, when I coughed, I raised red mud. Because of the dust problem, we did not take as long a trip as we had planned.

One of the places we visited on that trip was our station at Tchollire. A day or two previously, Ernie Johnson had shot a cheetah. Because a venomous snake had attached itself to the animal's body, when Ernie came to pick up the animal, the snake struck. Mrs. Johnson promptly treated the bite, making knife-slits around the site, and then sucking out the venom.

Ernie skinned the chetah and gave the hide to our girls. Later, Carole had it tanned and mounted on felt. It was displayed on her living-room wall for many years.

THE SADLER CONFERENCE

In January of 1962, when we brought our girls back to school at Garoua-Boulai, we stayed on for three weeks, because Lloyd had a herniotomy. He recovered rapidly, but, because our roads are so bad, we did not try to drive back sooner.

Coming back as far as Meiganga, Lloyd remained there—he always had mission business, interviews, etc. This time, he was also involved in preparations for the intermission conference on literacy for which a very experienced missionary from Liberia, Dr. Sadler, was coming.[3]

---

[3] See Roslyn Sadler's autobiography (Bolivar, Quiet Waters Publications, 2001).

It was the end of the month—payday—so I drove up to Djohong by myself to pay the help, spending the night at our home. The next day, I developed the most dreadful headache I had ever had, but I had to get back to Meiganga. I attended the first sessions of the literacy conference, together with other missionaries from our mission and from several other missions.

Because there were so many guests for the conference, the lodging facilities were over-taxed. Lloyd and I were assigned to a room on one side of the building which housed the orphanage laundry.

I soon realized that that dreadful headache was the beginning of a bout of infectious hepatitis. That year, many of our missionaries got it, including Dr. Mandsager. My case was not one of the worst—one of our nurses had to have intravenous treatment. I did have to stay in bed—a camp cot set up in the room next to the laundry. The gasoline-powered washing machine gave off exhaust fumes which floated easily over the dividing wall, since there was no ceiling which did not help my headache much.

Dr. Sadler had developed a system of teaching reading which was based on the "Each One Teach One" system which Dr. Frank Laubach had originated. This method was used very successfully in the Philippines, and adapted to use in many languages. We found this system to work quite well for Gbaya. Each of the vowels in Gbaya was used with a set of the consonants to line up a series of words. Gbaya has many two-letter words, and many of them could easily be illustrated.

Our missionaries were very enthusiastic about this system of teaching reading, and, subsequently, a series of textbooks were written, with appropriate illustrations, and printed by The Graphic Publishing Company in Lake Mills, Iowa. Eventually, many people learned to read Gbaya using this system, which lead to their ability to read the New Testament in their mother tongue.

Lloyd and Margaret Smith developed a system for teaching teachers to teach. When Bible School was in session in Baboua, they would supervise the regular students as they taught others, perhaps their own wives or older children. They then sent the Bible School students out into the villages to teach reading. Later, the Smiths would pack up household supplies and move out to a remote village to conduct a literacy campaign. The people enjoyed it, as the prize for mastering the reading system was a copy of the New Testament with a bright red cover. Even many older people succeeded in learning to read.

Later, we discovered that the Gbaya language requires some special letters to express sounds that we had not recognized. So the reading system had to be revised, and when the revised New Testaments, and later the whole Bible, came out, special letters had been produced and included in the books, so they became much more readable.

Having been involved in literacy work, I had really anticipated taking in this "Sadler Conference." But the infectious hepatitis, known as yellow jaundice, kept me in our rather unpleasant quarters for the whole time. One of the mission nurses, who was attending the sessions, brought my low fat meals to me. Shortly after the conference, our hostess, Marge Jergenson, also came down with hepatitis.

After we returned home, and I was convalescing, I suffered after effects—very painful abscesses in a very sensitive part of my body. The Catholic nursing sister came and gave me some excellent treatment. So, in time, I recovered. Knowing that I had been assigned to be one of the hostesses for our mission conference to be held at Garoua-Boulai later that year, I gave up my teaching activities, trusting my dispensary assistant to do most of the medical work. I spent considerable time working in the garden, getting lots of fresh air and physical activity in order to rebuild my strength.

Being a hostess at the mission conference meant supervising the preparation of meals for 108 American missionaries and their children. The African cooks and their assistants, men who washed the dishes and did the cleaning, were under our supervision.

About the middle of May, Lloyd decided to take an evangelistic trip to the northeast edge of our mission territory. I had never accompanied him on such trips, but I had been getting some patients from that area, so I loaded up a box of medications and my microscope. Mark was still at home with us, not having started school yet, so he enjoyed the trip. He spoke Gbaya so well, and the Africans gave him so much attention that it was really a fun time. Our cook and house boy helped me with the medical work, as well as preparing our food and took care of setting up our camping quarters. With the aid of the microscope to assist in diagnosing illnesses, we found a number of patients who promised to come to Djohong for more thorough treatment in the near future.

The African pastor, who was directing the expedition, had planned to be out for a week, but later he decided to do it in five days. We were glad that the villagers go to bed with the chickens, as we were all woofed when bed-time came.

At that time, we had a spring-wound phonograph, made in Australia, on which we played several records that had been prepared in Gbaya by a visiting team who had come from the Gospel Recordings organization in California. So, while I was examining patients and Lloyd was having personal talks with catechumens who presented themselves for baptism, one of our helpers gathered quite an audience who were fascinated by the recordings. Someone remarked, when hearing these records: "It must be true. He says the same thing every time!"

Back at Djohong, we had a boarding school for boys who came in from other villages where there were no schools. It was often quite a problem to get enough food for them. They were expected to do some work in exchange for their food. At one time, we had them make adobe bricks for building a new, bigger dispensary. The Brockmans, our good friends in Minneapolis, had sent us money to pay for cement for the floor of that dispensary.

With the bricks which the boys made, we built a three-room dispensary. As a base for the cement floors, they laid rocks, the porous, red laterite which was abundant in that area. At the time, we had only enough cement for two of the rooms and my dispensary assistant got pretty tired of walking across those sharp rocks. When he complained about it one day, I reminded him that he did want a drain, so he was willing to wait.

From my letter written June 5, 1962:

It was a good thing we had decided not to try to do the cement work now, as Lloyd had to be away again. He went to Meiganga on Thursday, planned to buy some lumber on Friday to make new doors for our school houses; go to Garoua-Boulai for a hasty committee meeting on Saturday; return to Meiganga that night, and come home again Sunday or Monday. Yesterday (Monday) he was on the way, having loaded up the lumber, a barrel of gasoline (no service station up here), eight passengers, and two sacks of flour for the pastor's wife. This afternoon I heard that, about twelve miles out of Meiganga, a spring broke, so he had to unload everything and go back to have it repaired. Lloyd is just too kind-hearted, and our International Travelall is old and "tired." With the lumber and gasoline, he should not have accepted any passengers, but as long as they can see any sitting space, they do not realize that the rest of the load may already be too heavy. They all have legitimate reasons why they must have a free ride. There is daily bus service most of the way up to Djohong, and a bus comes all the way three times a week, but usually they have just missed the bus, or they have no money—mostly that.

It rains almost every afternoon now, so my garden is doing well. I'll have to make a few pickles tomorrow, as the cucumbers and tomatoes will ripen and spoil while we are away at conference. Since I recovered from my bout with hepatitis, I have not taken on any class work nor dispensary work. I have deliberately chosen to do gardening—vegetables and flowers. This physical work in the fresh air has really meant a lot to me, so I feel normal again.

Africans have a tremendous sense of the dramatic. At Christmas time, they put on a Nativity pageant. When they came to the story of the slaughter of Bethlehem's baby boys, they followed that by a dramatic portrayal of God's judgment on King Herod for having committed such an atrocity! The one who played the part of Herod died in great agony!

For several years, Verna Syverson, who was in charge of women's work in the Gbaya church, wrote a Christmas program which could be used in the congregations, similar to a Sunday School program. But we had many adults who also wanted to participate. One year, an older woman took a brief part in which she was to recite a verse about the Wise Men who came to see the Baby Jesus. The Gbaya words for three Wise Men are "oHayawi tar." But she said "Haya Gbaya tar" (Wise Gbayas three). She never heard the last of that! They called her "Haya Gbaya" (Wise Gbaya) ever after.

FORTY
Empty Nest/American School
"Jesus Took My Burden And Left Me With A Song"

When our girls were little, they loved to snuggle down and listen to me read to them. But Mark was too busy! He liked best to be out playing with his Gbaya friends, which often meant eating "kam" and even drinking un-boiled water. Of course I didn't know that at the time, but he told me years later that that water tasted much better than what we had boiled, even though we stored it in the kerosene-operated refrigerator.

Mark's birthday came in August, so he was barely six years old when it was time to start school. The girls were always so glad to be going back to be with their American friends at school, and Mark had not expressed either anticipation or dread as the time approached. So I really was not prepared for his reaction: this was the end of his childhood freedom!

We took the children to Garoua-Boulai for the opening of school, and of course, Mark had to be in the boys' wing of the dormitory, which must have seemed to be miles from his sisters!

Lloyd and I stayed on in Garoua-Boulai for a few days, because, as usual, Lloyd had mission business. That should have helped Mark adjust, but it just seemed to make it worse. Those first days in the dorm were difficult, but, as is true in life, he lived through it.

Reubin and Millie Johnson were the house parents—a new job for them, too, for which they had moved from their previous station at Woumbou, to Garoua-Boulai.

About a month into the school year, on September 28, 1962, Millie sent out a form letter to all of us parents:

People come and go, hours come and go, days, weeks, and now the first month (of school) is just about over.

The new schedule is really a rush at noon, but it seems to be working out. The first and second graders eat promptly at 11:30, then begin their rest hour before the others, as, at 1:20 they must all be on their way again. No matter how you look at this, it makes a pretty short rest hour, but we are trying to get them all settled just a little bit earlier in the evening than last year.

The older ones start studying at 7 p.m. This means that Uncle Reubin and Aunt Millie help the little ones get ready for bed. With 15 little ones in my corridor, this is no small task. Wash up time is really quite a riot! Sometimes I think I should put on a huge plastic apron, or maybe a bathing suit would be better. Well, it would be quite a "fun time" if it weren't for the fact that we have to try to keep it fairly quiet for the older ones who are studying. So many little ones need many different things: cough medicine, a band aid for a little sore, or an aspirin, or just a little extra loving, some one to talk to. From 6 p.m. to 8 p.m. is really the "children's hour" here, and the time when we need the most strength and patience, and the most love to meet all the demands. Could you remember to pray especially for us in the early evening, and on rainy weekends? These are the times we feel the need of an extra lift. We are thankful to God that His strength has been sufficient for each day, and we know that is because each one of you and many others are faithfully remembering us in prayer.

As you read this, forty years later, remember that many of the things Millie said still apply to life at the American School at Garoua-Boulai, where children of the missionaries who work in the ELCA fields in Cameroon and the Central African Republic bring their grade school children for boarding school. Remember them in your prayers.

Millie continued in her letter:

The Bredfelts came to wait for their new baby (not a long wait, either, only a couple of days)—They came to Garoua-Boulai because our American doctor was there, and he would deliver the baby. ...

Now Ellertsons have been here for a couple of weeks, too, and Joan has been inviting a few of the dorm-ites over for supper each day, much to their delight. 'Variety is the spice of life,' they say.

In my 1962 file, I found a copy of the little newspaper, "Harmony Notes," put out by Grades 3-6 of the American School in Garoua-Boulai, dated December 21, 1962. Here are some of the articles in the paper:

Ruth Larsen wrote about Thanksgiving in 1962:

On Thanksgiving Day at the dorm the little kids ate with the big kids. We had eight chickens, potatoes, buns, salad, gravy, and pumpkin pie with whipped cream on top. We ate so long that we had to sleep just ten minutes. The Awads, who own a store in town, ate with us.

Conrad Mandsager wrote:

A Gbaya man was bitten by a spitting cobra on Tuesday, November 20. He was working in his garden when the cobra jumped out of the grass. He picked up a stick and tried to fight it, but its mate jumped out and bit him on the hip. It was raining that day, and his sons brought him in after the rain. He died that night.

Our Wanda wrote:

FRENCH SCHOOL REPAIRS

On Saturday, Nov. 17, the Rodney Ellertson family came to fix the school buildings here. By Monday morning, Joan Ellertson was ready to begin. She had women mix the mud and slap it on the buildings. They whitewashed the buildings, too. A soccer game was scheduled for Nov. 23; therefore, a field had to be made. Joan had workers do that, also. A trench was dug around the ball field. The goalposts were painted blue. In the trench there was whitewash. The doors of all the school houses were painted salmon. Some of the roofs were grassed.

Becky Johnson wrote:

The first and second graders have been doing experiments. They have been learning how plants grow. They have been planting bean seeds, corn, and sunflower seeds...In Mark's class in reading, they are reading We Come and Go. Paulette's class is reading Fun with Dick and Jane. Debbie's class will finish Friends and Neighbors before vacation and Philip's class is reading More Friends and Neighbors.

My 1963 file contains several letters. Ladies in one of our supporting churches duplicated and mailed out form letters to a mailing list we provided. Here are excerpts from our letter written February 15, 1963, while we were living in Djohong:

"When the cares of my heart are many, thy consolations cheer my soul." Ps. 94:19. We all have our cares—be they great or small—but to each comes the same assurance: "My grace is sufficient for thee."

Many things have happened since I wrote my last general letter two years ago. One of the most momentous, as far as our family was concerned, was the departure of our fourth child to enter school. You folks in the U.S. send yours away when they enter college—at eighteen or so. Ours leave us at the tender age of six, and believe me, when it is your first or your last one, it is especially heart-rending. I have never considered missionary life as one of sacrifice, but this came the closest to it that I have ever experienced.

And now we face another: our two oldest girls must leave us, as there is no provision for senior high school on the field. Out here our children live at the boarding school, where the Lord has provided wonderful, consecrated houseparents and teachers. But this means we have had very little time with our children since they were six years old. (A few years later we discovered that we were eligible to send our high school students to the interdenominational mission school at Jos, Nigeria. Wanda and Mark both graduated from Hillcrest.)

We want the girls to attend one of the Church-operated academies, which provide supervised dormitory facilities, so we will send them home just in time *to enter school. But then comes the problem of the summer vacation, when they can not be in the dormitory. We considered the possibility of my going to the U.S. in May of 1964, to set up a home for them during the summer, and to remain with them during their senior year of high school. That would leave Lloyd alone out here just one year, which would not be too bad. (As it worked out, the girls got summer jobs, so I did not go home early. More about that later.)*

Last summer (1962) we were very happy to have the Sigurd Larsen family join us at the Djohong station to take over the work of the station and the district. This means that Lloyd can again give his full time (?) to translation work. However, he still takes his share of committee responsibilities. Last fall he was elected by the south-east synod of our newly organized church, to be their synodical president. This involves some traveling, but Lloyd enjoys his work with the African brethren. We now have several ordained pastors among them, and it is a thrill to note their spiritual growth and discernment.

Last summer at our annual mission conference, I was again asked to teach the Gbaya language school for new missionaries. This time we have one new couple: Rev. and Mrs. Donald Peterson, of Menomonie, Wisconsin. Their three older children: Douglas, Karla, and Anne, are at school in Garoua-Boulai; the two little ones, Cathie and Meg, are here with them. Mrs. Peterson had had polio as a child, so she walks with a distinct limp, but she handles it well, and is a very sweet person. At the end of their six months of language study, they are scheduled to move to the Dir station. ...

When my language school assignment is over, I expect to give much time to literature work, typing manuscripts for Lloyd, etc. Women at Djohong have asked me to teach sewing classes; the African pastor wants to learn to type, and both he and the French School teacher want lessons in English. Now that all my children are away at boarding school, I do have more time for mission activities, but there are so many things we could do that it is a problem of setting priorities. I still supervise the dispensary, but my African assistant is now capable of doing the work with a minimum of help from me.

Since my bout of infectious hepatitis last year, I have not had the endurance I used to have, but I have learned to live with this. We still cling to the Lord's promise from Phil. 4:19: "My God will supply every need of yours, according to His riches in glory in Christ Jesus.

WOMEN'S CONFERENCE

At one time, when Madel Nostbakken was at our station working with Lloyd and their Gbaya informants on Bible translation, we were invited to participate in a conference of the women of the Mbere District, to be held at the village of Mbarang. Some of these women came from great distances, walking and carrying their baggage on their heads, and many brought a baby tied on her back. Of course, none of them had cars, and it was something of a surprise to them to see me, a woman, driving—the market trucks and buses were, of course, all driven by men.

Going to conference was a tremendous experience for them: a respite from their daily work routine and an opportunity to have fellowship with women from other villages. As they walked, they would sing! Sometimes, by the time they arrived at their destination, they had composed and memorized a new song, which they volunteered to perform during the gathering. People in the villages along their route who could not attend provided meals for them, and, if they had come far, they might stay overnight, rising early the next morning to be on their way again.

This conference had been planned by leaders of the Church, and we were amazed to find that 21 women had been assigned topics on which they spoke! It was interesting to notice that the more literate women were on the program first. One of the later speakers, when she rose to speak, held her New Testament high and read her text. Then she admitted: "I really can't read, you know, so I asked the pastor to teach me the words, so I could recite them for you," which she did, by memory! Then she took off on her sermon. One woman used a very impressive object lesson: she was wearing a beautiful, colorful two-piece outfit. As she spoke, she peeled off one wrap-around skirt after another. Finally, the last one was a faded, dirty skirt, a symbol of the sin which might be hidden under a very attractive exterior!

Going to spend a weekend in a village was quite a major operation at that time. We would take our camp cots with bedding and mosquito nets, a supply of boiled drinking water, and food for the time we would be there, plus a cook to build a fire and prepare our meals. It was dry season, so he could prepare our meals on an open fire outside the house which we occupied. This conference had been planned some time in advance, so many new houses had been built to accommodate the anticipated guests. That meant that the family who had provided the guest house would have a new dwelling to move into after the meetings were over.

At that conference, the men of the village had taken on the task of preparing the meals for the conferees, but they did not expect us foreigners to eat with them. So, when our cook announced that the meal was ready and set on our camp table, we would eat by ourselves.

At that time, we still had our Green Beetle, the International Travelall, and Lloyd packed all our baggage into it for the trip. He was an expert packer. When the conference was over, I tried to get everything back into the car, but when it was full, there were still several items of baggage which I had to leave for him to pick up on his next trip through that area. He did not complain!

The summer of 1963 was the last one Carole and Linnea spent with us in Africa. During that time, a Gbaya women delivered a premature baby which I took to our house to care for until she should recover from the case of measles which had evidently caused the premature delivery. I asked the family what his name was, but they said, "We didn't know whether he would survive, so there would be anything to name." We called him Tiny Tim, and Carole loved to care for him.

GOODBYES

A missionary's life is punctuated with Good-byes. But, on the other hand, if one says Good-by, it stands to reason that "Hello" is just around the corner—hopefully with pleasant expectations.

Since our daughters, Carole and Linnea, had gone through school in the same grade thus far, they were now, in 1963, ready for their junior year of high school. Lloyd's sisters, Borghild Hofflander and Helen Feig, were planning a trip to Norway, so it was arranged that Carole and Linnea would meet them there and return to the U.S. with them, where they would enroll as juniors at Hillcrest (Lutheran Brethren) Academy in Fergus Falls, Minnesota. The Division of World Missions would underwrite their basic expenses as students there, since no equivalent facility was available for them in Cameroon.

We had no telephone service in Cameroon at that time, so we made travel arrangements by mail, well in advance.

We brought the girls to our mission station in N'Gaoundere and then to the airport there, where they boarded a small plane for Garoua, in northern Cameroon. The plane then went onto the West African country of Senegal, where they had a lay-over in Dakar before flying onto Rome. As they were flying along, they wondered out loud how they would find their way in Rome. A passenger behind them informed them that, upon arriving in Rome, he would direct them, though he, himself would be going on else-where. From Rome, they flew to Paris, where our new missionary couple,

Pastor and Mrs. Bohnhoff, were studying French. They enjoyed taking Carole and Linnea on several sight-seeing trips.

Though they enjoyed the sights of historic buildings, especially the majestic cathedrals, their enjoyment was tempered by the fact that they were wearing their high-heeled dress shoes and girdles. Some of their sight-seeing excursions were provided by our friend, Orloue Gisselquist, who was working on a doctorate in Medieval History, with special emphasis, also, on the great cathedrals there in Paris.

The girls remember that their hotel was adjacent to a police station and a neat little park. But one could not sit on the benches without paying a fee ("and we were warned that nice girls did not use those benches"), "but we got tired of walking around, and not seeing anyone to whom one would pay, we just sat down. In a matter of minutes two men approached and 'propositioned' us, but we first pretended that we did not understand French, and then explained that we were missionaries' daughters en route to the U.S." The girls were relieved to see a policeman come along, and the men retreated.

At that time, one could not get flights at just any time, so they had several layovers. When the time came for their departure for Norway, the Bohnhoffs took them to the airport. The flight to Oslo was short, and there they were met by their two aunts and taken to the apartment of Cousin Oydis Lid, whose husband worked with the Norwegian radio and television department.

Considerable time was spent at the Sand farm. They especially remember the festive occasion of the confirmation of a young male cousin. After the actual confirmation service, numerous relatives gathered at the home, and "we a-t-e and a-t-e and ate!" Linnea remembers being shocked to see that the special gift the young man received was an ornate chalice—strange for a family of teetotalers.

BECOMING AMERICANS

Though the girls were born in the U.S., they had spent little time there. In fact, when we had returned to the U.S. and they started first grade in Moorhead, MN., they could hardly speak English. Now, they would be juniors in high school, an awesome change.

After a few days in Minneapolis with their aunts, their Aunt Wava Valder, my sister, took them down to Joice to spend some time with Grandpa and Grandma Ramsey. One day Grandma invited many of her friends for a shower for the girls, when they received gifts of clothing—some new, and some, good, used items—plus linens which they would need in their dormitory room when they started school in Fergus Falls.

Perhaps their most outstanding school experience at Hillcrest was being accepted into the mixed choir, where Carole was soon given soprano solo parts, with Linnea doing well in the alto section. In the spring, the choir took a tour to the West Coast.

FORTY-ONE
Back To Work Again; Medical Evangelism
"Little Is Much When God Is In It"

From my letter of September 13, 1963, written to our daughters:

Sig Larsen, who is in charge of the Mbere district now, had planned to make an evangelistic trip out into the area, but Mrs. Larsen wasn't well, so Lloyd and I took the trip instead. (Wanda and Mark were back at Garoua-Boulai at school).

The road—just one track made by a bulldozer that simply pushed away the trees, bushes, and sod, had no ditches for drainage, and of course nothing like gravel. Part of the way, where it ran on ridges, it was all right. But most of the way was through an area which would make excellent farm land: deep, soft, black DIRT! Since the road was opened, big trucks with dual wheels had hauled loads of lumber and cement 'way out to the end of the line for construction of a veterinarian center. Since it had rained (and it was raining part of the time during our trip) the ruts were mostly full of water, too. Our International Travelall looked high, wide, and clumsy on paved streets in the U.S., but several times it took a regular nose-dive into the mud and had to be dug out. On one stretch, it took us nearly three hours to go six miles! We could have gotten there faster on foot, but with no accommodations along the way, we were carrying all our camping equipment. On the way home again, though the food and medicine supplies were lighter, we had acquired eight chickens and two puppies, which our cook and laundry man bought from the white builder out there.

On Friday, the first night, we slept in a Gbaya village and gave Communion there the next morning. It was the first time some of those people had seen the sacrament given, so Lloyd spent some time explaining the rite. After the service, I had clinic. Then we went on—that grueling six miles—to the next Gbaya village, where we spent the second night. Early Sunday morning, another Communion service, then onto a new Mbororo village right in the midst of their cornfields. The chief was away, so we didn't ask permission to have a service, but I had clinic (yes, on Sunday) and met a number of people who have been in to Djohong for medical care. We did witness briefly, but it was market day, with the noise and clatter of open-air selling. Then we went on to

Ngaoi, where the veterinarian center is being built. There Lloyd counseled
with some Gbayas who have heard the Gospel at other missions.

On Monday morning, I treated many patients. Then Lloyd heard that it
had taken some men only two hours to walk over from Diyel, a Mbororo center we had very much wanted to reach, but we had been told that the road was
impassable. So, at three that afternoon, after rearranging our baggage so it
could be carried by porters, we set out in the car to the edge of the mountain.
We left the car there and walked, possibly eight miles, to Diyel. There we
have a Gbaya Christian who is conducting a primary school and has succeeded in getting five Mbororo boys, besides 17 boys and girls of other tribes.
My heart went out to his young wife who was rather lonely there. We slept
two nights in a guest house in the chief's compound. The chief's three wives,
the minister of public works, and another substitute for the chief bustled
around making us comfortable. They brought us a chicken, some uncooked
rice, and a nice, big onion. Our cook prepared the food. We had no vegetables
with us, but I had noticed many sweet-potato gardens, so I asked for some of
the leaves, which make a good substitute for spinach.

The second morning we had breakfast at six o'clock, took care of a few
patients, and left at 9:30 for our return hike. After crossing the stream and
climbing a long hill, we sat down for coffee and a snack. We got back to our
car by noon. When we drove in to the village, we were met by a Mbororo who
had just brought his brother in from a remote encampment. He had had measles three months ago, and complications had set in. They wanted us to take
him back with us, but he was in no condition for a trip over those awful
roads. So I left a supply of sigmamycin capsules, anti-malarial and aspirin
with the chief, who seems very intelligent. He had a Moslem teacher take
down the directions for the dosages, etc., in his "shorthand"—Arabic, then
they all repeated the directions several times, to be sure they understood. I hope
the young man will recover.

Going on after lunch, this time we knew what to expect from the road, yet
it was six o'clock by the time we reached Bafuk, where we had spent the first
night. When the people heard our car coming, the family in whose house we
had slept the first night, hurriedly moved out, so we could eat and sleep there.
After a short service, we were really ready to sleep. The next morning we got
up at 5:30 to resume our homeward journey. At nine, we reached a Mbororo
encampment, where we visited our old friends, the Ardo Djai family.

After our return home, Ardo Djai's wife came in with milk again, and I
sat down and read to her (Fulani) and had a good visit. She said her husband had said he wants to build a good, big house, make two beds in it, and
put some nice blankets on them. Then he wants us to come out there and have
a service and stay over night with them. (This did not materialize, but it was
a good thought, anyway.)

Next week, Sept. 18-22, we plan to go with the Larsens to the district conference at Mbarang. There, too, we must bring all our camping equipment, and I will take medicines along. But the Bible studies will occupy most of the time, so the medical work will be mostly of an emergency nature—not like on this other trip.

The Larsens got word that a short-term surgeon has come to our hospital in N'Garoundere, so they planned to go there for surgery for Florence.

On Monday a Mbororo man was brought in from Diyel, having been attacked by the husband of a woman who had been stolen by another man, the brother of the victim. When the enraged husband found his wife in that compound, he did not care which man he attacked. The guilty man was away, so his brother got it. He had ten big gashes, and his right arm was broken just above the wrist. I could see a tip of bone sticking out of the wound. His people brought him to the government dispensary, so I didn't go over, though I heard about it. The next afternoon a delegation came to ask me to take him to Meiganga. By that time I knew that the Larsens planned to leave the very next morning for N'Gaoundere, so I said I would go and ask them, and then come to let them know. When I came over to the dispensary to tell them that they could go with the Larsens, I was horrified to find that none of the wounds had even been bandaged. They were very clean, but open. The relatives wanted me to give him a shot. So I went home for penicillin and bandaging materials. The government (male) nurse was away—I heard that he had simply left the patient there and went hunting. So I got Reubin, my assistant, and Philip to help me. The patient was lying on a mat on the floor. We worked from 4:30 until 7:30. Reubin helped me pull the wounds together with adhesive tape, so they were almost like they had been stitched. One wound had such a big hunk of flesh sticking out that I wasn't able to get it shut. Also, the one over the broken bones I just covered with bandage, since the doctor would have to open it again, anyway. He had one especially nasty, deep gash behind his ear. If it had come a little lower, it could have severed the jugular vein, and he would have died. It was a miracle he didn't die, anyway, from loss of blood. (Our doctor told me later that my treatment of the many wounds had been successful; he had not reopened them to suture them. The compound fracture did become infected and took a long time to heal. I never saw the man again.)

I wish you could see our "Tiny Tim" now. He is so fat he can hardly see. The women call him "Carton," because he sleeps in a paper box. I bet that will be his name all his life!

There is a Fulani man who brings me eggs and chickens often. He brought his 5-yr. old daughter for medicine yesterday, and will be coming in each afternoon for about a week. Today he asked me to read to him. I sold him a Gospel of John which has French on one side of the page and Arabic on the *other. Books like that are called "diglot". One can get French and English that way, and we even have the Gospel of John in French and Gbaya, too.*

NEWS OF PRESIDENT KENNEDY'S DEATH

When we lived at Djohong we did not have a radio. One evening Sig Larsen came running down the hill from their house. (It must have been Nov. 22, 1963) "We just heard on the radio, something about the late President Kennedy. It seems that he has been assassinated." Soon we heard all the sordid details of the loss of our youthful president. When we told our African friends about it, their immediate reaction was: "The vice-president must have done it!" reflecting on the likely turn of events in their culture.

When the time came for the international broadcast of President Kennedy's funeral, we were attending a district conference in a Gbaya village. The local French Catholic priest heard that the Larsen's radio was not portable, so he brought his radio to make it possible for us to follow the impressive procession leading to Kennedy's burial at Arlington National Cemetery.

From a letter containing interesting medical cases:

The rains have been heavier than usual, and it is very chilly and raw. This usually leads to more bad colds, malaria, etc. Also, several patients have been carried in from distant villages with serious ailments that have required much of my personal care. One little boy, just our Mark's age, though he is much smaller, and quite delicate looking, had three kinds of worms. The people from a distance always have a hard time buying food for a long stay here, so we try to give the treatments as quickly as possible. I guess we went at it too hard with this boy, as his legs suddenly became paralyzed. I wished I could have sent him to a doctor, but the roads are so terrible now, that I feared the trip would be too hard on him. So we have been praying much that the Lord will heal him, also that God will give me guidance as to further treatment. First I had to stimulate his appetite. I have given him, besides lots of vitamins, rice, milk, and eggnogs. Somehow, these people seem to be afraid to feed sick people the things that would be the most beneficial: bananas, eggs, and milk. But they are beginning to have confidence in my teaching. Now this little boy just can't get enough bananas. This morning his father came in with the good news that the little boy is beginning to move his bad leg. The other one began to move last week, and now the second one. So they are encouraged. I had to find work for the father, so he could buy food, as I stressed the importance of good nutrition for the boy's recovery. This couple have been through much persecution in the area they came from. About a year ago they lost their other child, so they have just this one. Consequently, I felt that the Lord just couldn't let this boy die. Steeped as they are—even the Christians—in old heathen superstitions, if this boy had died here, seemingly as a result of my treatment, it would have been almost more than their faith could stand.

Last week a woman was carried in, just all skin and bones. She had had diarrhea with blood for three months, and was so weak she couldn't even hold a glass to drink water for swallowing her pills. She has two kinds of worms, too, but I don't dare give her the rather drastic cures until she gains some strength. She got over the diarrhea right away, and now her appetite is improving, so I hope I can soon start the worm cures. But I told her people that they would have to expect to stay here at least two months, as she is not in condition to take the treatment she needs yet. They are from a different tribe, but they do understand Fulani, not Gbaya.

Last Sunday morning, instead of going to church, I took a copy of the Gospels in Fulani, and, together with medicines, went the rounds of our inpatients. After giving one message in Gbaya and two in Fulani, I was really tired. But what a joy it is to see the response of some of these people. I feel that there must be some of these Fulani-speaking people who will soon make a confession of faith. This is very difficult for them because of the Moslem influence. They could be just whisked away into the wilderness, never to be seen again.

Next week Lloyd goes to Garoua-Boulai for a meeting, and then our children will get out for fall vacation. They will most likely stay over night at Meiganga, as the road from Meiganga to Djohong is so bad now that Lloyd won't drive it after dark. Rumors are out that the government has promised to do something about it when the rains quit.

FORTY-TWO
Brooklyn Dentist
"He's Everything To Me"

Our Missionary from Brooklyn, Ruth Christiansen, had a dentist friend who had long been interested in the work in Cameroon. So he and his wife decided to take time off from his practice to do some hands-on missionary work. He sent money out to have an addition built on the dispensary building at Meiganga to house the dental equipment he also shipped out.

When they arrived in Douala, he and his wife rented a car for the drive to Meiganga. But they found that the rent of the car was prohibitive, so Tack Braaten, our field treasurer, arranged for the chauffeur to take the car back to Douala, and to lend the Olsons Dr. Eastvold's Land Rover that was resting in N'Gaoundere during the Eastvolds' furlough. Dr. Olson, who was perfectly at home driving in New York traffic, was hesitant to drive a strange car on strange roads. So I was drafted to chauffeur for them.

Consequently, I got to make an unexpected visit to Wanda and Mark at the American School in Garoua-Boulai when the dentist took a trip to visit the children and the missionaries there. It was a different experience, indeed, to drive that lumbering English vehicle. And, to make matters worse, it had a malady which made it necessary to add almost as much oil as one did gasoline when making service stops!

During their stay in Meiganga, Dr. Olson trained an African to do simple dental work, and when they returned to the U.S., they contributed the equipment to the mission.

BABOUA AGAIN

From a form letter written May 13, 1964:
Now Carole and Linnea have completed their junior year at Hillcrest Academy in Fergus Falls. Recently we received glowing accounts of their trip

as members of the mixed choir, traveling for three weeks in the Upper Midwest and into Canada.

In February, Linnea wrote that Prof. and Mrs. C. F. Erickson, music teachers at Hillcrest, had invited the girls to make their summer home with them, between work time at a resort near Fergus where they expect to secure employment. This made it unnecessary for me to go home for their sake, but it made Wanda very unhappy, as she had set her heart on going. We assured her that we would continue to pray about the problem, as we realize that she is very lonesome at school this year with so few young people left, now that we have no high school at Garoua-Boulai. We wrote to the school at Jos, Nigeria, where Ingrid Larsen, daughter of our co-workers, a sophomore, is attending, asking if they would take Wanda in their 8th grade this next term. But before we received their answer, my brother, Lynn wrote, suggesting that we send Wanda home to live with them this coming year. This seemed the best answer yet, so we have asked for plane passage for Wanda in company with Myrtle Noss, one of our missionary nurses, who goes on furlough this summer. They are booked for June 22nd, earlier than we like, but as we don't want to send her alone, this is next best.

School at Garoua-Boulai will close on June 5th, and the next day our annual mission conference begins. As this usually lasts for two weeks, Wanda will have no time at home with us before she leaves. But we hope that she will be coming back to Africa with us after our furlough, as it looks hopeful for our missionaries' children to take their high school work in Nigeria in the future. This school has been established by American missionaries from several different missions working in West Africa, including the group from the former Danish Lutheran Church now a part of ALC with us. It is a long drive to Jos, but there is a possibility that a mission pilot may get permission to come to N'Gaoundere to pick up our students, which would be much less expensive (and wearing.)

Now I can continue the typing of manuscripts for the New Testament without the pressure of trying to finish in a very limited time. I can also continue to teach part time at the Bible School here in Baboua—not to mention the joy of staying on with Lloyd. Hazel Bredfeldt, who is also a nurse, will take over the supervision of the dispensary while I do the typing.

We moved here to Baboua in February. It was hard to leave Djohong, as it meant closing the mission dispensary, since there was no nurse to take my place. But the government dispensary there, with a Catholic sister in charge, is doing good work, and the Sig Larsens are carrying on the work on the station and in the district.

Wanda arrived safely in the U.S. and became a member of Uncle Lynn's family. His daughter, Bonnie, is Wanda's age, but the youngest daughter, Rhonda, somewhat handicapped because of multiple sclerosis, became Wanda's closest "sister." Wanda took her eighth grade school work at Lake

Mills, riding the bus to and from school with her cousins and neighbor kids each day. She became an active participant at Bethel Lutheran Brethren Church, where she took instruction for confirmation. (All the other members of the class were boys!)

From a letter written November 23, 1964 to members of the church at Morris, Minnesota, who had taken on our support:

Lloyd's translation work on the Gbaya New Testament is now in the final state of checking, and I have typed the manuscripts for the Gospels of Matthew and Mark, I and II Corinthians, Galatians, Ephesians, Philippians, and Colossians. Each page must be typed in five copies, which means that if I make a mistake, I must erase five times! (It is amazing what stupid mistakes the machine makes sometimes!) For this work I use a large, long-carriage machine which has the French accept marks and special keys needed for Gbaya.

Though Lloyd is considered a full-time translator, he has various church responsibilities. This morning he left for a two-day district conference. Next week we go to the annual conference of the South-East Region, of which he is president.

FORTY-THREE
Confirmation At Baboua
"Oh Jesus, I Have Promised"

Confirmation services were still somewhat of a rarity on our Sudan Mission field, as many of our congregations were barely old enough to have had children of confirmation age.

Shortly after we moved back to Baboua, after an absence—at 5 different stations, plus furlough—of nine years, the African pastor, Elie Barbou, announced that he would be having the first confirmation service since he was installed in this, his first parish. Pastor Barbou, a native of Baboua, was one of the first group of teen-age boys who came to meet Laura and me when we first arrived in 1944. He was trained by Catechist Paul Sippison and baptized by Pastor Trygstad in 1947.

This time around, as Pastor Sand was in full-time translation work, we had no responsibilities in the local congregation except as communicant members. So we were not aware of the constituency of this confirmation class.

As the young people came forward, and their names were read off, I recognized most of them as young people who had been baptized by Pastor Sand, either as infants or as small children, when their parents were baptized. I remembered one especially large baptismal group which included a couple with five children. How curious our two little girls were to see what Daddy was doing: pouring water on the heads of some of their playmates!

Three of those young people were in this confirmation class. Then there was "Butterball," a slim teenager now, even though her mother was still calling her "Buttabahl." That was what I had dubbed her when she was a roly-poly chocolate drop, and our girls loved to take turns carrying her around, tied on their backs, like the Gbaya mothers do.

The confirmation service was held in the ramshackle mud-walled church, with its leaky grass roof. But we took pictures outside, and in the background was the new church—its sturdy brick walls still without a roof. Pastor Bredfeldt, who was building the church, had charge of the mission station and the Bible School, so he had little time left over to do building.

Also, the local congregation was financing the building on a pay-as-you-go basis. They paid for a neat, aluminum-roofed residence for their pastor and had gotten thus far on the church with only a little help by way of personal gifts from missionaries. We all hoped that the old church would not collapse before the roof got on the new one. As it was, no services could be held there if it rained.

Most of these young people in the class, even the girls, have been attending the government French school. So it is our prayer that they may all be kept for the Lord and His Church and become leaders in the Kingdom.

From a letter written December 30, 1964:

BIBLE SCHOOL GRADUATION

The last two weeks have been especially busy and interesting, as the closing activities of this year's Bible School term culminated in the graduation exercises for the three-year students yesterday morning at the Sunday services.

Madel Nostbakken, Marie Mundfrom and I have been conducting classes for the wives of the students and a few women from the village, since many of these women had never had a chance to go to school as children. In fact, at one time, a delegation of student-wives came to me, saying, "When our husbands graduate from Bible School, we will be assigned to live and work in a village. He will be the catechist, and people will expect us wives to teach the women. So, please give us some instruction, so we can 'do school' when we get settled in our villages.' A set of books had been prepared for teaching adult illiterates."

These new books came from the printers just in time to begin the school year in March. Now many women have learned to read. Madel and Marie taught the reading classes and I taught writing. Then on Wednesday afternoons I had all the women for health and hygiene, and on Fridays we had an inspirational meeting. Sometimes I gave a Bible lesson, and sometimes one of the Gbaya women would speak. We had a lot of singing, too.

Some time before school was out, Madel and Marie got the great idea of having closing programs for the women (to correspond in a small way for the highlight experience for their husbands when they graduated.) They made attractive head-bands for all of them. On each head-band was an open book, of a color corresponding to the book from which each woman was now reading. On it was superimposed a lighted lantern, symbolizing the light of knowledge. Each woman's name was inscribed on the book, and also the page to which she had progressed in her studies. Madel had composed a literacy song which the women learned. We had a parade early Saturday morning before the sun got too hot, and then we went to the church, where Madel and Marie and their students put on a 2-hour program. As we knew it would get to be too much for one session, I had planned my program for the afternoon. All the women wanted to take part in the health program, so I had made out short skits in which each woman made some statement about a particular preventable illness or some kind of intestinal parasites which are so common among them. I had made posters, too, so almost every woman had something to hold up to illustrate what she was saying. This, together with several of the songs they had learned, made up another one-hour program. About 50 women took part. (The paper for the head-bands and the posters came from the shipment of "mill-end" paper which had been donated to our work by publisher Gordon Aasgaard of Lake Mills, Iowa. This was before recycling.)

Some time ago Lloyd got a neat little booklet from the Dept. of Stewardship called A Primer on Proportionate Giving (In simple English: Tithing.) He translated it and I added some little sketches, and we mimeographed about 1200 copies (again using some of the Aasgaard "mill-end" paper for covers). We set our goal to get them sent out when the people came to get the students at the close of the Bible School this week-end. Did we ever work on Saturday!! I got a man and three women to help me to assemble them. We plan to take the rest of them along to the conference next week. We put the Gbaya version of the song "Trust and Obey" into it as the conference song. We won't be charging for this.

One of the frustrations of printing a book on a mimeograph machine is that one never seems to come out even: we ran out of covers while we still had pages left. Then we would run out of one of the pages, so I would be putting the stencil back on the machine and running off more copies, — etc.

Later we translated a little brochure on the ill effects of smoking cigarettes. This is especially appropriate here, because, since tobacco is raised locally, cigarettes are actually given to children to get them addicted. The production of that little booklet was even more frustrating, because our stencils were evidently defective, so they would split and smear ink on the paper.

With all these other activities, my manuscript typing doesn't go very fast! I begged Lloyd to let me stay home to work on it when he goes to the conference at Dir next week, but I guess he feels that he needs me along to bolster his morale.

There was a lot of excitement around here early this morning. Three missionaries with trucks loaded up Bible School students, wives, and families, to bring them home for vacation.

How I have enjoyed the Bible School work! Teaching here, plus some literature work is, I believe, what I would really enjoy doing "siti siti." (Gbaya for "right along.") I suppose I shouldn't say that out loud, for sure as anything our conference will decide to move Lloyd somewhere else, so I will have to adjust to something completely different again. I told Cliff one day: "I wish the conference would consider what I like to do for once when they station my husband!"

Next on the program will be preparation for the Christmas program. I am working with a group of teen-age girls who are such "eager beavers," they would be here to practice every day if I had the time. Using the music of the Christmas carol "O How Beautiful the Sky," originally from the Danish, I wrote the whole Christmas story in Gbaya. It got to be about 25 verses! (That would never do for a group of American teen-agers, but to these girls, the longer it became, the better they liked it.)

From my letter written December 30, 1964:

CHRISTMAS PAGEANT

And now I can tell you about our Christmas pageant—something that had never been done here. We started with the nine girls who had been coming to sing, and then we sent out word that we needed boys. Each time we practiced, we got a few more participants. At last I had more than I could use—of course one could always have more shepherds. I almost had four wise men! And we had six or seven priests and scribes who came in at Herod's call to consult the Scriptures concerning the birthplace of the Messiah. We had only one dress rehearsal, on Saturday afternoon. That did not go very well, but we realized that, since no one here had seen anything like this before, we couldn't have a less critical audience!

That (Saturday) night, at 1 a.m., I woke up with flu symptoms, so I skipped Sunday morning service.. That afternoon, during one of my naps, I dreamed that 5:30 rolled around, and suddenly I had strength to go to the church for the pageant. So I took that as God's answer. Lloyd went to get the chief, who sat in our brown car-seat in the aisle. The aisles were so full that the wise men had a hard time getting through. And when Mary climbed on the donkey (two boys under an army blanket) they had to clear the children out of the aisle, so the donkey could carry her out the side door, wait a while, and bring her back in (to the door of the stable). The audience howled with laughter over that! Also, King Herod brought down the house with his violent reaction to the question about a new king! Because of the crowd, some men stood outside a window where they could watch what was going on behind the curtain—very amusing.

You should have heard the thanks I got after the pageant was over! It really was worth all the hard work. Now I wish I could make use of this as the beginning of something new—a young people's society, Luther League, or whatever. You know how desperately the young people here need something interesting to do! (Where have I heard that before?) At least we don't have to compete with TV!

FORTY-FOUR
Furlough Plans, 1965
"He Leadeth Me"

This was going to be a biggie! Carole and Linnea, who would have been in the U.S. for school two years, and would be graduating from the Hillcrest Academy in Fergus Falls on May 31st, and Wanda, taking her eighth grade work in Iowa, was preparing for her confirmation early in June. We needed to do something together as a family—for the last time before the girls would reach that rite of passage and be grown up. We were hearing news about the 1965 World's Fair in New York, and we wanted to attend. That would be a big expense. What kind of plan could we work out to make it possible?

When missionaries come on furlough, they are expected to do deputation work to spread the word among the churches about what is being done on their respective fields of service. So, why not plan an itinerary that would bring us to New York and back? I wrote to the Mission Office and asked for permission to do this. We were given permission, providing we would do the preparatory work ourselves. So, Lloyd and I sat down with road maps and the ALC almanac. Having laid out a tentative route, we wrote letters telling of our plans, and suggesting that the "Singing Sands" could present a program on a suggested date in June, 1965.

It was customary for a congregation to take up an offering for the presenters and to provide food and lodging. We knew we could not expect to make much money at this, but we would be getting room and board, plus enough for traveling expenses. We got very favorable responses, especially from churches in the East, where our mission work had not been presented before. One church secretary responded: "Imagine a missionary actually asking to come to present the work. We usually have to beg them to come." The pastor of a rural church in New York state wrote that that would be haying time, but the farmers had responded, saying: "Oh, we will just leave our work a little early that evening."

At that time, the Lutheran Church in Morris, Mn. was under-writing most of our support, so we wrote to tell Pastor Grindland what we were planning. He invited us to come to Morris after having attended the girls' graduation in Fergus Falls. The people there realized that our plans for giving mission programs en route to New York would not involve bookings for every day (or evening). That would have been too much for all of us. So, we needed a trailer to provide sleeping accommodations for those open nights. Somebody in the congregation had a friend who owned a Bethany fold-down trailer. They rented it for our use for the summer. It was light and easy to pull behind the Chevrolet station wagon which we were able to buy shortly after our arrival in Minneapolis.

But there still was much to do before our departure date in the middle of May.

DR. SCHIOTZ' VISIT

Because of the recent merger of several Lutheran synods into the American Lutheran Church, the Presiding Bishop, Dr. Frederick Schiotz planned a visit to our field, following a conference in Nigeria. He met with us who worked in the southern part of the field and then went on for a similar meeting with those in the north. What a wealth of experience he had! He had been all over the world, and could talk about most church leaders and many government and U.N. officials by their first names.

When I took on the typing of the New Testament manuscript, I turned the medical work over to Hazel Bredfelt. But she, in turn, took time out to have a baby: their fifth, the second boy.

From my letter written March 2, 1965:

Thank you, Linnea, for the wonderful Christmas package. You had packed it so well, whoever tried to open it gave up.

Recently all the missionaries' children at the American School had stool and blood tests. Mark and Holly were found to have schistosomiasis, but now the treatment can be given in pill form, instead of the painful injections which Wanda had to take.

Good news from your letter, Carole and Linnea, about plans for choir tour to California, where the choir is to participate in the Easter service at the Hollywood Bowl.

When we were in N'Gaoundere last week, people were excited about the prospects of having President Ahijo of Cameroon and Dako of R.C.A. visit there. In preparation, people have been carrying rocks to line up along the road, painting them white. The problem is that they made the driving space so narrow, one can hardly meet a car.

We had an interesting guest the other day, a French gendarme, wearing one of those snappy, flat, black hats. He said he is Catholic, and had received a Bible from a missionary, "But I don't have time to read it." Lloyd advised him to take time. He admitted that Catholics are beginning to encourage their people to read the Bible more.

There is an older Gbaya widow lady who visits occasionally. It is a rather long walk up here from the village, so she often lies down on the verandah and sleeps a while. Then I go out to visit with her—mostly listen, though she is hard to understand, first, because her teeth are gone, and also she uses the Tongo dialect. But she is a happy Christian, and it doesn't seem to bother her much that I don't understand her.

We just returned from a trip to Tchollire, where Ernie Johnson made some repairs on our car. It was very hot and dry there, but here, at Baboua, spring had come, and today friends brought us lovely, crip lettuce, carrots, little spring onions, and some greens like spinach.

I am back at work typing the N.T. manuscript again. Really, I have gotten so I actually enjoy it. There is a challenge in doing something difficult, different and exacting which always appeals to me. So often the thing I dreaded gets to be what I really enjoy when I have committed it to the Lord and know it is His will for me.

We still don't have confirmation on our plane passage from Bouar. As soon as we get our passports, we plan to go over to Bouar to check. Yellow fever vaccinations are given the first Thursday of each month. Lloyd may hop a bus or truck to Bangui to get the visas, as our mail service has been so bad lately that we don't dare trust mailing the passports to Bangui.

From my letter of April 29, 1965:

TRAVEL PLANS

When we leave here on May 15th, Bouar on May 16th, and Bangui on May 18th, we will stop only an hour in Paris, and go onto Amsterdam that same evening. The Netherlands Bible Society has promised to print our Gbaya New Testament. (What I did not know then: we stopped briefly in Ft. Lamy, Chad, en route to Paris. I was hungry, so I ate a ham sandwich—neither Mark nor Lloyd ate. I have reason to believe that that food was contaminated, as several months later, I developed symptoms of dysentery.)

ORGAN FOR MEIGANGA CHURCH?

When Ruth Christianson's dentist friend from Brooklyn, N.Y., Dr. Olson and his wife were in Cameroon for their second visit, they talked with the missionaries at Meiganga about the idea of donating an electric organ for the church there. Since we had had a Wurlitzer organ in our home for four years then, I was asked my opinion on the wisdom of this gift.

First of all, our churches were open, with no glass in the windows. Although they were sheltered from rain, the humidity during the rainy season was very high. Also, since there were no public utilities, no regular supply of electricity was available, either to power the instrument, or, especially to keep it dry. Moisture is very hard on an organ. We had a special drying element built into ours, but since our electricity was available at most four hours in the evening, it was not adequate. Then, mice got into it and chewed off the plastic coating of some of the tiny wires with the result that adjacent keys would sound at the same time, and many keys just did not sound, although the organ never went out of tune.

In writing the Olsons about my negative reaction to the provision of this organ, I also raised the question of the training of an organist. Anyway, nothing came of it, so they evidently accepted my pessimistic reaction to the idea. I guess the use of indigenous music was best for the Church in Africa, anyway, at least for then.

For me, personally, I was not sorry that I had gone to the effort and expense of buying, shipping out, and moving the organ whenever we changed station. I often said that, to me, having music was almost as important as food. The climatic conditions were very hard on it, but it did hold out for the duration of our ministry in Africa.

FORTY-FIVE
Our New Testament Manuscript To the Netherlands "Saved By Grace"

From Paris, we had just a short flight to Amsterdam. In Lloyd's briefcase was the manuscript of the New Testament in the Gbaya language which I had typed. (When it was done, it was as big as a full ream of typing paper.)

The personnel at the Netherlands Bible Society welcomed us as if we were royalty. When we had turned the precious package over to them, we were entertained for meals at several of their private homes. Mr. Kijne, the CEO, took us to his apartment, to which we had to climb a long, very narrow stairway. His teen-aged son showed us his garret where he had a collection of model airplanes, of special interest to our Mark. They explained that one could never move furniture up those stairways, so the problem was solved by placing a very sturdy hook under the eaves of the roof. A pulley on the hook was used to hoist furniture to the desired level, then the chair, sofa, or whatever, was let into the apartment through a window. They were very proud of the fact that these buildings were five or six hundred years old and were under the surveillance of the historical society.

Amsterdam, like Venice, has many canals instead of streets. Not many people drive cars; cars are parked alongside the canals, and our host mentioned that few days pass without a car having to be pulled out of the water. There are hundreds of bicycles which allow riders easy access to the ferries.

They took us sight-seeing on a boat, and we also walked along some of the dikes and saw old-fashioned windmills. The windmills are mostly just tourist attractions now, as the pumping of water from the fields is done by electric motors. The people shared space with some of the biggest mosquitoes I had ever seen—at least they were not "anopheles" (malaria-carrying) which we had left behind in Africa!

Though the old things in Europe were interesting, our hearts were keyed to meeting the members of our family who were awaiting us in Iowa and Minnesota. We stayed in Minneapolis long enough to locate a commodious Chevrolet station wagon, which served us well for that furlough.

Stopping by my brother Lynn's home, we first picked up Wanda and then drove onto Fergus Falls, Minnesota. What a thrill it was to meet up with our two graduating seniors, as well as some members of the faculty who had been on the staff when I had graduated thirty years before! It was great to hear the choir, with our Carole singing solos, and then to see them march up to receive their high school diplomas.

We then returned to Iowa, where Wanda joined her class for confirmation at Bethel Lutheran Brethren Church.

DEPUTATION AND WORLD'S FAIR

The planning we had done while in Africa for a deputation trip which would give us opportunities to share our mission news with many ALC churches, as well as bringing us to New York to attend the 1965 World's Fair, was now about to become a reality.

Our sponsoring church in Morris, Minnesota, had invited us to visit them first. They had done some preparatory work and had already rented the Bethany fold-down trailer for us to use during the trip. Those days in Morris also gave us some time to become reacquainted with our daughters and to do some rehearsing and preparing for the programs we had planned to give along the way to New York.

It wasn't all fun: the girls had matured, and were not now accustomed to taking orders from us as their parents. Some time ago one of them remembered "We gave you a hard time, Mom." But, at the time "the grace of God was sufficient."

We discovered that we should have done more route planning, such as making reservations in advance for places to park our trailer. When we got to Washington, D.C., we did not give a program, but the pastor of one of the Lutheran churches there let us bring the mattresses in from our trailer and lay them on the carpet in their lounge. We were then also able to use the restrooms, and we prepared some meals in the church kitchen between sightseeing trips to the famous points of interest in the capitol.

When we got to the Lutheran Bible School in Teaneck, N.J., we were told that their zoning laws forbade them to let us park our trailer on their grounds, so we "camped" again in the building as we had in that Washington church. They had contacted friends in

Brooklyn and arranged for the girls to stay with our dentist friend and Mrs. Olson in their apartment. Lloyd, Mark, and I stayed with Pastor and Mrs. Theodore Maakestad, pastor of the church connected with the Deaconness Hospital where Laura and I had stayed when en route to Africa. We also made contacts with friends from Minnesota: Rev. & Mrs. Roger Ose, then living in the east, who made helpful arrangements for us for visiting the World's Fair.

After an interesting week there, we struck out again, visiting churches in Upper New York, through the picturesque Finger Lake area, and onto Tonawanda, where our Wurlitzer organ had been built. But we were saddened to find that the once beautiful factory was almost abandoned, with weeds in the flower beds, a result of the electric organ industry being taken over by Japanese companies. We did meet and visit with the man who had arranged the purchase and shipping of our organ five years earlier.

Then we visited Niagara Falls, and drove across Michigan, traversing one of the very longest bridges in the world, leading to the historic settlements on Mackinaw Island.

One day, while driving through a scenic area, we stopped for a picnic lunch. As usual, we sang our table prayer before eating. There was another group picnicking not far from us—it turned out to be a Sunday School group. They were impressed to hear our singing, so they took up a collection, and presented it to us.

Driving around the North Shore of Lake Superior, we came to Duluth, then traversed northern Minnesota, coming to visit the Ose family on their farm near Thief River Falls. Mrs. Ose was the woman who had so enjoyed packing boxes to mail to us during the early years of our mission work. Several years later, one of her sons told me: "Mom always saved the best Karo Syrup pails to put into the boxes for the Sands. We had to use the dented ones for carrying our school lunches."

Mark had a good time climbing the windmill tower with the youngest Ose boy. Of course windmills were things he had never seen in Africa.

FORTY-SIX
Furlough In Minneapolis (Just Off Franklin)
"I Will Sing Of The Mercies Of the Lord Forever"

For furlough housing, we had been assigned to a large older home on 3lst Ave., just off Franklin Avenue, which had belonged to the Lutheran Free Church. It had previously been used for a family home, plus a tiny apartment for a single girl. They gave us the use of the whole house, though, plus a two-car garage in back.

Carole got a job as a nursing assistant at Swedish Hospital, Linnea enrolled at Augsburg College, Wanda began her freshman year at Minnehaha Academy, and Mark entered fourth grade at the nearby elementary school. Lloyd was soon involved in traveling, and I worked nights at Swedish Hospital. The old B building had been replaced by a parking lot, and upper floors had been added to the A building. However, I was glad to find familiar territory on the second floor when I went back to work there. Usually, all the fifty beds on that floor were occupied. I had one LPN and an aid to assist me, so we were busy.

Carole usually worked the evening shift with me. The bus service was good, so we seldom drove. One night I did drive the car, and when I came off duty at seven a.m., from force of habit, I climbed on the first bus that came by. When I got home I realized that I had left the car near the hospital!

One evening when Carole came off duty, she told me: "Mom, I admitted a young man (as a patient) this evening, and I know he fell for me." Ron Gabrielson had come in for minor surgery for plantar's warts, and he did fall for Carole.

That fall, before we went back to Africa, Carole had arranged to attend Waldorf College, but Ron had gotten a job in Chicago and was lonely. So he persuaded her to give up college, even though she was soprano soloist in the college choir, and they were married at Thanksgiving time and moved into a small apartment in Chicago.

Linnea arranged to continue at Augsburg College, and since she planned to major in French, she got a room with other girls who were studying French, at the old house which was called "Chez Nous."

BACK TO AFRICA AGAIN, 1966

When Lloyd's year of furlough expired, he went back to Africa alone, leaving me to spend a little more time with the girls, and allowing me to keep Wanda and Mark with me in Minneapolis. I also continued to work nights at Swedish Hospital until just a few days before my return flight to Africa.

In spite of an airline strike, we took off on schedule on one of the hottest days of August, flying by way of New York, then via Paris, to Kano, Nigeria.

We had bought Wanda a neat little piano-accordion, which she was doing very well playing. It did present a problem, baggage-wise, though. She also had a foot-locker trunk of things she would need at Jos. At the airport, they told me that, within the continental U.S., these items would not exceed the weight limit, so, when we got to New York, I pulled the locker-trunk off the baggage conveyor, hailed a cab, and took the trunk to the freight office of Air-France. I told the cabbie: "Now wait for me, as I must get back to the terminal to make my flight!" There I paid the freight, which was less than it would have been as excess baggage. (It probably went on the same plane with us. I got back to the boarding area just in the nick of time, finding Wanda and Mark a little anxious. What a relief to get our seats and find ourselves winging over the Atlantic to Paris!

Arriving at Kano, Nigeria, we sensed a strange atmosphere of guarded suspense. Later, we heard that the president of Nigeria had been assassinated the night before. Planes were grounded for three days, but the small, private plane belonging to the Sudan Interior Mission was permitted to pick us up and take us to Jos, where Wanda would enter Hillcrest Academy as a sophomore and live at the Lutheran hostel. It had been so hot the day we left Minneapolis that it did not occur to us to carry sweaters. So, when we arrived in Jos, which is on a highland, we were surprised to find that the weather was chilly. But the housemother where Wanda would be staying found a sweater for her to use until her baggage should arrive. We had a chance to see the school and the dormitory and to meet some of the staff. The other students from our mission had not yet arrived, so we didn't get to meet them.

The Missionary Aviation pilot had been assigned to fly to N'Gaoundere, in Cameroon, to pick up those students from our mission, so Mark and I got to fly with him. It was awesome to fly in that little plane, winging between jagged mountain peaks, and sometimes over wispy white clouds.

Our friend, Pastor Jergenson, was in N'Gaoundere, so we got a ride with him as far as Meiganga, where we found Pastor Earl Peterson, who took us along to Garoua-Boulai. There was Lloyd, awaiting us in our slightly revitalized Green Beetle which was being prepared to serve us for another term. We stayed on over the weekend to give him time to put on two new tires.

When we got to Baboua, we found that Lloyd, besides opening the Bible School, had taken time to unpack enough of our household equipment so that he could set up housekeeping during the month he awaited my return.

The first night we were back, as I was putting Mark to bed, he sighed and remarked, "Oh, Mom, isn't it good to be home again?!"

Since the Bredfeldts were unable to return to the Bible School, Lloyd had to lay aside his plans to do literature work in order to run the Bible School. It took me a long time to get settled, because I was constantly being interrupted by friends who came to welcome me back. They don't invite us to eat with them, but they brought fixings for meals: eggs, tomatoes, peanuts, bananas, an occasional chicken, and one man went fishing and brought us a lovely, big fish. He apologized: "I didn't have a chicken to bring you, but the Lord gave me this fish."

Twenty-six families made up the school village. Only the men attended the classes, but we did have separate classes for the women, many of whom had had no previous opportunity to learn to read. So they had to be divided according to their level of readiness. They begged me to have a class for them each morning at 6:15, the time when the men come for their first class. They have no concept of baby-sitters, so the little tykes wandered or crawled around on the floor—or maybe got Mama to take time out to suckle. As a nurse, I have struggled with a way to teach hygiene, but how was I to do it properly with the babies crawling around on the dirt floor? And, in their homes, where they had neither stove nor table, they had to cook over an open fire. Fortunately, the water supply there was clean, coming from a spring down in the valley. When it rained, they brought their big, wide, enamelware pans and lined them up under the eaves of our aluminum roof. We had a trough which ran the nice clean rain water into barrels. Even at that, we did boil the water, as it could have become contaminated in the barrel. I always had three large aluminum kettles that I used exclusively for the boiling of drinking water. This water was poured into containers in the refrigerator, being aerated in the process. So, when the cook emptied one water kettle, he knew it was time to refill and boil up another again.

Our cooks became quite responsible for these routine duties. Often, he would make the long walk to the market to buy meat for us. Vegetables and fruit were usually brought to our back door by local growers. As there was no bakery in the village, our cooks learned to make bread, cakes, and cookies. At one time, I had a cook who had worked for French people, and he knew how to prepare tasty meats. One of his specialties was spicy, boiled, chilled tongue which reminded me of the delicious head cheese which my mother used to make.

From a letter of December 1966:

> *Yesterday and today have been two of those frustrating days when one sort of goes around in circles and wonders what will come next. Our laundry man reported that his wife, who had gone to Abbo Bogrima to recuperate from a previous illness had had a relapse so we should go to get her! Last time we were at Garoua-Boulai we couldn't buy gasoline, as the attendant had broken the key off in the lock for the pump. We got enough from Cliff and some army men to get us home (and back there again) with a little left over to run our light plants (ours and the girls'). The government has an ambulance, but since the sous-prefet has no car, he uses the ambulance, so now, when it was needed for a patient, it was not available. Yesterday afternoon we were called to see a seriously ill sister-in-law of Ruth Pendo, Pastor Elie's wife, so we brought her up here. Then two German fellows drove in, only asking for a place to park their Volkswagen. We always enjoy conversation with these "tourists," so we invited them to come in for meals. One of them is a linguist, and spoke good English. Consequently, he monopolized the conversation at supper, the evening, and breakfast. It was casually mentioned that his companion is a doctor. So this morning I asked him if he would see this woman. He thought she might have meningitis, and advised us to get her to the doctor. He also examined Samuel Loba, who had just staggered up the hill en route to the dispensary. I have long advised him to go for an X-ray, as he looks like T.B., but he always says he doesn't have money. When I relayed the words of this doctor, that no "now and then" treatment here would help him, but he should get to the hospital for "long term therapy"; in about an hour, one of his relatives came to ask me if we couldn't take him along to G.B., too. In the meantime Lloyd got ten litres of gas from these German guys, and some from the girls, so he went to Abbo to get our laundry-man's wife. We were already planning to go to G.B. on Saturday morning, but we may have*

to go this afternoon instead. The girls will have to ride with us, too, as there won't be enough gas for two cars—not even Marie's wee little Peugeot.

BIBLE SCHOOL ACTIVITIES

For the opening of school, in order to get acquainted with the students, I made out a questionnaire, mimeographed it, and passed the sheets out to all of the students. As they were writing in the answers, I walked around, looking over their shoulders as they wrote. When I looked at Enoch Aoudou's paper, I made the remark: "You write very well." He looked up at me with a surprised look on his face and answered: "You know who taught me, don't you?" My mind flashed back at least 25 years to the group of little boys who came to my classes in Abba that first year I was there, and I guided those grimy little hands to teach them to write.

I believe it was during Enoch's second year at Bible school that he came to me at the dispensary, showing me an eruption on the skin on one of his feet. After trying unsuccessfully to treat it, the next time someone went to Garoua-Goulai, I sent him along to see the doctor. But, at the time, the new government official at the border chose to demonstrate his authority, and he did so by refusing to permit Enoch to cross the border and go onto Garoua-Boulai. By the time Enoch finally did get to the doctor, the skin condition had developed into cancer. In its early stages, skin cancer can be treated easily, but by this time, it was necessary to amputate his foot in order to save his life. Later, when Lloyd and Margaret Smith had received some unspecified monetary gifts, they paid for Enoch's trip to the Presbyterian Hospital at Elat, where he was fitted with a prosthesis. He walked well with that, and went on to graduate from Bible School, becoming a good catechist and the father of a large family.

Along in October, we got the idea of inviting some of the Bible School couples to eat dinner with us. We had four couples at a time. Most of the women had never eaten a meal at a table, using separate dishes and silverware for each individual. So they naturally were quite timid and ill-at-ease. We started with some who had had a little more social background. When they got back home from this encounter, of course these first ones had to fill in everything to the rest, so the next ones knew a little more what to expect! I always wished I could have been a mouse in the corner to hear what they said.

In connection with this, I could also mention that we had heard via the grapevine that each of us "Nasara" as they called us, also had a nickname, something perhaps like the name Jesus gave James and John, when He called them "Sons of Thunder." I always wished I knew what they called me, but perhaps I would rather not know! Even our children, who spoke Gbaya better than we did, and who were well accepted, could never get their friends to divulge the nicknames by which they called us. We all had our foibles, and they very likely picked up on those tendencies with nicknames that they used surreptitiously among themselves.

From a letter written February 13, 1967:

Our biggest news is the arrival of the first 100 pages of galley proofs from our Gbaya New Testament. Lloyd and I started in right after supper and checked twelve pages without even looking at the clock. Suddenly Lloyd asked, 'What time is it, anyway?' The Dutch printers have done very well, especially as they must work with a language totally strange to them. It is the special diacritical markings which they slip up on.

Mark has been back at school in Garoua-Boulai. He has a new, male teacher, Lew Hille, who teaches the lower grades. His wife, Marian, is a nurse, so she volunteers, caring especially for the premature babies born at the hospital. She also teaches piano for some of the American children.

The Mission Board could not find a teacher for the upper grades, so they asked Pastor Earl Peterson to fill that vacancy this year. His wife is also teaching piano. The two, Marian and Lorraine, presented their piano students in a recital on Dec.21st, before the regular Christmas program. We were happy to see Mark doing well in this. In fact, Mrs. Hille remarked to me once: "Mark surely has an ear for music. Once he was to play a piece in the Key of C. He got started wrong, and played the whole thing in D, sharps and all!"

Wanda came with the other high school students by Sudan Interior Mission plane to N'Gaoundere on Dec. 20, so we met her at Garoua-Boulai when we went for the Christmas program there.

Our high school students, attending at Jos, had had quite a traumatic experience when they were asked to help give emergency "first aid" to victims of the Ibo uprising in Jos. The combatants did not have guns, so they went after each other with knives and machetes—a mess! News from Nigeria indicates that the government is trying to patch things up, but as TIME magazine stated, "Nigeria will never be the same." (Writing this now, 30 years later, we have seen how this trend of inter-tribal violence has escalated almost all over Africa.)

As in any institution, building upkeep and improvement takes time and energy. Conrad Jergenson, who was involved with the Bible School from its inception, and is now at the seminary at Meiganga in Cameroon, came to Baboua to supervise the improvements on the student housing. The rectangular houses, built of adobe bricks, had thatched grass roofs, which would now be replaced by aluminum sheets. It had been decided to construct these roofs on a slant, instead of a 'gable' style. So all the old roofs were removed, the rafters saved to use again. Cement blocks were added to the back wall to give the roof a slight pitch. Because of this construction project, the school will not open in March, but (hopefully) in July.

Changes are being made in housing in the Gbaya (Tongo) village, as well. The government issued an edict that all residences in the village are now to be rectangular, instead of the traditional circular houses with grass roofs. This edict had come out some time ago, but the people had pretty much ignored it. So military police came and rammed many of the houses, enforcing the rule. There were complaints, but no open rebellion. It is still dry season, so there is time for rebuilding. If the old houses were built of blocks, they salvaged them, as well as the reusable rafters. A village plan was laid down, so these houses would be constructed in straight lines, with room for streets and open spaces (parks?) They will also supervise the construction of out-houses, to improve sanitation. (There can be no such things as plumbing, since there is neither water nor sewer.)

While Wanda was home for Christmas vacation (until Jan.29) she enjoyed meeting with the youth, about a hundred of them, who had been organized by the African pastor who teaches at the Bible School. There are several young men who can assume leadership, one of them the son of a relative of the chief. George had had an opportunity to take training as a veterinarian, but his father advised him to stay in the village and be involved in the Church. Pierre had observed that so many men who were employed by the government, with much better incomes than the ordinary people, were still always running out of money by the 20th of the month, then going around borrowing from their neighbors. Later, George did enroll at the seminary in Meiganga, but he was not led to be ordained.

Yesterday was one of those terrific Sundays. (The dispensary is closed on Sunday, so patients come to my verandah.) Before breakfast a Mbororo woman came with a stinky, abscessed hand: her co-wife had bitten her, and how true it is that a human bite is worse than most animal bites! So I had her come three times yesterday to soak her hand in hot epsom salts solution. I gave her a shot of penicillin. Today her hand is better, but she'll have to keep coming three times a day to soak it before we can start bandaging it.

At 2:40, as I was biking toward the church, I met a family with a very sick baby, so I turned around, went into the house and prepared an injection for the baby. It didn't even move when the needle went in. The mother tapped the baby's mouth with the back of her hand, as they do to get its attention, and I knew she realized that it was dead. She said it had just gotten sick during the night, but relatives told me later that the baby, her 10th child, had been sick for some time. The mother said softly: "The Lord gave, and the Lord has taken away." As they walked back to town, weeping, they stopped at the pastor's house. Their mourning is always so loud; this time it interfered with the youth meeting just beginning in the church. So the boys left, but several of the girls stayed, and we had a good visit.

Then Pastor Eli came in and called the people together for the funeral. After the funeral we invited Marie (Mundfrom) to have waffles with us. (Our

Onan generator can produce just enough electricity to heat the waffle iron, so we eat by candle light.)

After supper, I played the organ a while, and we had a short devotion. I was really ready for sleep when I rolled in to bed!

In a letter from Linnea recently, she mentioned that our Mission Board has increased the grants-in-aid to college students recently. Dr. Fricke said he had failed to get a raise in salaries for the missionaries, but he did get this increase in aid for our children in college.

FORTY-SEVEN
"The Song Of Ruth"

Carole and Ron sent us a tape recording of their wedding service, in which she sang "The Song of Ruth" to Ron. I had a copy of that song, and, from time to time, I had worked on singing it. So I got the idea of singing it at one of the evening sessions at our annual conference. So Marian Hille and I worked it up. Joyce Martinson helped me create atmosphere, with flowers and candle-light. So, after Jeanette Engesather had given her little devotional message, I announced: "When our daughter, Carole, was married last Thanksgiving, she sang 'The Song of Ruth' for her prospective husband. I decided to sing it for my husband tonight. We lack something in the way of atmosphere (Joyce piped up: "We're working on it.") so imagine yourself in a church. Also, imagine the singer about thirty years younger."

Marian played well, and, if I say so myself, I sang well, too. Then I said, "Some time ago, in one of her letters, Carole said, 'Mom, I wish you wouldn't worry about us, because when we know you worry about us, we worry about you.' Isn't that rather ridiculous? I had found a song based on Matt. 10:29-31, where Jesus tells of God's care of sparrows. My next song is based on that: 'Not a Sparrow Falleth, but its God Doth Know.'" When the song was over, you could have heard a pin drop! They all enjoyed it, but I think I enjoyed it most. I told Marian I had waited 23 years to do this, as I had never had an accompanist out here who could play this type of music.

MICHELLE/RENAULT

And then we were grandparents! Michelle Renee Gabrielson was born in Chicago on Aug. 17. We found out later that she had a congenital hip—she was born with her hip out of joint. But the nurse who did her first check-up discovered it; it was treated by putting the baby in a cast, so Michelle now has a normal hip and learned to walk correctly in proper time.

Our two-term, old International Travelall, which we called "The Green Beetle," was causing more and more trouble, so when Marie Mundfrom left for furlough, we bought her little 4-passenger Renault, which was very economical on gas.

CAR ACCIDENT

The Renault is considered a 4-passenger car, but when we went over to Garoua-Boulai to attend the Christmas program at the American School, we crowded five into it. As usual, the program was good, and we had a great time visiting around until eleven that night. We should have stayed over-night, but the trip back to Baboua was a short one. I had so much on my agenda for the next day, so I wanted very much to get home that night—which we thought would be about midnight.

We were not far from Baboua, going down a long descending curve toward a river, when Lloyd evidently dropped off to sleep. With a frightening "scruntch" we found ourselves in the shallow ditch, wedged up against the opposite bank! Lloyd banged his head against the support between the doors and was temporarily knocked out. My left knee struck the heater, breaking the heater to smithereens. We don't need a heater in Africa, anyway, but my knee was somewhat the worse for the encounter.

Madel Nostbakken, sitting in the back seat, knocked her head against the back of Lloyd's seat, so the next day her forehead was black-and-blue. Wanda and Mark were shaken, but unhurt. After trying in vain to get help from neighboring villagers, Madel, Wanda, and Mark walked in to town to the Catholic Mission. The Sister took them home first, then came out to get Lloyd and me. In the daylight, we could see that the car was not badly damaged: the front fender was 'wrinkled', the two right doors were somewhat out of shape, and the right wheel was slanted outward a bit. It was subsequently repaired and put into service again.

From a letter Wanda wrote to Carole:

As soon as I got out of the car, I started praying. I found out how calming it is to put one's faith in Him. It could have been much worse if it had happened near enough to the bridge for us to have fallen in the river. When the rest of us had crawled out of the car, I saw that Dad was sitting, slumped over the steering wheel. For a moment I thought he was dead, but then he began to rub his neck slowly, and then he climbed out, too. We were really scared for him because he asked four or five times where we were. He kept on repeating, "I must have been asleep when we came to that curve." I think we all feel that God has spared us to continue to work for Him.

Wanda continued:

In church on Sunday a group of young people sang a song in French...on Christmas Eve our family was alone, a rare thing. But every once in a while we were greeted with a "Bon Noel!" (Merry Christmas in French). After we had finished opening our gifts and finished our devotions, another group came. It was the youth group. After they left, I felt so...well, out of it. I wondered if they would let me join them. Dad took me over to the African pastor's house, and I was accepted!

I really enjoyed myself. I got to know the kids a lot better, and also the first verse of "Angels We Have Heard On High" in French...We went all over town singing. At midnight, the church bell rang, and all the groups of carolers met there. It was wonderful to hear the carols sung so whole-heartedly (in French or in Gbaya). Pastor Eli gave a wonderful Christmas message, our group sang our song, accompanied by rhythmic clapping. After the service, some of the kids escorted me home.

I got the idea of inviting them to our house for coffee the next day. They came at 5:30 on Christmas afternoon. We sang carols and looked at slides....One of the guys knows English quite well, so we had a good time visiting.... I'll be here until Feb. 2nd, so I'll get to be here for Mom's birthday."

When the time came, Wanda returned to school at Jos.

From a letter I sent to our family back in the US:

Remodeling of the students' houses is almost done, at least enough so they can move in: 38 families. Then three more families came from Woumbou, a remote area in Cameroon. They walked cross country, not even by way of the motor road. Two of the couples have five children each; the third have six. The refurbished houses have no furniture, so Lloyd and I had to hunt for mats, etc., which could be spread on the dirt floors for them. Naturally they were dead tired, though very cheerful and happy to have arrived.

This morning one of those women came to greet me. She was one who had been very sick last year, so I had spent considerable time treating her. Now she appears to be in perfect health, and she brought me a nice, big rooster as a gift, having carried it on top of all the other necessary baggage—on foot—all the way from Woumbou. I nearly cried when I accepted it!

I have a lot of other young roosters now, so I don't dare let this one loose in their midst—they would kill it—so I'll take it along over to Garoua-Boulai when we take Mark over to start school tomorrow. We'll take another rooster along, too, and give them to the house mother and ask her to prepare them for Mark's birthday.

We plan to drive the little Renault when we go over there, (Lloyd will take it to N'Gaoundere to have some repairs made on it) and then drive the old

Green Beetle back to use it for hauling sand for cement for the houses whose floors have not been laid.

The Green Beetle has been standing idle over there a long time. When that happens the Gbayas call a car Nabua (mother of mushrooms) because they grow in its shade. It "revived" all right, as Lloyd hauled 10 sacks of cement, and brought 4 women with 5 children as passengers."

In a subsequent letter, I shared my burden for the many children of those students who had nothing to do. The public school did not have room for them. So we decided to hire Joseph Moury, our former cook, who had also been a catechist, to have some simple reading classes for the children. We were not equipped to give classes in other subjects, but at least we could teach them to read in Gbaya, give them Bible lessons, and teach them songs to sing.

I had our carpenter build some display boards with slats across them on which to set flash cards, said cards made from some of that same mill end paper that came from Lake Mills.

From a letter written January 20, 1968:

Cliff Michelson, housefather at the American School in Garoua-Boulai, brought a load of the upper grade school children in his LandRover (including Mark). They ate their picnic supper on our porch. He then took them down to Abba for a week-end excursion.

The Smiths returned last night from a vacation trip to Gode and Tchollire, having spent Christmas at Gode. Beulah (Mathre) sent us two White Leghorn hens. They (Mathres) will leave for furlough this spring, so they are giving away some of their flock. Beulah has seventy turkeys and just about countless chickens. They order baby chicks from France once in a while and have them sent by air to Garoua. When the chicks are due, the Mathres rush up there to get them, and then rush home with them.

From a letter of February 11, 1968:

On Feb. 1st, Wanda, Lloyd and I left Baboua in the Green Beetle. This may be our last trip in it, as Lloyd has a couple prospective buyers. The motor is good, but the floor is so full of holes that we almost choke from the dust during the dry season.

While he was home for vacation, Mark got a couple guinea pigs. He took the male with him when he returned to school, but he left the pregnant female with me. She gave birth to three cute little piglets. I put them in a carton and took them over to G.B. You can imagine the squeals of delight when the children saw them. They all love pets, and Aunt Lil, their house mother, is so patient with them. They did have to fix up a cage for them outside, as it got pretty stinky having them in a dorm room.

We got in to Meiganga about 7:30 Thursday evening, looking, of course, like the brownest of Indians. On Friday Marge and Sharon gave a birthday party for me (special, because it was my 50th). The Flatens are in Meiganga now, too, and Grace came to the party, but Don was working on his car, as his son had crashed it against a tree about a week ago. There have been many accidents involving missionaries lately. The Norwegian dentist, whose services we need, was on a trip up north. Going down a long hill, his steering rod broke off. His assistant, who was riding with him, said they rolled three times. The assistant's arm was broken, but the dentist was not hurt—even his portable dental equipment. But now many patients are impatiently awaiting his return.

When we got Wanda to N'Gaoundere where she and the other six students from our mission expected to take the mission plane, they found that the four-passenger plane was forbidden to make the second trip necessary to transport the rest of the young people. In spite of radioing back and forth, it took a long time to get the permission to get out of Cameroon again. In the meantime people back in Nigeria were waiting for the pilot to take them on previously arranged flights.

So the Flatens, who were planning to go to Poli and Balkossa anyway, decided to take three of the students and go the "back road," which is open now during the dry season. Wanda enjoyed the trip, and the students were able to overcome the disadvantage of arriving at school a week late."

FORTY-EIGHT
Visit Of the "Death Angel"
"I'll Fly Away"

Lisel Waechter, a French teacher who came from Alsace-Lorraine, and had taught at our Bible School, and, at this time, at the College in N'Garoundere, was on vacation from her teaching duties, so she arranged to give a refresher course in practical French for us missionaries in the Central African Republic. She arranged for us to come to Garoua-Boulai for the classes.

We had barely begun when the young missionary couple now at Djohong, Ron and Carol Sagness, came to Garoua-Boulai. They had a bouncing baby boy whom they named Hans. Soon after, she became seriously ill with infectious hepatitis. The Hilles took the Sagnesses into their home, and Marian, who is a nurse, took over her care. But her illness went from bad to worse, and soon she died. Her death was a shock to all of us. Several other missionaries were having or had had hepatitis, but her resistance was undoubtedly lower, having so recently given birth to a child.

As I had my Wurlitzer electric organ in the American School building at G.B. at the time, I recorded some suitable funeral music on a tape. So, before, during, and after the service, I played some of this music which I had recorded.

Soon after the funeral, the grieving husband and father packed up and took his infant son back to the U.S. for a time. Several years later, a single lady doctor came to Garoua-Boulai; she married Ron and they worked for a while in Africa.

TENDER LOVING CARE (George and Pauline)

The town of Baboua was made up of several large divisions: our mission, which was located some distance south of the main part of town; the Gbaya village, known as Tongo to the western world, whose people speak a different dialect of Gbaya; the business district, where there are a number of Hausa, the butchers; people who keep tiny stores where they sell a remarkable variety of merchandise; the douane, or customs, the government "fonctionaires;" and the Catholic mission, where a priest and usually two sisters from France lived and worked. One of the sisters ran the government dispensary where there were houses for in-patients. There was also the settlement of Sango-speaking people who had come from farther east; they were another kind of Gbaya. Many of these Sango-speaking people were Christians, having been evangelized by missionaries of the Baptist or Brethren missions. Most of them have been in Baboua long enough to have learned to speak our kind of Gbaya. (Africans are natural linguists. Most of them can speak six or seven languages.)

Among these people was a man named George, who had a sewing machine, a small, portable Singer operated by a hand-crank. He came one day to tell me that his wife, Pauline Yado, had been taken to the hospital in Garoua-Boulai. When we went to see her, I found that she was paralyzed from the neck down. Treatment given her there did not seem to be helping her, so George got her on a truck and took her to an herbalist who practiced in a little village on the main road east of Baboua. This woman heated a certain kind of leaves and applied them as a hot pack to Pauline's body. This reminded me of Sister Kenney's hot pack treatment which we gave for polio back in 1943. Pauline did regain some feeling, but was not able to move herself nor sit up. Eventually, we were able to install them in one of the student houses at our Bible School which was vacant during the summer vacation. Getting her history, I discovered that Pauline had been out gathering up a load of cassava roots in her basket. With her baby tied on her back, she had been descending a steep path which was slippery from rain, and she fell. When I first saw her at the hospital, I noticed that she had blisters on the top of her feet just behind the toes. I thought to myself: "She has been struck by lightning!" But I never voiced that idea to any of the Africans, knowing how extremely superstitious they were about lightning.

Because of her paralysis, she was incontinent—she couldn't hold her urine. So I got a Foley catheter from the hospital and inserted it. Later, I found that they had pulled it out, because it had gotten plugged up. I obtained another one, put it in, and told George that he must see that Pauline drank a lot of water. Gbayas do not habitually drink much water, so I thought of a way to solve that. I got some lemons, extracted the juice, and then cooked it up with a lot of sugar, making a syrup. Giving it to George, I told him: "This is medicine. Mix a tablespoon of it in a glass of water and have

Pauline drink it four times a day." That solved the problem. She put out a large volume of urine, and the catheter stayed open indefinitely.

Pauline could not do anything for herself: she had to be fed and her husband had to turn her two or three times a night. He dressed her in the morning and carried her out to sit in the "chaisse longue", the lounging chair that we brought her. Friends came to see her, and she witnessed to them. People who came to sympathize with her left inspired by her faith.

When some unspecified monetary gifts came, George and his children made adobe blocks to build a new, three-room house, and we provided the money to buy cement for the floor.

Pauline lived, a paraplegic, and George was an unusually faithful husband. People who observed them would go away shaking their heads, and saying, "Most men would walk out on a woman who was no longer useful to him." Eventually, though, she lost her will to live. When she died, we went to visit the family. Among those people, the degree of love and respect of the neighbors is indicated by the amount of firewood that they will carry in and deposit in the "begara," the front yard of the home. It was customary for friends and relatives to sit around several small bonfires in the yard most of the night for a wake, sometimes more than one night, especially if relatives came from a distance. Heathens brought and drank beer, but the Christians drank coffee (with lots of sugar) and sat quietly and visited, singing hymns. There were many words of commendation for George's faithful, tender, loving care for his beautiful, paralyzed wife, and their five children.

FORTY-NINE
Agricultural Missions
"There Is Something About That Name"

As the lifestyle of the Gbayas was dependent upon their subsistence farming, though they did not go hungry, they were able to produce little more cash or trade crops than they needed for food and to pay for the clothing necessary for their warm climate, or perhaps cement for the floor of a house, aluminum roofing, or a Singer sewing machine. So, with the hopes that the members of the Church community could become self-supporting, our mission leaders decided to send out a missionary who could teach the Gbayas how to farm more efficiently. Bill Peters, a graduate of the University of Minnesota School of Agriculture, and his wife, Nancy, who had a degree in Home Economics, joined our staff, and came to Baboua to learn the Gbaya language with the help of Madel Nostbakken.

Later, Bill found that his modern methods were not practical in the Gbaya culture. There was no way that the Gbayas could, even as a co-op, finance a tractor and the other implements considered necessary in the U.S. So, eventually, he bought and trained oxen for plowing. Oxen required neither gasoline nor spare parts, and the extra boy needed to lead them was readily available. Women and children followed the plow and chopped up the furrows to prepare the small fields for planting. Later, Bill was able to import some of the small, diesel-powered, Self Help tractors which were simpler to repair and took a minimum of fuel to run.

With his 5-ton truck, he established a route for gathering the produce which the people wanted to haul to the markets in the larger centers. In the past, they would simply have had to walk, carrying a sack of peanuts or cassava on their heads.

He was able to train several leaders, who, in turn gave instruction to prospective farmers. So, by the time he left Africa, there were a number of Christians who were qualified to teach others.

FIFTY
Fire!
"Oh How He Loves You And Me!"

From a letter written February 5, 1969:

Sunday was a happy day here. Corrine and Doris had come over on Saturday, so they joined in my birthday party. I had intended to invite the Bible School wives in for coffee, but when Communion was announced for the afternoon, we decided to invite them on Monday morning instead.

Shortly after the women had left, I went out on our back porch and saw clouds of smoke rising from the Tongo village. (There is a wooded valley between that village and ours.) Soon sheets of flame erupted from houses just in front of the chief's compound. Our Gbaya help were watching, too, and as the flames leaped toward the direction of Raymond's house, I said, "Run!" Then I ran down to the Bible School, which is located below our house, in the other direction, so they had not seen the fire. It didn't take long for them to get into action when I yelled: "The town is on fire!"

When we arrived at the village, we were horrified to find that the fire, which had begun as a grass-fire north of the town, and driven by a high wind, had already wiped out about 150 houses before we knew what was going on. Then it jumped that big open space in front of the chief's compound and went around behind it. Men were busy splashing water on the roofs in his compound. That, together with the protection of the big, mud walls around it, saved his place. George and his father, and Joseph Moury were among those whose homes were destroyed. But they had seen it coming so long before it reached them, that they got all their belongings out of their houses. Children were taken to the wooded area by the stream. Because of the wind, the fire cut a clean swath right across the town: 230 houses wiped out. But fortunately no lives were lost. Many of the people were out in the wilderness, hunting, or gathering building materials, so there were actually few present to fight the fire. Some of the people who were there carried things out of their houses, but they didn't take them far enough away, so the fire licked them up, too. As we approached the town, we met crowds of people carrying all their simple possessions and depositing them at the church (made of brick, with a metal roof).

When the fire had spent its fury, we heard screaming back in the direction of the church. From a very low area there, flames were creeping toward the part of town that had been spared so far. So the men hurried down there. The students broke branches off trees and beat out the flames as they approached the houses. One man climbed up on a roof and put out sparks that had lit on it. So the rest of the town was saved.

We had three Bible School houses vacant, so we invited three families to move into them. Yesterday many were busy scooping the charred remains out of their blackened walls, putting poles over the tops of them and spreading grass over them, so they can have a place for shelter. (The walls are constructed of adobe blocks, so they did not burn.) This is dry season, so they won't get wet, but it is bitterly cold at night (about 50 degrees, which is cold for here, where everyone runs around barefoot much of the time.)

There is nothing like insurance here, but today government officials came and were listing losses. I surely hope they will get some help. (I never heard that they did.)

FIFTY-ONE
Annual Conferences

After the new dormitory was built at the American School in Garoua-Boulai, we gathered for our missionary conferences there—either at the close of school, when we would be coming to get our children, or just before school would open. The second, larger school room was a good place for business sessions, and the dorm kitchen served well for the preparation of meals, planned by a committee of missionary wives.

In later years we always designated one of the last nights of conference for FUN NIGHT. We were blessed with some very talented people, so we enjoyed much wit and music. It turned out that, right after each conference, we would begin to plan what we would do next year, God willing.

The American School teachers always coached groups of children in music and drama pieces to perform. One year, I wrote to a music company in the U.S. and ordered something funny, but the first things I got were either corny or downright vulgar. I did get three sheet music pieces from Rodgers and Hammerstein operettas, though. I made appropriate costumes, and Lloyd and I sang "People Will Say We're in Love." Tom Christianson was the Master of Ceremonies, and he introduced us as the entertainers called "The Flower and the Flame."

Bill Weldon, a short term elementary teacher, could play almost anything, and could transpose from key to key. So the next year, I wrote a parody on "He's Got the Whole Wide World in His Hands," putting the names of all the missionaries in the song, with something appropriate (or funny) about each one. Lloyd and I started the first verse in as low a key as possible, then, with each succeeding verse, Bill would raise the pitch half a step, so, by the time the song ended, we were practically on the roof!

Since they had recently resigned, Connie and Marj Jergenson sang a duet about going home. At the end of each verse, Connie sang: "And you pack the trunks..." Three of the men, dressed as girls, sang as a trio (?). Two of them were good singers, but the third one really messed it up—which became more and more hilarious, and nobody cared! Luther Flugstad gave a demonstration of how to sew a button on your pants without taking them off! Of course the contortions he went through made it all the funnier!

In Col.3:17 we read: "And whatever you do in word or deed, do everything in the name of the Lord Jesus, giving thanks to God the Father through Him." I believe that includes having fun.

One year, two of the single girls wrote and sang a very good, entertaining song entitled "When I Retire."

FIFTY-TWO
The Biafran Crisis In Nigeria

Wanda's graduation from Hillcrest Academy in Jos, Nigeria, was coming up early in June, 1969. Naturally, we hoped to attend. But the political situation in Nigeria was getting worse. We were warned that we would have to request special visa permission in order to be admitted into the country. Lloyd hitch-hiked to Bangui, the capital of R.C.A., but discovered that Nigeria had no embassy there. Then he went to Garoua-Boulai to catch a bus to go to Yaounde to contact someone at the Nigerian Embassy. Lew Hille, who was in charge at G.B. in the absence of Paul Nostbakken, asked him to stay over because they were expecting a group of Germans coming through. They spoke French, and they wanted Lloyd to interpret for them in consultation with Gbaya leaders in the Church.

One of the Germans had been a missionary in West Cameroon some years ago. The driver of the Volkswagen in which they were traveling ran a safari service. One of the passengers, a committed Christian, was a jet pilot. Another was a woman doctor who wanted to see what it is like out here, maybe with the idea of coming out to work, though what she saw convinced her that she would have to get training in surgery. So Lloyd rode with the Germans to Yaounde. They stopped off on the way at Bertoua to spend Sunday at the mission which was then run by a fine African pastor who had once been a French School teacher at our mission in Djohong.

That Sunday morning, they had a very festive service: baptism of both adults and infants, confirmation, re-affirmation of faith on the part of two women who evidently had been out of fellowship, and now had come back; then Communion—all this besides a sermon and songs by at least five different choirs.

Reaching Yaounde, the Germans took Lloyd to the American Embassy, where he was given some blanks to fill out and present to the Nigerian office. The officials there provided him with a permit which seemed to be what he would need to get us in to Nigeria in good time.

Leaving Yaounde on Tuesday morning, he got a bus that took him only about 45 kilometers. Then he boarded a truck with a chauffeur who was not as careful as he should be. After dark that night, they met a truck on a narrow stretch of road. To avoid a collision, the driver of the truck in which Lloyd was traveling took to the ditch and rolled his vehicle. Fortunately, Lloyd was not injured; another car soon came along and the driver dropped him off at the home of an Armenian who invited him to spend the night in his spare bedroom. The next day, Lloyd boarded a bus which got him back to Garoua-Boulai about 9:30 p.m. The day after that, he planned to take the bus back to Baboua, but a nice sedan came along, and the driver picked him up and brought him right up to our house. The driver, who was from Bangui, had been at our hospital in G.B. being treated for diabetes. Nula, one of the African nurses at G.B., having the day off, was riding with the driver. He was doing this in order to learn how to drive, since he was planning to buy a car.

After all that effort, though, we did not get into Nigeria for Wanda's graduation! It turned out that one of her classmates whose parents were coming from the opposite direction, in Sierra Leone, were also forbidden to enter Nigeria.

Here are some of the details of our attempt. The mission plane that we had planned to take could not get permission to land in Nigeria. Lee Bohnhoff was then conscripted to take us in his Land Rover. When we got to the border town of Mubi, Nigeria, we were refused permission to enter—in spite of the permit that Lloyd had received in Yaounde. The immigration officer showed Lloyd the circular which had recently come from the capital in Lagos, forbidding border control officers from admitting any foreigners except recognized business men—and they were given only 48 hours to come and go. At first, he would not even let us sleep at the mission in Mubi. He said, "You must turn right around and go back to Cameroon!" It had been a long, hot drive from N'Gaoundere that day, and we were tired and dusty. He finally agreed to accompany us to the mission. There we were received kindly by the American couple, Rev. and Mrs. Stern, who also had a son attending Hillcrest Academy at Jos. They agreed to contact Jos by short-wave radio in the morning, to ask that someone transport our six high school students as far as the border. Then Lee would meet them and bring them down to N'Gaoundere.

The Sterns lent us air-mattresses, bedding, and gave us some food, and they agreed to come out to the border in the morning after they had conversed with Jos. So we made our way back through the three check-points where we had registered earlier in the evening. There is a nice customs house on the Cameroon side, and the guards there let us in to sleep. By the time we settled down, it was almost two a.m.

In addition to our own woes, we had with us an eleven-year old Norwegian boy whose father is a builder at the mission in Nigeria. The boy attended the Norwegian school in N'Gaoundere, and went to visit his parents in Nigeria when someone from our mission went to get students from our mission who are there. This Norwegian boy was born in Nigeria, so he did not have a visa in his passport. The border official also refused to let him in.

Undoubtedly, his father was successful in getting him through later. Lee took us back to the Lutheran Brethren Mission in Garoua. Since Mark had come with us for the trip having just completed his school year, we were having some time with him while we waited. He and Lloyd took a picnic lunch with them and went hiking in the mountains behind the mission at Garoua. But we decided not to wait for Wanda in Garoua. There was little guest space, and it is very hot! The mission at N'Gaoundere was wall-to-wall people at that time. A new builder, Earl Christianson, his wife, and two teenage sons arrived from Albert Lea, Minnesota. They worked in Meiganga the next three months.

On the same plane with the builder and his family were the Mundshenk family and Madel Nostbakken's sister, Marie, who had come out for a visit. An unsung part of mission work is the hosting of traveling co-workers. The Dressens hosted Lew and Marian Hille, who were leaving for study at the seminary. Lew had been one of the elementary teachers at Garoua-Boulai for three years.

The Dressens were going to the US, too, but he had to first orient James Noss to the duties of mission treasurer. Bill had worked very hard that year. When Joan Ellertson got sick, and the family had to leave, Bill took over the administration of the College, where he was already on the staff as a professor, as well as served as mission treasurer, and as chaplain at the French army camp outside of town.

To be station hostess there at that time was really a strain on all of one's ingenuity. Besides missionary families coming and going, the six high school students were coming in late from Jos, hungry, and tired. Besides the missionary families already listed, Earl and Lorraine Peterson were en route back to the U.S. where he hoped to work on a doctorate. Their son, Tim, was with them then, and Becky was coming in from Jos.

FIFTY-THREE
Mbalang

"I Heard the Voice of Jesus say: Come unto Me and rest."

Several years ago, two Frenchmen came out to the N'Gaoundere area. They had heard about the bottomless crater lake known as Mbalang, and that the volcanic soil near the lake would be great for vegetable gardening. Each man had built a house on the hill south of the lake and proceeded to prepare their gardens.

With the help of African laborers, they dug a channel from the lake to their gardens to provide irrigation in the dry season. Eventually, they produced wonderful vegetables. But the European community in N'Gaoundere was not large enough to provide a profitable market for their vegetables, and the Africans had their own lifestyle, foods, and system of farming and barter, so they were unwilling to pay the higher prices which these Europeans needed to make a profit.

First one, and then the other family gave up and returned to France. Later, some of the missionaries from Norway discovered that the place was for sale. Africans who had been trained to do the actual work were available, so some of the missionaries began to produce vegetables on a smaller scale.

It was also possible to reserve the house, so that a family could spend a week or two of vacation camping there. The lake water was clear and clean, but there was no beach, so Rod Ellertson built a raft which the missionary families used to get out into the center of the lake. There they would dive off the raft and swim in the uncomtaminated, deep water. Africans had discovered that it was fun to play along the edge of the lake, and people who were infected with Schistosomiasis (Bilharzie) parasites deposited their larva-infested excrements there. One could not see them, but, since we knew that the disease was spread in that way, we all resisted the temptation to swim or play along the edge of any of the lakes in the area. That was why they would take the raft out into the deep water in the center of the lake, where the water had not been contaminated.

Since both the missionaries from Norway and our American workers cooperated in building and staffing the hospital, a secondary school and the radio studio, there was a large settlement of missionaries stationed there in N'Gaoundere. The climate was ideal, so missionaries from hotter areas often came there for vacations, to get physical exams and treatment, and to have their babies. The Norwegian missionaries also established their elementary boarding school for their children on the mission grounds. Most of the Norwegian missionaries spoke English, and we had good fellowship with them. Sometimes a large group would go out to Mbalang for a picnic and a ride on the raft. Because they had become good friends while working together in Cameroon, many of our American missionaries would stop off in Norway to visit on their way to the U.S. for furlough.

Lloyd had a cousin, Helge Sand, in Norway who was the traveling secretary for the Norwegian Mission Society. Two of their sons, Aage and Sven, and their wives spent several years in medical mission work in Cameroon. Aage was a physician and, as I mentioned earlier, Sven was a "diakon," one who does many kinds of auxiliary medical work, similar to an American "paramedic."

TRAVEL AGAIN

After Wanda's graduation, she returned to our home in Baboua in the Central African Republic for a short visit.

Word got around among the Gbayas that we were leaving for furlough again. Because of this, Lloyd was kept busy with umpteen kinds of counseling, etc., so there was always a lot of last minute bookkeeping to do. I remember one thing vividly: at our church services, the Gbayas got into the habit of bringing their most tattered currency to put into the offering plate, because they knew we could exchange it. So, when we were ready to go, I had packed all this old money—mostly metal coins—in a bright red train case which had a mirror in the lid.

This time, we went home by way of Bangui, the capital of the Central African Republic, instead of through Cameroon. It was rainy season, and we were told that, on what passed for the highway toward Bangui, there were two bridges that had been completely washed out. One of our more prosperous Gbaya friends, Andre Nagbata, had two trucks. So, he kept one on the Baboua side of the wash-outs, and the other on the Bangui side. The problem was that the two wash-outs were about five miles apart!

Because our departure had been delayed, we actually left Baboua after dark. Andre took us in his Baboua truck to the first wash-out. The moon was shining, and our Gbaya carriers were all in good spirits, so we rather enjoyed the walk. At one time it actually rained a bit, but we took shelter in an African house until it subsided. Then the moon came out, and we walked again. The African who was carrying my money box found it rather heavy. In fact, he asked, "What have you got in this box? Money?" I did not tell him. At one time, he set it down in the road and sat on it. When we got to our destination, I found that the mirror had been broken! Finally, we arrived at the second stream, and with the help of our African carriers, were able to cross. We then climbed into the second truck, which took us safely to the American Baptist mission in Bangui. We had communicated with them by telegram, so they knew we were coming. Having lived in Africa, our hosts were not surprised when we knocked at the door in the wee hours of the morning.

FIFTY-FOUR
Tourists
"All The Way My Savior Leads Me"

As Baboua was the first government post in the Central African Republic and was situated on African Highway #1, we got some very interesting visitors. Actually, the mission was located about two miles off the highway, but when trucks stopped at the government post where police and customs offices were located, if there were European passengers who needed lodging, the customs people would often direct them to appeal to us. So we entertained some people from different countries who had come to Africa with varying purposes. There were even white girls who had the courage to travel alone!

At one time, we entertained two American couples in Land Rovers who were practically out of cash. They had thought they would find a bank at the border town of Baboua. They would need to buy gasoline in Bouar, 75 miles farther on. We knew they would not find a bank until they arrived in Bangui, the capital.

So we lent them the amount of cash which we thought would get them to Bangui, with the request that, when they got cash in Bangui, they would turn it in at the mission for us. They were simply astounded! They carried through on it, and really lauded us to our missionary friends in Bangui who accepted the money on our behalf!

At one time we were brought to our door by the roar of two immense motorcycles. Each one was ridden by two swarthy turbaned Indians (Hindus?). They told us that they were professional surveyors hired by the Cameroon and RCA governments to chart a route for a railroad which would run from Douala, Cameroon, to Bangui, RCA. Whether they did or not, we never heard any more of the project.

We kept a small guest house which was always set up and ready for unexpected company. I don't remember ever having a guest take undue advantage of this hospitality. Also, among ourselves, when one family had been away, it was understood that those on the station would welcome the ones returning and provide their first meal. Often it would be more than one meal. How we did appreciate this Christian hospitality, because travel was very tiring. It was so nice to have a meal prepared, and probably a loaf of bread and some boiled water to start the first meal the next day! Remember, there were no motels nor cafes in that area then.

FIFTY-FIVE
International Travel Adventures
"Seek Ye First The Kingdom Of God"

The last time we traveled back to Africa as a family, we had a stop-over in New York. At that time, the airlines permitted each passenger to bring two carry-ons. Someone had given Mark a bow and arrow just before we left, and there was no way we could pack it up, so that was what he was carrying. As we sat waiting, with baggage all around us, a stewardess came over to me. She asked, "Are all these things yours?!" When I said they were, she kindly offered to take care of some of them, and when we arrived at our destination, we gathered it all up again.

At one time when Mark was attending Hillcrest Academy in Jos, Nigeria, he took the jet from Kano to London by himself. En route, a stewardess offered him a small glass of wine, which he graciously accepted. Later, when she presented the bill, surprised, he remonstrated: "I thought you were giving it to me. I have absolutely no money of any kind!"

At another time, Wanda and I were traveling by ourselves, and we arrived in Rome in the wee hours of the morning. Evidently, all the other passengers got connecting flights or lived in Rome, so we found ourselves alone in the cavernous building with only the night-time cleaning personnel. Early in the morning, when the place came to life again, we walked around, looking at the interesting things for sale. There was a beautiful, pink sea-shell made into a lamp. It was about ten or twelve inches tall and set on a sturdy base. When we got it home and unwrapped it, we found that the salesgirl had removed the bulb. I was never able to find one that fit that socket.

While we were working in Poli and Lloyd was Field Superintendent, he was asked to take two representatives from LUTHERAN WORLD ACTION in Switzerland for a tour of our mission field. Arne Sovik, an American, had been a missionary in China, and Sigurd Aske, was from Norway. I accompanied Lloyd as he took them around on one part of their tour, when we visited one of the

Norwegian mission stations. The missionaries had their school children all dressed up in uniforms and trained to sing and do gymnastics for the visiting dignitaries. During the course of the visit, we mentioned to them that we hoped to stop off in Europe a little on our next trip for furlough. Mr. Aske told us that he has an apartment in Geneva, Switzerland, and he would be glad to entertain us while we were there. It turned out that he was actually at home in Norway when we arrived, but he had left the key for us, so we saved hotel money and prepared our own meals between sightseeing excursions. He also had given us the name and address of a German deaconess mission in Rome with whom we corresponded, and who provided us with inexpensive accommodations. No matter that it was third class. They also spoke enough English to give us directions.

Taxi drivers in Rome gave us unofficial, guided tours, pointing out the various ruins sticking up here and there in the modern city. (In Europe many people can speak either English or French, which was helpful to us as tourists.) Seeing the remains of the once-magnificent Coliseum stirred our imaginations, as we remembered its history of the Christians thrown to the lions who had been kept in cages in a subterranean area where all the floors had, since then, caved in. The building had been severely damaged by earthquakes, and it would take a fortune to restore it. Our outstanding experience in Rome was attending a performance of the opera "Aida." this was performed by a group of students in the part of the Arena which had been restored so there was seating for the audience. The stage was large enough so that, at the appointed time in the story, a double team of white horses came charging up a ramp, across the stage, and out a side exit!

DENMARK—NORWAY—LONDON

Wanda had a friend at school in Jos who was from Denmark. The family had gone back to Denmark, and when the girl heard that we would be traveling through Europe, they invited us to stop off to visit them in Aarhus. Denmark reminded us so much of Iowa. When we were there, the farmers were harvesting wheat, using a tractor pulling a binder like the one my Dad used when I was a running the tractor for him back in the thirties.

Lloyd had gotten word that his cousin, Olga, who lived just north of Oslo, Norway, had cancer, so he decided to forgo the visit in

Denmark to go to see her. So Mark and I went with Wanda to Denmark, arranging to meet Lloyd at Heathrow airport in London.

We had toyed with the idea of doing some more traveling, and sight-seeing in Europe, but Carole's second baby was due, and we were so eager to get home. Ronnie was born before we got there, but by only a short time.

From a "circular letter" written from St. Paul on November 13, 1969:

> Three months ago our family alighted at Minneapolis-St.Paul airport and were welcomed by members of our family and Pastor Hesterman of our Division of World Missions. Good news they brought: our Carole (Gabrielson) had given birth to baby Ronnie. Bad news: Mrs. Lee Bohnhoff, one of our missionaries in Cameroon, had died suddenly on July 30, after we left Africa.
>
> The first few days we were welcomed—as during each previous furlough— to stay with Lloyd's oldest sister, Borghild Hofflander.
>
> His brother Rolfe helped us choose a good, used car at Larson Chevrolet. Then we went to Iowa, where it was good to see Mom and Dad Ramsey (Dad is 83) looking so well. Coming back, we moved in to the "pink house" on Fulham and did some hasty shopping for Wanda.
>
> On Aug. 26, we drove as far as Morris, Mn., where we visited friends, Rev. & Mrs. Clifford Grindland on our way to Moorhead. After getting Wanda's things into her lovely room in the new dormitory: East Complex at Concordia College, we went to call on neighbors from our 1953-'54 furlough spent in Moorhead.
>
> The day after Labor Day, Mark entered 8th grade at Murray. Right now he is having the "time of his life" in swimming class. On Dec. 19th, Linnea will get her Bachelor of Arts degree, French major, from the U. of Minn. But she has decided to teach 4th grade, so she plans to go back to Augsburg College for Elementary Education. By the time she is through, she expects to have three majors: French, English, and Elementary Education.
>
> Ron and Carole live at 4532 Xerxes Ave., Minneapolis. He is fortunate that he has his military service out of the way. He works very hard at the Sun printing Co. in Edina, but they are happy to have a home of their own with a back yard where their 2-yr. old daughter, Michelle and their gray poodle, Tabor, can tumble around on the grass (or snow). We are so thankful that the defect in Michelle's hip (a congenital dislocation) has been completely corrected, so she walks normally.
>
> Lloyd has been booked most Sundays for deputation, and when his destination has not been too far away, Beryl has enjoyed going along to speak and sing. We enjoy sharing news of what the Lord has been doing in Cameroon and the Central African Republic. We only wish words could express the tremendous joy, the deep satisfaction gained from the many-faceted, never boring work of an "Ambassador for the King."

FURLOUGH IN ST. PAUL

The system for missionaries' furloughs had been changed: instead of staying on the field for five years, and then going to the U.S. for a year, we would stay two years and then have a home leave of two months, or three years, with three months. This came about especially because there were more and more of the missionaries' children being left in the U.S. for higher education.

So, it was possible for us to go with Wanda to Moorhead and get her established as a freshman at Concordia College. Later, Ron and Carole found a better house on Park Avenue, owned by an aging lady doctor. We were assigned to a furlough home in St. Paul, referred to as the pink house, not far from Luther Seminary. Our friends, Dr. and Mrs. Bernard Christianson, lived just across the street. He was an invalid, but we had some good visits with them.

During that time, we also celebrated our silver wedding twenty-fifth anniversary, gathering with other Sands at the Wapagasset Bible Camp, at Amery, Wisconsin, which was only a short drive from St. Paul.

In preparation for our return to Africa, we bought, with some financial help from the Mission Board, a bright blue Chevrolet pick-up. Knowing how bad the roads were, Lloyd asked the company to replace the tires with more heavy duty ones. They did, but they must have used some old stock, as we discovered when traveling on the sometimes rocky roads because often they would go flat simply from a stone bruise. Some of our African helpers became quite adept at changing tires, but Lloyd always had to be there to supervise. So, of course, we always needed to have a good spare or two on hand. Speaking of help: at one time when we were visiting in Abba, Lloyd asked a man to check the water in the radiator. Instead, the man poured water into the oil receptacle. So, they had to drain out all the oil. Fortunately, Lloyd Smith, whom we were visiting, had a supply of new oil, so Lloyd was able to refill it.

A couple days after we took delivery of the pick-up in Minneapolis, I was driving it near the garage where we had bought it. As I pulled into an intersection, something in the clutch mechanism simply fell apart, so I could not move it. I put on the warning flasher and walked the two blocks back to the garage. When I got there, I announced: "Something in the pick-up we bought here two days ago fell apart in the middle of the intersection." A man ran down there and somehow got it back to the garage where they repaired it.

My brother, Lynn Ramsey, who was working at Winnebego, gave us a white camper top for the pick-up which transformed it almost into a van.

Wanda had just completed her first year of college at Concordia in Moorhead, Minnesota, and, together with a girl-friend, had found a summer job at Ballagh's Big Bear Resort in a forested area in northern Wisconsin, 14 miles out of Winter, Wisc. So, en route to New York to put our car on a freighter to go to Africa, we took her up there and got to see the place where she would be spending the summer. Driving along that winding, black-top road after dark, we nearly ran down a family of deer. The forest area reminded us of Africa, except for the smooth road.

Wanda had decided to take a year off from college studies to go to the Lutheran Bible Institute in Seattle, beginning that fall, which she did after spending the summer working in Wisconsin. That summer proved to be a new and different experience, being a part of a working team, most of whom had had a very different background from hers. It wasn't pleasant to have the girls make fun of her for bowing her head for grace before meals, but she was victorious, and they admired her for it. We were thankful for her openness, as she told about an evening spent with girls who had used too much liquor. I have the copy of the letter I wrote to her in response!!

After her year at L.B.I., Wanda transferred to Winona State College, a branch of the University of Minnesota, where she earned her degree in nursing.

A letter of September 8, 1970 in regard to the pick-up:

On Aug. 19, James Noss drove our blue Chevrolet pick-up from Douala, the seaport in Cameroon. He had had a terrible trip up country, as the roads were so muddy. The Bible School students who washed the caked red mud off it were surprised to find that the wheels were white! When I asked one of them to wash it (as the kids were already scrawling their names in the muddy surface) he answered: "Of course! It's ours, isn't it?" which means that we belong to them, and they know they can expect many free rides while we live and work here.

FIFTY-SIX
Evangelism-In-Depth »Key 73«
"How Firm a Foundation!"

A movement had started among missions and churches in Central America often referred to as Evangelism in Depth. Missionaries returning for furlough in the U.S. had shared their enthusiasm about it; missionaries then going back to their work in Africa spread the news. The missions east of us in the Central African Republic invited us to participate in a conference entitled "New Life for All," where material was shared. Among these things was a new song book, lively Gospel songs written in the Sango language and set to melodies familiar to missionaries from all the missions. Our Gbaya leaders knew Sango, so they helped Madel translate these songs and we mimeographed a little song book. At that time, I had acquired a huge piano-accordion from a Swedish missionary at Bouar, and I learned to play the piano part to teach the melodies to our church people. I put the songs on audio tapes and lent out tape players to go with the song books.

Since that time, the African Christians have developed their own hymns. Often, they will take the words of our songs and set them to their own melodies. I was amazed at how readily they had learned the American music because I could not master theirs. At first the music annoyed me, for it seemed so irreverent, but since we have been back in the U.S., we have become accustomed to contemporary Gospel music, which is quite similar, and which is being used by the Lord in evangelism.

This Evangelism-in-Depth movement spread to most missions in Africa and then back to the U.S. where it became known as "Key 73" because it became well known in 1973. It was a movement where people of many denominations gathered in small groups, especially in homes, for neighborhood Bible Studies.

In Africa, the movement was called "New Life for All" and someone produced a logo, a sketch of a green cornstalk with a sturdy ear of corn sticking out on each side. Mr. Beaver of the Brethren Mission was put in charge. We were invited to participate in a conference in preparation for this movement. Representatives from five missions attended. Mr. Beaver and his staff did a good job in producing literature for the leaders. The fact that all of the Central African Republic uses the same language, Sango, was a unifying force. Actually the Central African Republic was unique in this respect: although the people speak many different tribal languages, the trade language, Sango is used by all of them throughout the country. and is now the official language, along with French.

A group with musical ability wrote 27 lively hymns to use at the gatherings. They set them to familiar American Gospel melodies, so Madel and some of the other church leaders who know Sango well translated them into Gbaya, and I mimeographed the words and put them out in a little book. Then Lloyd and I put them on audio tapes—I played the music on our Wurlitzer organ, and he sang the words into a microphone to make the tapes. We had purchased several small tape players which we put in the hands of some of our leaders, so that they could teach these songs. This is something they really enjoy, so the songs became a good evangelistic tool. Since they don't read music, they are accustomed to learning songs by rote, None of them type, and since they have no copy machines, they painstakingly hand-copy the words of songs in their notebooks. So, when a choir rises to sing, you will see them looking over the shoulder of the singer in front of them to follow the words. They are good at improvising parts without music to follow. And, in many of the churches, each age-group will organize a choir; you won't see a director standing up in front of the choir, but there will be designated leaders to whom all the rest look for direction. They have no musical instruments as we know them, but they may use a drum, a tambourine, or shakers to lead the time and rhythm.

Several of our missionaries had learned to operate a mimeograph machine (A.B.Dick, or Gestetner), but we were always short on paper, so none of us dared to risk using supplies for teaching Africans to type and mimeograph. When we visited the Brethren mission, we saw the Multigraph which they had trained Africans to operate. Also, they had the printing press which they had bought from our mission. One of our missionaries had brought it out, but was unable to operate it, so it was sold to the Brethren. At the time we were there, they were waiting for a vital replacement part, but they had hopes of getting it in use again, soon. Some of their Bible teachers had written and reproduced study guides which were kept in supply from year to year for their students.

This was one of the things I had tried to do at our Bible School, but, to my disappointment, when we returned for a visit in 1984, nobody knew anything about the material I thought I had left for posterity. I did find that one of the men who had been one of my students and now is a pastor still had one of my commentaries to which he referred from time to time. They still have no library, but now that the complete Bible has been printed in the Gbaya language, more study material should also follow.

When the Jergensons were quite new in Baboua, he felt led to put in a large orchard of citrus trees. In fact, in our contract with the government when the French were in control, our mission had agreed to establish an orchard, utilizing a certain percentage of the concession. So he supervised the digging of holes one meter square, filling them with fertile soil and planting citrus trees. They grew and bore well, but eventually a fungus growth took over, killing most of the trees. When we had returned to Baboua, we tried to reestablish the orchard. On one of our business trips to Bouar, we found a nursery where we were able to buy 40 citrus trees. We gave some of them to the chief, and then we planted the rest of them in the holes we had dug last year. This project did not turn out to be very successful.

Fortunately guava trees and the little limes grew and produced well. Making guava jelly was so much fun, because guavas have much natural pectin. I discovered that, if I used about fifty percent rather green guavas, they had more pectin. Then I used very ripe fruit for flavor and color. Later, one of the last years we were in Africa, while we were in Meiganga, one of the older catechists Jean Hamboa, had many guava trees. He heard that I knew how to make the jelly, so he managed to collect empty jars and even the tin oatmeal cans which had replaceable lids. He brought the containers and the fruit, and bought sugar at the store, and we made jelly!!! I found out that he actually sold some of it. Well, why not?

In RCA, most of the people raised cotton. When they picked the cotton, they would pack it into huge baskets. Some of these baskets were too big to go through their doors, so they would store them on raised platforms outside. The platforms kept the termites from eating the bottoms out of the baskets. However, if an early rain came, there was no way to protect the cotton, and it would be ruined. Sometimes that one big basket represented their entire crop for the year, so the income they had anticipated was lost. Too bad they didn't have a tarp.

The cotton crop usually provided some extra income to help pay their taxes In fact, often the tax collector would sit beside the treasurer who paid for the cotton and collect the year's tax assessment on the spot. Some people managed to save that money to buy something special like a bicycle, a sewing machine, or aluminum sheeting for the roof of a new house—maybe even cement for a floor.

MISCELLANEOUS REGARDING BIBLE SCHOOL

From a letter to Carole and family, Jan. 20, 1971:

Now I have to tell you something that really thrilled me! Yesterday after-noon three of the students came up on our back porch to get some medicine. One fellow came to ask if we would be having a confirmation service soon, as his oldest daughter would like to be confirmed before school is out. She will be married this summer, so she won't be coming back with her parents next fall. That girl is just darling; intelligent, sweet, and unusually capable. She can read and sew, etc. So I remarked to all the guys: "That fellow will really get a good wife!" Then they said that the young man wants to go onto the seminary, but he is so young, so they think he should come to the Bible School first. As I was talking about a seminarian getting a good wife, one of the men said, "You should have heard Pastor Sand talk about you this morning. He said we should pray that all of our sons would be very careful in choosing wives, hoping that they would all be blessed with a good wife like the one he got!" I had just brought in a stack of papers that I had run off for him on the dupli-cator, for their study of Joshua, and when he thanked me for helping him that way, after I had gone out, he was inspired to give them a little talk about what a blessing a good, helpful wife is! When they recounted this to me, I could see that they really admired him for it. Later in the evening, I thanked him for praising me so before the students.

From another letter written August 29, 1971:

Tomorrow we expect Bill Peters (our agricultural missionary) to drive his huge Mercedes-Benz truck (printed on the door is: FOKPAYONO-Badan-Nandeke) full of Bible School students who are coming from the Cameroon. The students are so eager this year: three families came from Woumbou area last week with the Myklejords, who came to teach during our New Life For All retreat for all the workers in our church in RCA. We had over 60, in-cluding the Baboua people. Quite a number of men from here in RCA have arrived. When we were over in Garoua-Boulai last week, the men from Mei-ganga and Djohong had already arrived there and were having their physicals, getting worm cures, etc.

We are getting several men this year who have had Moyen Cours II (the equivalent of Middle School). It will be great to have students who know a little more. We have made it known that we want them to be able to read well. We were too soft-hearted last year, so there were 5 men who were told not to return, as they just were not getting enough out of the course—only what they retained by hearing—as they couldn't take notes, and if they knew the material, they couldn't express themselves in writing for tests. It looks like we'll have full houses. The Smiths are giving a literacy course, employing some of the Bible School wives and some of the older children who can read. Since the new town was built so far north and east, it is too far for those people to walk out here to take the classes, so Lloyd Smith will hold some classes out there.

Lloyd (Sand) is going to travel quite a bit in the district this month, since I will be teaching—Acts one hour each morning, and Bible for the women who can read well enough to take that in the afternoon: one group on Mondays and Wednesdays and the other on Tuesdays and Thursdays. On Friday I plan to have all of them in a class for health. Pray that I will be able to get some kind-hearted fathers to entertain the pre-school kiddies during the time I have classes, as I just haven't the endurance to try to teach the mothers while their tots are running in and out.

Your father went to Kounde yesterday afternoon, taking Pastor Zama and Antoine Zehoa, the evangelist, with him. The Kounde chief, who was also the Chef de Canton, died suddenly in Bouar last Saturday—sounded like a stroke. He had not been well for some time. All the other Chefs de Canton had been called to Bangui (the capital) for a meeting with Pres. Bokassa. He does that instead of having a Parliament, which is a good idea—more economical, and he gets actual representation. Many of these men (Chefs de Canton) are actually illiterate, but they are wise. Though they are from various tribes, speaking various dialects of Gbaya, they all know Sango, the official language used all over the Central African Republic. This is unique in Africa, where there is a multiplicity of languages. More and more of our missionaries are learning Sango. The Protestant missions east of ours do all their work in Sango, and have the entire Bible and some study material in that language, which they are happy to share with our missionaries.

FIFTY-SEVEN
Names

An old hymn says:
> *"Is my name written there*
> *On the page white and fair,*
> *In the book of God's Kingdom,*
> *—Is my name written there?"*

It would make an interesting topical Bible study to look up verses about names. Many children, especially in the Old Testament, where given long, heavy names with significant meanings. We found that many Gbaya names had meanings, such as a child born during a time of great oppression whose name was Hard Work.

When a believer was ready to be baptized into the Christian faith, he would often choose a Bible name, or sometimes they would take the name of a missionary who had had a special influence on their lives.

Our missionary co-worker, Sig Larson, had a gift for remembering names. At one time Lloyd and I accompanied him to a conference at one of our remote out-stations. When one of the participants came to greet him, Sig called him Kolyna instead of his Christian name. Later, during one of the open sessions, Kolyna rose, and in tears, confessed that he had been out of fellowship, and the Holy Spirit had spoken to him that he had, indeed, lost the privilege of using his Christian name.

DR. EASTWOLD'S STROKE

From a letter written August 30, 1971:
> *We in our mission are having a chance to experience Rom.8:18 again: "All things work together for good to them who love the Lord," as our beloved and faithful Dr. Eastwold suffered a stroke two weeks ago today, and by Friday he was on his way to the U.S. He had been working entirely too hard, the only doctor for a large hospital. We had seen him the previous Thursday, when he gave Lloyd and me our annual physical examinations.*

Less than two weeks previously, Dr. Lila Yaouk, a Canadian woman who had been out here as a volunteer for a year, in 1968, had come to N'Gaoundere to help out for six months. Now it fell on her to decide that Dr. Eastwold would have to be evacuated. The missionaries said that he was very unhappy to think that he would have to leave, but I am sure that he realized that the sooner he would get to the U.S., the sooner he could expect to recover.

PanAmerican Airlines has the most direct flight from Douala, one on Wednesday, and one on Friday. There was no flight scheduled from N'Gaoundere to connect with it on time.

On Thursday morning, the telephone system which has been under construction for over a year, was opened for service. (Isn't that miracle #1?) Cliff Michelsen, our mission superintendent, telephoned the American Embassy in Yaounde. They went to work on the problem. A plane going from Garoua to Yaounde was notified to stop at N'Gaoundere to pick up the patient and family. He was taken out that same evening on a stretcher. The Prefet at N'Gaoundere, a Moslem, came out to see him off. Dr. Eastwold's speech had, by that time, returned, and he said, "I'll be back!" Dr. Lila, Connie Nelson, our newest nurse, and Cliff Michelsen went with Conrad, Alice and Rolf to Douala (James and Philip Noss made a strenuous drive to Jos, Nigeria, to fetch AnneMarie and Sonya Eastwold from school there.) The Embassy sent an ambulance to bring Conrad and Dr. Lila right to the hospital. The rest of them were put up at the Embassy (like royalty!). Dr. Lila returned to N'Gaoundere on the next plane, but the nurse went along to the States.

In Douala, Cliff telephoned Minneapolis and talked to Pastor Sorenson, our Mission Executive Secretary. They decided that Cliff should accompany Rolf, as there wasn't room for him on the plane with his parents. AnneMarie and Sonya went the next week, and the Embassy people promised to meet them in Douala and see them off safely for the U.S., too. Of course Pastor Sorenson began to make arrangements immediately for the best of medical care for Dr. Eastwold.

MISSION AIMS

Early in 1972, Pastors Sorenson and Hesterman, from the home mission office, made a visit to Baboua and the area served by the Lutheran Church of the Central African Republic. Up until about this time, the field in CAR had been included with the area served in the Cameroon. The CAR government had objected to that arrangement, so it became advisable to make the western part of CAR, our area, a separate field. In order to promote interest in this new field for the people of the American Lutheran Church, the men asked for our suggestions for topics of interest. We lined up the following items:

1. We needed to develop a campus ministry. In the past, many of our young people had gone to Cameroon for secondary and advanced study. Since the CAR government now forbade that, more were going for advanced study in CAR, especially in Bouar and Bangui, so we needed to follow them. The Midmission and American Baptist missions were reaching them, but that meant that the possible leadership for our Lutheran churches in CAR would be lost to us.

Now, in 2000, we have a flourishing Lutheran church in Bangui, the capital, where there is a university.

2. We needed to develop a ministry program among Moslems. They hear the radio broadcast taped in the Fulani language in N'Gaoundere and aired from Ethiopia, but the missionaries of the above-mentioned missions admitted that they have no work among Moslems.

Now, in 2000, Philip and June Nelson work in Gallo, in CAR. They know the Fulani language, and they started a good ministry among the Moslem Mbororo, a cattle raising people.

3. Agriculture needed to be added as another means to spread the Lord's Word. This was of special interest to President Bokassa.

Now, in 2000, the ELCA has a full-time agricultural missionary, Rev. Tom Olson.

4. Medical work needed to be improved and extended, with special emphasis on public health. We suggested a mobile unit, set up in a rugged vehicle for bush travel. This did not work out in the way we thought, but during the years that Carl and Paula Stecker worked at Gallo and the surrounding area, they trained many Africans in simple, basic, medical ministry.

5. Pastoral training needed to be added to our curriculum.

About 1958 the government nationalized all schools, so our mission schools were closed, but the curriculum calls for an hour for "morale" for each class, during which time leaders of any religion were encouraged to gather the children of their adherents for classes. A seminary has now been running in Baboua, and a number of graduates are out in the Church field.

FIFTY-EIGHT
Baboua Station Electrification—Broderious

In 1971, each of the three missionary households, the two single ladies, the Smith family, and we Sands, had a small gasoline powered electric generator. We realized that the Bible School and the student camp needed lights as well. From time to time in our Bible School teaching, we wanted to show Bible films, which we had done by setting up a projector on our front porch, but that was not very successful. So, when the mission station at Garoua-Bouai outgrew their diesel-operated generator, we found it possible to get it for our purposes.

During one of our furloughs, Lloyd and I had visited with a couple in Hector, MN., Harold and Edna Broderious. He was a semiretired electrician, and they expressed an interest in coming to Africa to install a generating system for our station. So, in early 1972, they came. Lloyd and I took them to Bangui, the capital of the Central African Republic, and the men made the rounds of the stores to purchase the supplies Harold needed for the installation. He set the generator on a concrete base, and built a house around it. This turned out to be much more economical to operate, and it included the Bible School building and a pole light in the center of the student camp. We had talked about putting electricity in each of the students' houses, but then we realized that, when they finished their course and were appointed to work in a village, they would not have electricity. We did find that, with the pole light in the center of the camp, students would often bring their little study tables out under the one big bulb and study there, instead of in their own houses, where they only had kerosene lanterns. At times, it was hard to find kerosene for sale in the market, so the light was especially helpful to them.

When Harold and Edna Broderius first came to do the electrical work at Baboua, they took their meals with either the Smiths or with us. When we were in Bangui shopping, I had bought some packets of dried soup mixes. Some of them had weevils in them. We had been in Africa long enough, so they didn't bother us—

cooked, maybe they even provided a little extra protein! But they were offensive to Edna, and I don't think she appreciated the joke: "A first-term missionary who finds a bug in his soup will throw away the whole thing; a second-term missionary will dip out the bug and calmly eat the soup; a third term missionary will throw out the soup and eat the bugs!" After a while, Edna wanted to set up her own household, and as the residence of the single girls, Marie Mundfrom and Madel Nostbakken, was empty while they were on furlough, the Broderius' moved in there.

As Lloyd had turned 65 in 1971, he could have retired. But Philip Noss, who had earned his doctorate in African languages and had been asked to set up a translations office in Meiganga, wanted Lloyd to help him. The Gbayas who had been hired as informants were translating faster than Philip could keep up in checking; also, he needed Lloyd to be sure that their work was theologically correct. So it was decided that we should take a quick home leave and then return for two years more. Mark would be out of school at Jos on June 15, and the other Sudan Mission kids would be brought to N'Gaoundere in two plane loads. So Lloyd and I drove to N'Gaoundere to fly to Jos with the mission pilot when he went back for the second load. Then Mark joined us for the flight from Kano, Nigeria, to London, where we spent a few days with Linnea. After graduating from Augsburg College with a degree in elementary education, she had had trouble finding a teaching position. She flew to London, then, where she got a position in a private school teaching art, French, and literature at the junior high level.

We had heard about the internationally famous Keswick Conference, held in the beautiful Keswick area in England. So we decided to take about a week there before going onto the U.S. As Linnea was in London, she came up to participate, too. Lloyd and I were assigned to a room in a private home, but Mark was given a cot in a tent out on a field. Though it was already July, the nights were cold and the bedding was inadequate, so we did manage to get him in to spend the rest of the nights with us.

Before the week was up, we got notice from Lynn and Norma that my Dad was seriously ill, so I should cut my stay short in England. Consequently, I left before Lloyd and Mark did. When I got home, I found that Dad had recovered and was very glad to welcome me.

After a quick home leave, we exchanged housing with Tom and Sharon Christianson, who had lived in Meiganga and now would move to Baboua to teach at the Bible School. Sharon worried about replacing me because of the years I had spent doing medical work in Baboua. But I told her something like this: "You are Sharon. Don't try to be Beryl." So she never tried to do medical work, and the people loved her for herself.

Though we were making our home in Meiganga, I made a point to take a trip back to Baboua once a month to do medical work. There were medical supplies locked up in the dispensary, and Michel, my assistant, was only too happy to spend a couple days helping me. There always seemed to be an accumulation of emergencies to make those visits memorable. I shall never forget one of the very last side-trips I made. Word always got around when I was there, and people expected me to respond.

A messenger came rushing in (on a bicycle, I suppose) from a village about 30 kilometers south of Baboua, on the Abba road. I don't remember now what the problem was, but they needed help! It was rainy season, and the bridge over one of the streams had washed out. It was evident that this had happened some time ago, and that the market trucks had simply bypassed the ruined bridge by driving down into the stream bed and then up the steep incline and up the hill. I had the pick-up full of patients, with the inevitable family members who always needed to accompany them.

As we contemplated the feat before us, I told all the able-bodied passengers that they would have to dismount and be prepared to push if the truck should get stuck. The road ahead of us, up that hill, was crisscrossed by eroded ruts that were deep! One of the men made the observation: "Madame, if the car slips into one of those ruts, there is no way we will be able to get it out!" So I said, "Well, we'll all have to do an extra amount of praying!"

The pick-up did not have 4-wheel drive, or I surely would have used it. I gunned the motor, in super-low, and did a lot of powerful praying. I don't usually pray out loud, but that time I'm sure I did, and the truck made it to the top of the hill, where we just sat and waited for the passengers to catch up with us. Then it started to rain, but we had made it to the top, and the rest of the way was smooth sailing; that is, as much so as it ever was on those roads.

FIFTY-NINE

From my letter of October 30, 1972:

After Lloyd's brief "home leave", he returned to Africa by himself, leaving me to do some "left over" family things before joining him again.

On Sept. 18, I took Wanda to Winona State College, where she entered the nursing course. She had applied to the U. of Minn., but that year they were limiting the class to 40, so her credits were transferred to Winona State.

Mark had flown back to Africa in company with the Cliff Michelson family, their two children being also students at the Hillcrest Academy in Jos, Nigeria.

I drove to Iowa for a quick visit with family, then, as I had been unable to sell our car, I took myself to the airport in Mason City. My sister-in-law, Norma Ramsey, drove our car back to Joice, taking also Mom and Dad, Aunt Ada Bang, and neighbor, Anne Slattum, home, too.

A night flight, Sept. 21st, brought me to London, where I spent the weekend with Linnea, then another night flight, Sept. 25, brought me to Kano, Nigeria, where a sharp-eyed official noticed that my cholera immunization was out-dated. A kindly doctor whisked me past a long line of Moslem pilgrims, waiting for the shots they would need before their flight to Mecca.

I appreciated a hotel room to change from the warm clothes I had needed in chilly London to a cotton dress appropriate for 95 degree temperature. At noon a short flight brought me to Jos, where Mark had not received my letter, so nobody came to meet me. But another missionary had come to meet someone, so he brought me to Elm House, our Lutheran hostel. At three p.m., I went along in the bus to fetch the children from Hillcrest School. It was fun to stand outside and to see the surprise on one face after another as our 12 Sudan Mission high school kids came out and exclaimed: "Aunt Beryl!" Mark was one of the last to emerge.

At the dormitory pool, I watched Mark take part in the Life Guard training class taught by Ollie Tovson. He got his certificate later, so now he is qualified to take his turn as a paid guard when people from other hostels have a turn in the Elm House pool. An interesting extra-curricular activity for Mark: he had a chance to buy an old motorcycle which the "house father" helped him rebuild. Actually, the project was not successful, but it did give him some good experience.

The visit at Jos was all too short, as I had to go on the next morning to get the weekly flight to Douala, Cameroon, to make the deadline of Sept. 30th for my re-entry permit.

The next day's flight from Douala to N'Gaoundere was cancelled to make repairs on the plane, so Lloyd had to wait another day there for me. The birthday cake Mrs. Ron Nelson had made for him the 28th tasted good the next day, as the other American missionaries at N'Gaoundere gathered to celebrate with us. The next day we returned to Meiganga, where Lloyd had been "batching it" for seven lonely weeks. (He had lost the 10-15 pounds which the Mayo clinic doctor had advised him to get rid of.)

Returning to Meiganga, Lloyd resumed his work as "technical counsellor" along with Dr. Philip Noss, to the Gbaya translators.

Most of the work on The Psalms is finished. He has also checked the translation of a booklet on prayer and a larger one on the Christian approach to Moslems.

One thing that impressed us during our brief stay in the States was the evidence of the moving of the Holy Spirit among the people of God. And now, since our return, we have been sharing the tape-recorded messages from the First International Conference on the Holy Spirit.

During the time spent in Meiganga in intensive translation work on the Old Testament, the team was joined by Dr. Wendell Frericks, an Old Testament instructor at Luther Seminary. It turned out that there was some problem with his papers, so we took him to Bangui. This must have been during Mark's Christmas vacation, as he accompanied us. As usual, we were short on time for the trip, and also, as usual, people at Baboua had given Lloyd letters to be carried to friends / relatives in villages along the road to Bangui. At one village, Lloyd simply slowed the vehicle, so Mark threw a letter out to villagers who, having heard the car approaching, had congregated along the way. To Dr. Frericks astonishment that we simply kept going, Mark explained: "African air mail." (African protocol is such that, had we stopped, we should have had to take up a protracted conversation: "Are you well? How is your family? How are the crops this year?" etc.)

Engaging "informants" for Bible translation work takes much grace and wisdom: men with a good command of their native language, a command of French or English (Nobody among the Gbaya knew any Biblical languages) as well as people in good standing in the Church.

It was necessary for Dr. Noss to return to the U.S. for a while to keep a commitment at the University of Wisconsin, so he left Lloyd in charge of the translation team. It came out that the main translator was having an affair with one of the teen-age girls in the orphanage. At that time the translators were hired by the mission, and this man, knowing that he was going against mission policy, let the word out that, if the missionary (Pastor Sand) should fire him, he would sue him for a large sum of money. (They seem to think that every American has access to limitless funds.) In order to avoid this con-frontation, leaders in the Church suggested that the Church take over the re-sponsibility of paying these workers, as they knew that he would realize that the Church's funds were limited. However, the Church leaders "dragged their feet" in taking action, so you can imagine that the "atmosphere" at the tables in the translation office was not really conducive to good spiritual study. We believed that 2 Tim.3:16: "All Scripture is given by inspiration of God (is God-breathed)" and that this should apply not only to the original writing of Scripture, but also to the translation and propagation of Scripture into other languages. So each day's work of translation was begun with prayer, and, on the part of the missionary, at least, an effort to keep the lines of communica-tion open for the very best expression of the Scripture in the language of the people—in this case, the Gbaya.

SIXTY
Spring, 1974, Lots Of Big Things!
"Make Me Clean"

Mark would be graduating from high school at Hillcrest Academy in Jos, so we were making preparations, winding up our activities, and packing for the trip back to the U.S. by way of Jos—this time to retire!

Having read this far, you realize that missionary life can be a series of interruptions. This time, they were very pleasant ones: (1) Dr. George Muedeking, the editor of The Lutheran Standard, and Mrs. Muedeking, came for a visit to our mission field. (2) An excited Gbaya messenger came hurrying in from Abba with the urgent news that Chief Abba wanted to be baptized, and, as Pastor Sand was the oldest missionary, the one the Chief had known the longest, it was logical that he should be the one to carry out the rite. So we all packed up, taking Pastor Andre Garba, the first ordained pastor in the Gbaya Church with us. We drove by way of Baboua, of course, and picked up Lloyd and Margaret Smith, who had been the latest resident missionaries at Abba. There was no missionary in residence at Abba, so we all had to take our camping equipment with us.

Though well into his 80's, the chief was alert and in good health. Ngoubou, his son, whom we all spoke of as the Crown Prince, had taken over the administration of the village and the Canton. Most older Gbayas had no definite idea of their age, but Chief Abba could tell us how old he was at the time of the Carnot Uprising, etc. When the first American missionaries had arrived to investigate the possibility of beginning work in the area, he had welcomed them and insisted that they make their headquarters at his village. Arthur and Bernice Anderson had taught him to read, and, though he encouraged the mission work, he had not made a commitment of faith. But now he told us an interesting story.

CLEANSE ME, O GOD

Approximately two months previously, he had had a vision: angels had come to him at night, announcing that they were taking him. But he responded:" I can't go. My heart is not clean." They left him, but later they returned two more times. Each time, he responded with the same words. The third time, they were more insistent, so he had decided that this was IT! "Give me time," he pled. "I must be baptized."

So he called for a messenger, who found us at Meiganga. Our guests, Dr. and Mrs. Meudeking, accompanied us. In all his years as a pastor and as editor of The Lutheran Standard, this was to Dr. Meudeking, the experience of a lifetime!

But this was not the end of the story. Ngoubou, the Crown Prince, was now the one in authority. As the missionaries sat down to talk with Ngoubou and his father, the Chief knew what he wanted. But Ngoubou reminded his father: "When I was young, I heard the Gospel which the missionaries were teaching. I accepted their teaching; I believed and wanted to be baptized, but you refused to give your permission. So, all these years we have been listening to the preaching of the Moslem teachers. Now you want to be baptized. I cannot accept this change. Do you really know what you are doing?"

When Ngoubou realized that his father really understood what it meant to be baptized, and that he had made up his mind to go through with it, he relented. The old chief rose and made his way to the waiting vehicle, our blue one-ton pick-up with its white camper top. Of course, the chief was seated in the cab, but the crowd around him wanted to ride, too. Even when the pick-up was completely filled, more and more men tried to get in, with the result that they tore the camper top to pieces. When they got to the mission, and I saw what had happened, I cried. But I think the Lord performed a miracle because in the morning, a group of men put it back together again, and it looked as good as new.

Dr. Meudeking wrote up the story and took pictures of Pastor Sand dipping water from a beaten-up wash basin on the bowed head of old Chief Abba, who had chosen the name Abraham. The picture made the front page of the Oct. 1, 1974 issue of The Lutheran Standard.

After our return to the U.S., we received the news that, three weeks after his baptism, the edge of Abraham's blanket had slipped into the smoldering fire beside his bed, and he had perished in the fire. But everyone is confident that he was then clean, and he was accepted into the presence of "Our Father who is in Heaven."

This, Lloyd's final pastoral act was perhaps the most climactic experience of his missionary career, reminiscent of Paul's words in I Cor. 3:6: "I planted; Apollos watered, but it is God who made it grow."

Dr. Meudeking also exclaimed that this was indeed the most outstanding experience in his whole career!

RETIREMENT 1974

Before we left Africa, Mark had indicated that he wanted to attended NIACC (North Iowa Area Community College) in Mason City. So I wrote to my life-long friend in Mason City, Edna Tweed Snell, asking her if she would look for a house for us to rent. Nothing was being advertised, so she consulted with Pastor Hanson at Trinity Lutheran Church. It so happened (God's arrangement, of course) that Trinity Church had just hired Al Gabel to be their head custodian, and they wanted him to live in the house just back of the church which had originally been the parsonage. The pastors now preferred to arrange their own housing, so the parsonage was unoccupied. Al had accepted the position at a considerable reduction in salary from his job with Decker's. He and Audrey owned a small house on Kentucky Ave. which they would be vacating. It had not been listed yet, so was available for us.

When a long-term missionary retires, the Mission Board pays house rent for a year, and they gave us also a $3000 bonus. When we arrived in Mason City, we moved into that neat, little house and proceeded to find the necessary furniture. We had not yet received the bonus, but we frequented estate sales, second-hand shops, etc. so we were able to manage with what money we had. After we had lived there for several months, we did get the bonus, and since we did not then need it for furniture, Lloyd took his half to pay for a trip to Israel, on his way back to Africa. He had promised to work for another year alone in giving training to some Gbaya men who were then to be ordained as Associate pastors—actually not associates, as we think of them, but as full-fledged pastors without having gone through seminary. I used my half of that bonus to buy a small electric organ.

One day while we were living in Mason City, a lady, a member of Trinity Church, made a courtesy call to welcome us to her church. She identified herself as Mrs. Vaage. In amazement, I asked her if her husband's name was LaVern, and if he had, as a child, lived north of Fertile. When she said that he had, I informed her that I had been his first grade teacher! Karen and I have been good friends ever since.

We enjoyed that little house until Mark and I moved up to the Asjel place south of Joice, which Mom and Dad had deeded to me as my retirement home. It was a blistering hot day in June when we made the move. The house was small and needed much remodeling, so I found two carpenters who proceeded to make a much larger house out of it.

That fall Mark took off with Paul Larson to attend the California LBI, and I took a nursing position at the newly opened Forest City Community Hospital, working nights. While we were living in Mason City, I had had the opportunity to take a refresher course in nursing at NIACC, so I could qualify to work as an R.N.

After a year at the California LBI, Mark spent the summer traveling with the singing team THE SALTERS. One of their first stops was to visit me. Mom put up several of them at her house in Joice.

I had hoped that the remodeling job would have been completed by the time Lloyd returned in the fall, but these carpenters were so much in demand that they would work a few days on my job and then disappear to work elsewhere. So it was far from done when Lloyd returned. But then he went to work—cleaning up after them, etc.

Many Lutheran churches, especially those in the country, have a custom of putting on a Mission Sunday in the fall. While Lloyd was still in Africa, I was invited to be the speaker at five of these, so I was kept very busy that fall. When I settled down there in Iowa, I joined Beaver Creek and became active there. One of the churches I spoke at was at my home church, Beaver Creek, just about a quarter of a mile from our home.

In January of 1976, Lloyd had a chance to ride with Pastor Dalen, of Salem church in Lake Mills, to the annual Luther Seminary convocation in St. Paul. The upshot of that trip was Lloyd's appointment as Visitation Pastor at Salem. Lloyd served in that capacity for ten years, retiring again in 1986.

We enjoyed life in our country home. One summer day, as Lloyd was mowing the lawn, he slipped and fell, and the mower took a bite out of his foot. I couldn't stop the bleeding, so I took him to the hospital in Forest City, where it was stitched up. He walked with crutches for some time. During that summer, Lloyd had been asked to serve as interpreter for two Cameroonian Christian leaders who had been invited to travel and speak to churches in the Illinois

District of the American Lutheran Church. They spoke French, so that is how Lloyd communicated with them. I enjoyed traveling with them.

As visitation pastor, Lloyd visited many Salem people who had entered the Care Center as residents. One day, I got a phone call from Thelma Stene, the Director of Nurses there, asking me to consider coming there to work nights. At first I declined, as I was happy in my work at Forest City. But, as we talked it over, Lloyd felt that it would be better for me to take that position. So, he visited many of the residents in his daytime work, and then I cared for them at night! I started working there in Nov., 1979, and continued until Jan. of 1997. I had had the secret hope of working until I was 80, but when the administrator told me that the powers-that-be had decided to assign my responsibilities to others, I said, "Well, there are other things I can do."

FIRE! TIMES THREE

It was a beautiful spring evening when we had our first fire. Lloyd and I were driving down Interstate 35, going to a meeting at the Holiday Inn in Clear Lake. Just as we were passing the rest stop, Lloyd said, "Bend down and see if you can dislodge the accelerator. It seems to be stuck." It was stuck, all right, and I could not dislodge it.

We were almost to the off ramp for Clear Lake. I said, "You'll just have to put the brakes on, even though the motor has you going 55 miles an hour." We got off the interstate and into the truck stop. I thought, with all that friction, there surely will be a fire. So I ran in to the truck stop and asked for a fire-extinguisher. There was a fire, but it was put out promptly. We walked over to the Holiday Inn, and after the meeting, asked for a ride home with a friend. The Chevrolet Cavalier was towed back to Lake Mills in the morning, and our insurance covered the cost of the repairs.

A year or two later, after we had traded the Cavalier in on a 1986 Dodge, we got a letter from the company, saying we should turn in that car because that particular model had had trouble like we had had—the fire had caused the accelerator to jam, not the other way around. Our insurance man asked me, "When you couldn't slow the motor down, why didn't you just turn off the motor and pull off to the side of the road?"

"Then the whole car would have burned up," I replied.

We lived in that remodeled house in the country near Joice for 9 years. Then, on Thursday evening, Jan. 17, 1984, one of the coldest nights of the year, the house burned down. It was so cold that the hoses on the fire trucks froze up, and the firemen had to stand watching in frustration, as the house and all contents were consumed. We came out well on insurance, so we bought a one-story rambler in Lake Mills, being able to pay cash for it from our insurance settlement.

Our third fire occurred when Wanda, Fred, and the children were spending the week-end with us. With only one bathroom, it takes a family a while to get ready in the morning for church. We were about to leave for the second service, when Fred opened the basement door and smelled smoke coming up. He grabbed my fire extinguisher and put out the small blaze which had started in the cheater, the connection for the water softener.

BACK TO AFRICA

At the time of our second fire, ten years had passed since we had left Africa to retire. In visiting us after the fire, Carole suggested, "Now, why don't you use some of your insurance money and take a trip back to Africa?" This was especially appropriate, as I had been asked to serve as interpreter for Martha Houma, the Gbaya woman who was the leader of the women's work in the Cameroon Lutheran Church. She had been invited to visit the American Church as a part of the Woman to Woman project being planned by the ALC women. I had wondered if I would be able to handle the language, having been away so long. The trip to Africa would provide me with a refresher course in the language.

The night the house burned, we went to stay with Mom in Joice (Dad had died in August of 1975, and she lived on there until Jan. 1990, when she fell and broke her hip. After that, she lived at the Lake Mills Care Center until her death in Sept.1992 at the age of 97.)

After the fire, we were provided with a rental house in Lake Mills. People at Salem Church put on a reception, really a sort of shower, for us, where we received beautiful and practical items of clothing, dishes, cooking utensils, and gifts of money. When it was over, Pastor Dalen loaded up his van twice to haul the gifts to our house. Then, looking around in town, we found the three-bedroom ranch house, made a down-payment on it, and took our trip to Africa. Upon our return, we had the closing and moved in. Twelve days

later, I took off on my six-week stint as interpreter for Martha
Houma in the WOMAN TO WOMAN project. We met first for
orientation at Augsburg College, and then dispersed with our hostesses.

TRAVEL WITH MARTHA HOUMA (WOMAN TO WOMAN)

The women of the American Lutheran Church, under the leadership of Bonnie Jensen, had prepared a wonderful project in which
they invited women in positions of leadership from each country
where the ALC had a mission field to come to the U.S. to meet
with women of the ALC to increase mission interest among the
women. Leaders of the women in each district of the ALC had
been chosen to arrange programs in strategic churches where these
women would speak.

This WOMAN TO WOMAN project turned out to be a 24-hour
job, quite strenuous, but very enjoyable, as we traveled among the
churches in the Southwestern Minnesota district. The climax of the
summer was a trip to the ALCW convention in Detroit, after which
we were taken for a debriefing session at a college campus near
Detroit. These women from so many countries and the American
church women who conducted the project were charming people. I
look upon that summer as a most memorable experience! At the
last evening meeting, we all sang "Blessed Assurance" in our particular language—a foretaste of heaven!

Quiet Waters Publications

Bolivar MO 65613-0034 www.quietwaterspub.com:

Touched By the African Soul

Compiled by Gloria Cunningham & Lois Okerstrom
In this collection of short stories, sixty-two missionary women recall their adventuresome years in Tanzania, Africa, from the 1940s to the 1990s. The stories tell of personal experiences of the writers and give insight into the culture and Christian faith of the Tanzanian people among whom they lived and worked.
ISBN 0-9663966-9-3

Daktari Yohana

By John Hult
This book is a compilation of stories, which grew out of the author's four years as a medical missionary to Tanzania from 1957-1961. John Hult is the husband of Adeline Lundquist Hult, one of the contributors to *Touched by the African Soul.* If you love Africa, you will enjoy this book.
ISBN 0-9663966-5-0

Miracle At Sea

By Eleanor Anderson
In 1941 about 140 American missionaries had embarked on the ill-fated Egyptian liner Zamzam, including Mrs. Danielson with her six children who planned to join her missionary husband in Tanzania. The vessel was sunk by a German raider off the African coast. Eleanor Anderson, one of the surviving Danielson daughters, tells the story of the events leading up to the sinking and of the family's miraculous rescue.
ISBN 0-9663966-3-4

On Our Way Rejoicing

By Ingrid Hult-Trobisch
Ralph Hult, one of the first American missionaries to Tanzania, was a passenger on the *Zamzam* as well. After returning to the US, he set out for Tanzania the following year, where he died unexpectedly. His daughter, Ingrid Trobisch, tells the story of what happens when God takes away the father of ten children. A whole family is called to service and sent into the world. The story surges

with movement, partings and reunion, sorrows and joys, adventure and romance, shining courage, and above all, the warm love that knits together a large Christian family.

ISBN 0-9663966-2-6

I Loved A Girl

By Walter Trobisch

'Last Friday, I loved a girl—or as you would put it, I committed adultery.' This deeply moving story of a young African couple has become a worldwide classic with its frank answers to frank questions about sex and love. Its tremendous success led Walter and Ingrid Trobisch to leave their missionary post in Cameroon and start an international ministry as marriage and family counselors.

ISBN 0-9663966-0-X

The Adventures Of Pumpelhoober

By David Trobisch, illustrated by Eva Bruchmann

"A Pumpelhoober is someone who has bad luck. I, too, often have bad luck, and that is why everyone calls me Pumpelhoober. My father is German and speaks German, my mother is American and speaks English but with my luck I was born in a country in Africa, where everyone speaks French." This humorous children's book tells the story of a missionary family in Africa from the perspective of a nine-year-old.

ISBN 0-9663966-4-2

I Married You

By Walter Trobisch

Set in a large African city, this story covers only four days in the life of Walter and Ingrid Trobisch. Nothing in this book is fiction. All the stories have really happened. The people involved are still living today. The direct, sensitive, and compassionate narrative presents Christian marriage as a dynamic triangle.

ISBN 0-9663966-6-9

Passport to Borneo

By Adeline Lundquist Hult

In 1951 the author was called as a missionary teacher to work with a Chinese church in British North Borneo. Her experiences of living abroad, the joys, frustrations, and adaptations necessary to cope with life in a multi-cultural colony, are all graphically portrayed. ISBN 1-931475-03-2